# SHORTERHAND SKILLS FOR THE FUTURE

## INTERMEDIATE COURSE IN WRITING AND TRANSCRIPTION SKILL DEVELOPMENT

GEORGE A. REID, B.Comm., B.Ed., M.A., F.C.C.T.
Associate Professor, Business and Commerce Department
The College of Education, University of Toronto

EVELINA J. THOMPSON, B.A., B.Ed.
Chairman, Secretarial Science Department
Ryerson Polytechnical Institute, Toronto

ESTHER M. SCOTT, B.A.
Director of Business & Commerce
Chinguacousy Secondary School, Bramalea

Sir Isaac Pitman (Canada), Ltd.
517 Wellington Street West, Toronto 135, Ontario

© Copyright Canada 1972, by Sir Isaac Pitman (Canada), Limited

**SIR ISAAC PITMAN (CANADA), LTD.**
Pitman House, 517 Wellington Street West, Toronto 135, Canada

**THE COPP CLARK PUBLISHING COMPANY**
517 Wellington Street West, Toronto 135, Canada

**SIR ISAAC PITMAN AND SONS LTD.**
Pitman House, 39 Parker Street, Kingsway, London, W.C.2
P.O. Box 6038, Portal Street, Nairobi, Kenya

**SIR ISAAC PITMAN (AUST.) PTY. LTD.**
Pitman House, Bouverie Street, Carlton, Victoria 3053, Australia

**PITMAN PUBLISHING COMPANY S.A. LTD.**
P.O. Box 9898, Johannesburg, S.Africa

**PITMAN PUBLISHING CORPORATION**
6 East 43rd Street, New York, N.Y. 10017, U.S.A.

Printed and bound in Canada by
The Hunter Rose Company, Toronto

1 2 3 4 5 6 — 75 74 73 72

ISBN 0-273-04126-6

# 1

## VOCABULARY BUILDING

Cannot be the word and.

delightful 1X — 1.

exciting — 2.

concerned — 3.

volume — 4.

supervision — 5.

Dark stroke

Cannot be "on the"

former — 6.

exceed — 7.

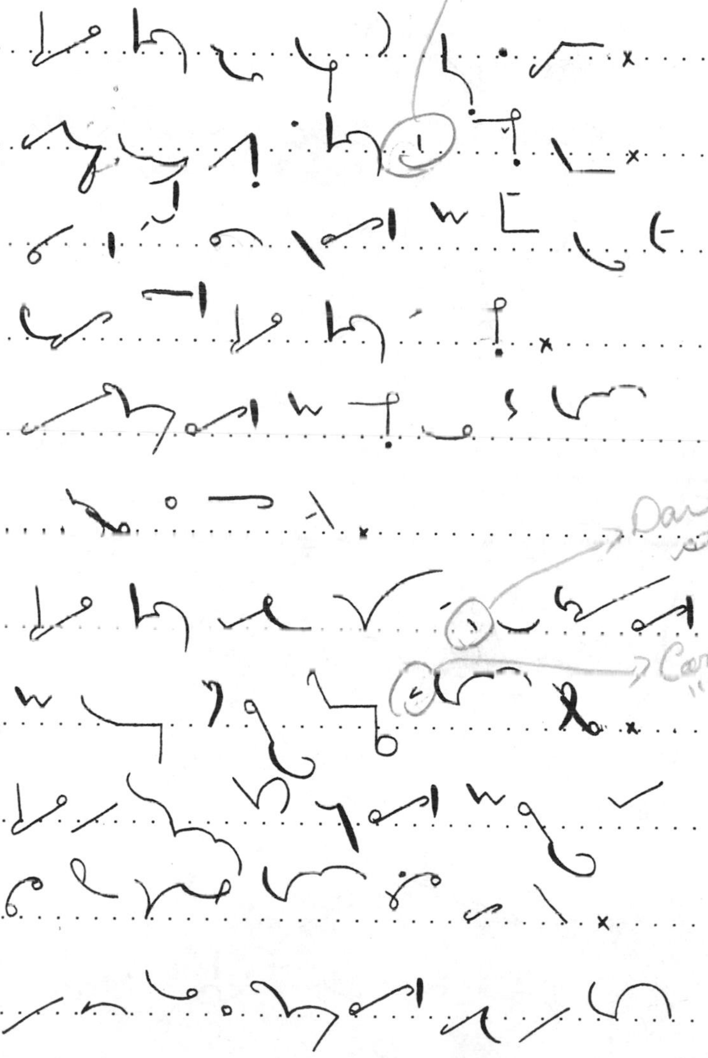

*Should be dark.*

substantial    8.

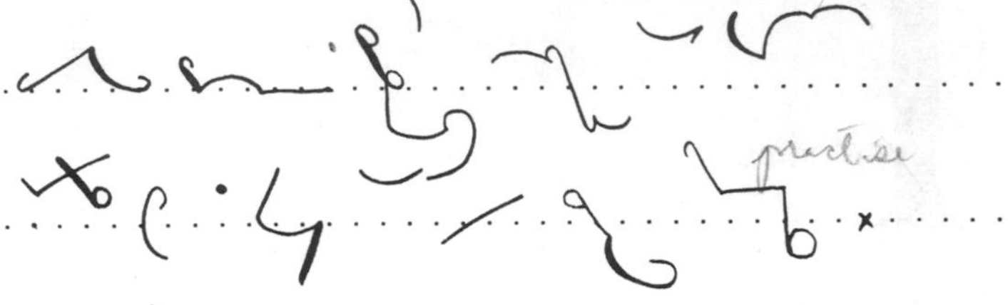

*practise*

**THEORY PRACTICE** — *full length*

*Should dark*

*Should be dark.*

*example*

**SPEED BUILDING PRACTICE**

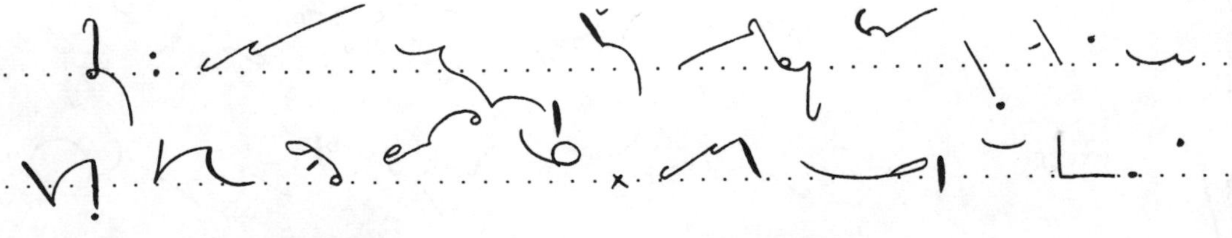

2

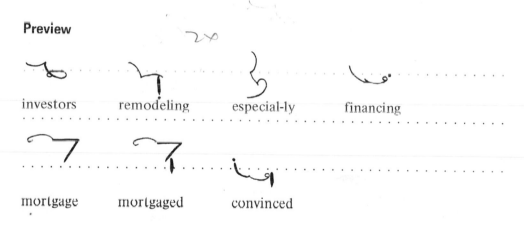

## TRANSCRIPTION LETTERS

**Preview**

investors     remodeling     especial-ly     financing

mortgage     mortgaged     convinced

Western Savings and Loan Association
58 Portage Avenue
Winnipeg, Manitoba

**Preview**

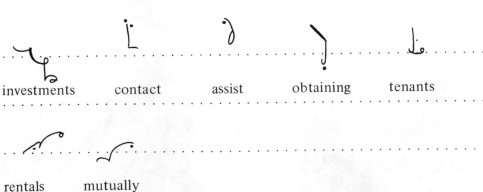

| investments | contact | assist | obtaining | tenants |

| rentals | mutually |

4

Mr. J.A. Holmes
1090 Don Mills Road
Don Mills, Ontario

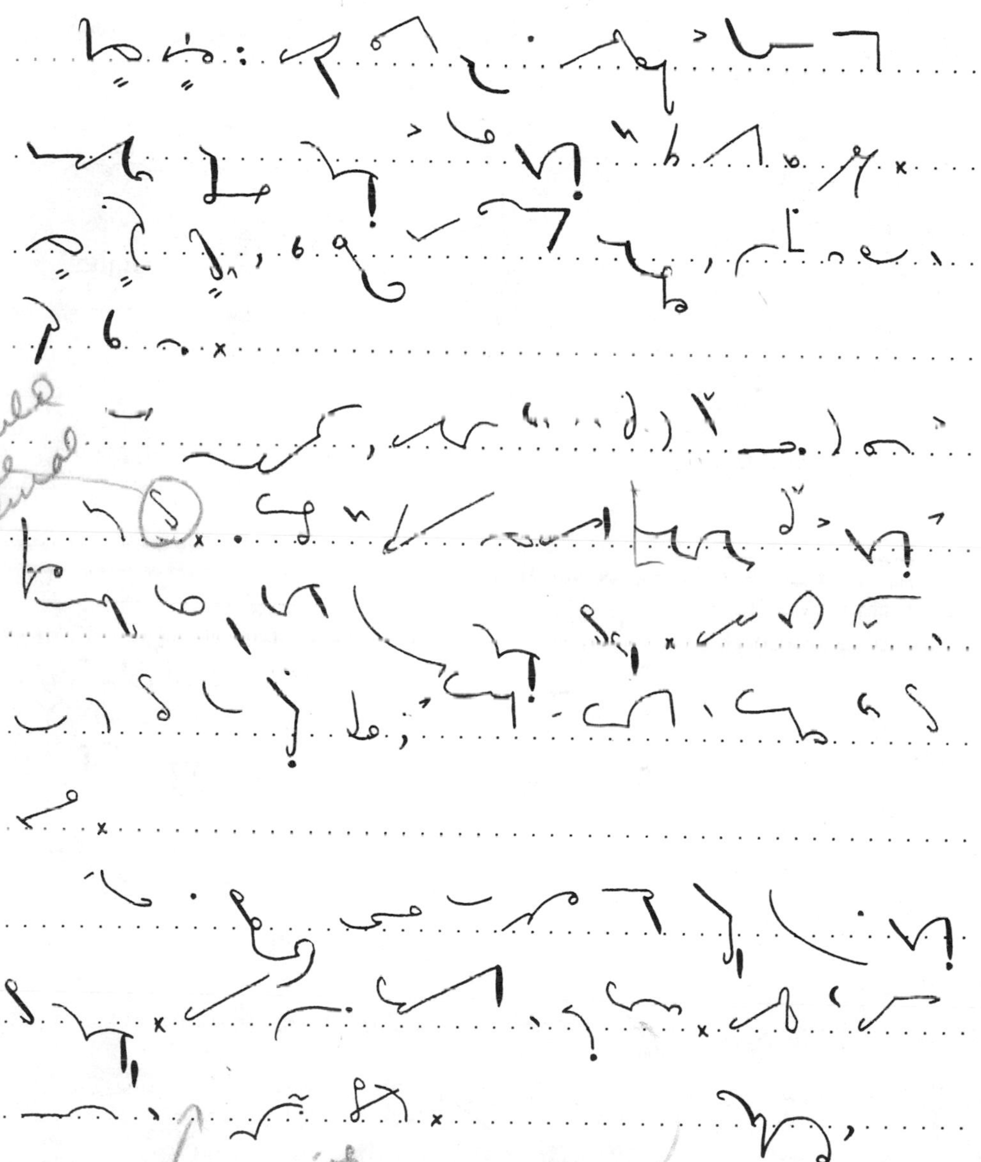

*should be plural*

*If a word is missing*

BUSINESS UNDERSTANDING

What is a "mortgage" and how is it used in the sale and purchase of real estate?

**Preview**

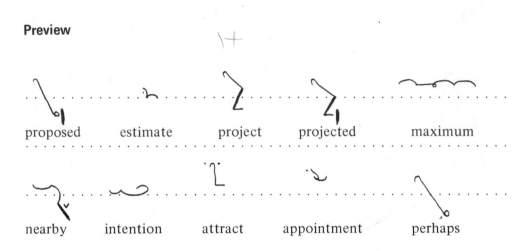

proposed    estimate    project    projected    maximum

nearby    intention    attract    appointment    perhaps

Western Savings and Loan Association
58 Portage Avenue
Winnipeg, Manitoba

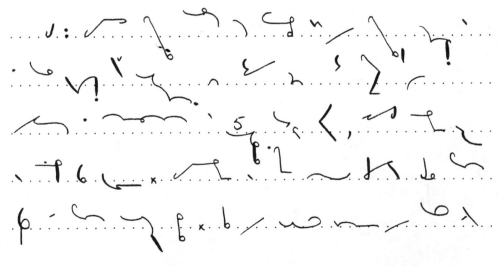

## TRANSCRIPTION SKILL DEVELOPMENT

**Spelling**

1. ............................................................................................

2. ............................................................................................

3. ............................................................................................

**Punctuation**

Punctuate the following:

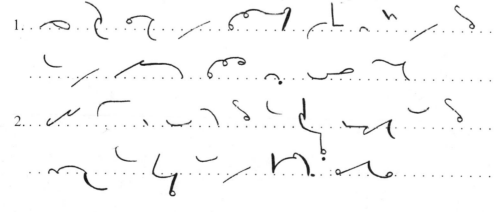

3.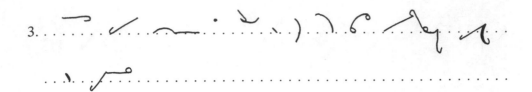

## Transcription Tips

If your employer dictates words that are new to you, find out what they mean so that you can use them properly in the future.

# 2

## VOCABULARY BUILDING

permission 1.

publicity 2.

examine 3.

render 4.

9

assistance     5.

supporting     6.

recognize     7.

**THEORY PRACTICE**

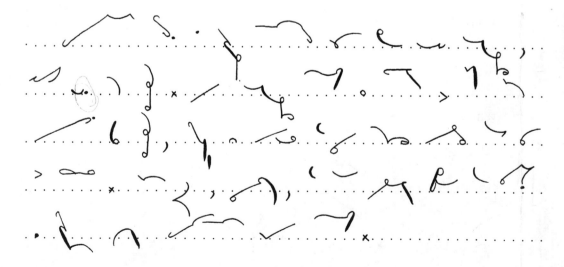

## SPEED BUILDING PRACTICE

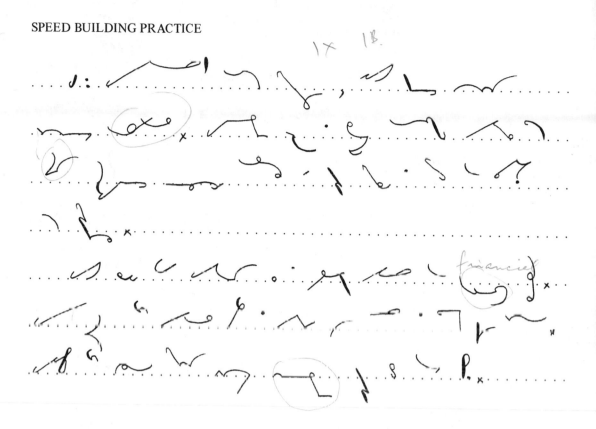

## TRANSCRIPTION LETTERS

### Preview

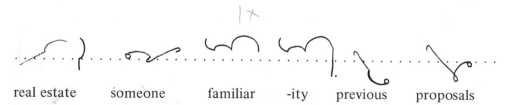

real estate    someone    familiar    -ity    previous    proposals

11

Standard Investment Corporation
56 Church Street
Toronto 1, Ontario

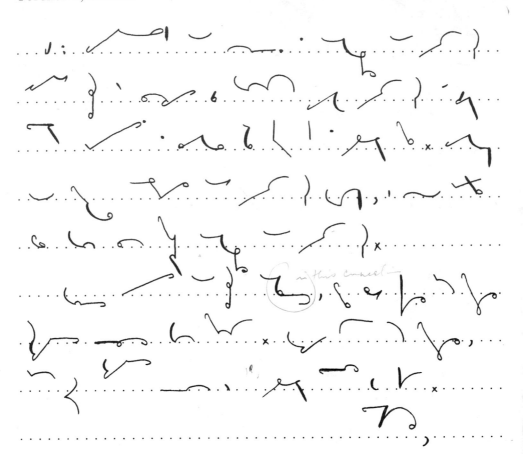

**Preview**

suitable        apartment        property        assure

12

Mr. Fred Williams
67 Willingdon Blvd.
Toronto 18, Ontario

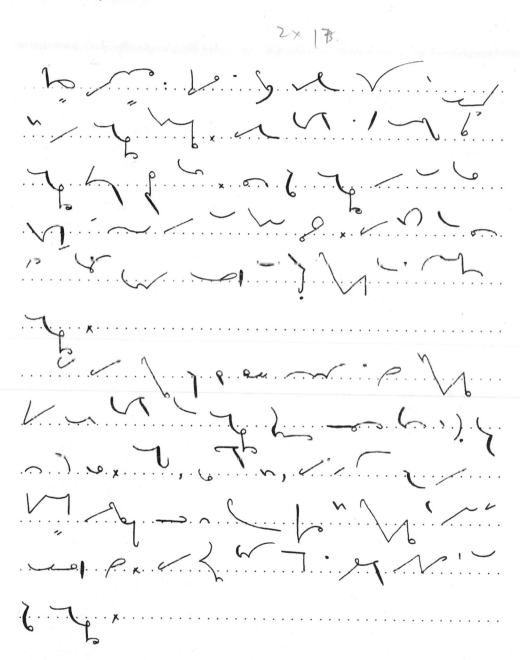

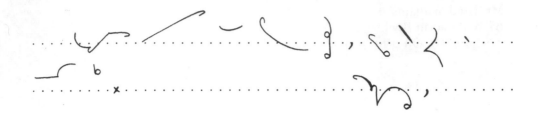

## BUSINESS UNDERSTANDING

What is meant by "real" property and how does it differ from "personal" property?

## Preview

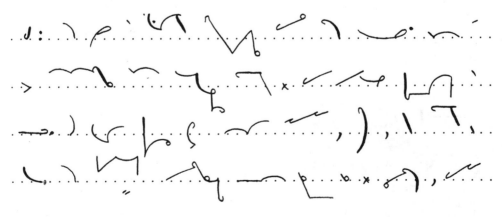

convenience      manager

Standard Investment Corporation
56 Church Street
Toronto 1, Ontario

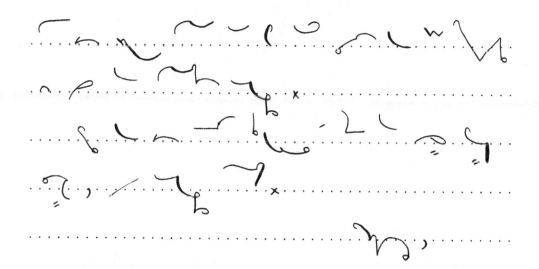

## TRANSCRIPTION SKILL DEVELOPMENT

**Spelling**

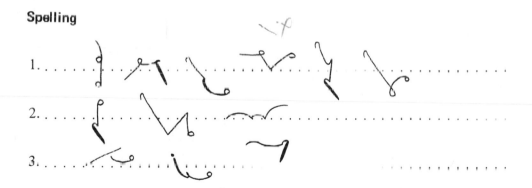

1. . . . . .

2. . . . . .

3. . . . . .

**Punctuation**

Punctuate the following:

1. . . . . .

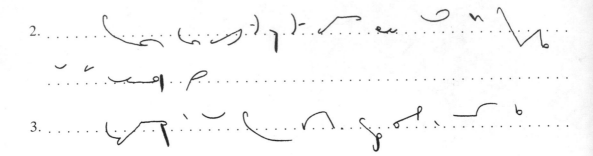

2. ......................................................................

.............................................................................

3. ......................................................................

## Transcription Tips

If during dictation you are handed enclosures to be included with letters, make sure that you indicate clearly (a light pencil mark will do) which enclosures and which letters belong together.

# 3

## VOCABULARY BUILDING

outstanding 1.

consult 2.

financial 3.

obligations 4.

adopted 5.

deferred 6.

personnel       7.

qualifications  8.

**THEORY PRACTICE**

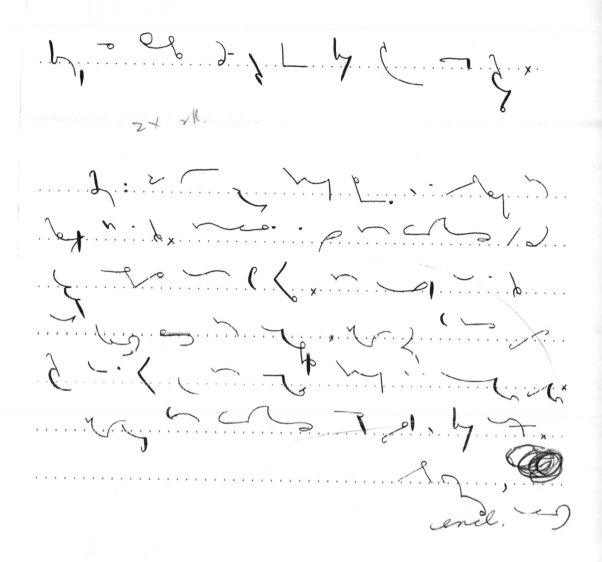

## TRANSCRIPTION LETTERS

**Preview**

cooperative    apartment    Jamaica    sections

beautiful      moderate      prefer      situation

Queens Realty Company
104 Main Street
Hamilton, Ontario

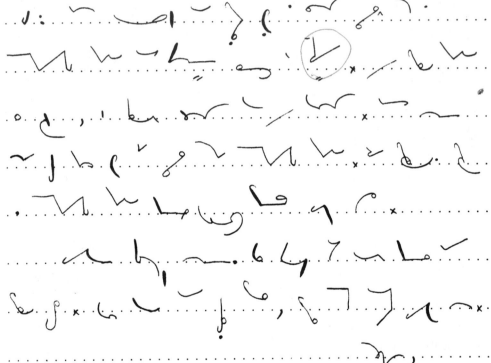

## Preview

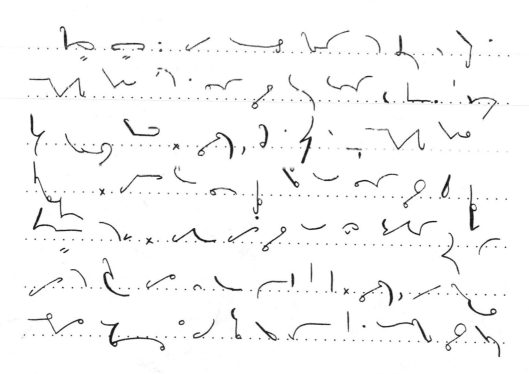

perfectly    additional    approval    previous    decision

appointment    privilege    assistance

Mr. Leslie Green
P.O. Box 36
Hamilton, Ontario

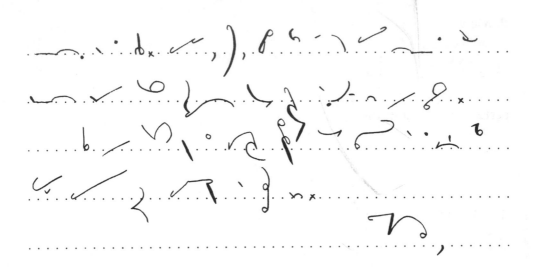

## BUSINESS UNDERSTANDING

What is meant by a "cooperative" apartment and what are its advantages and disadvantages?

**Preview**

disappointed       decided

Queens Realty Company
104 Main Street
Hamilton, Ontario

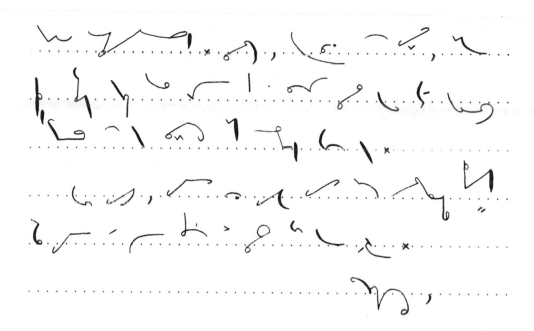

## TRANSCRIPTION SKILL DEVELOPMENT

**Spelling**

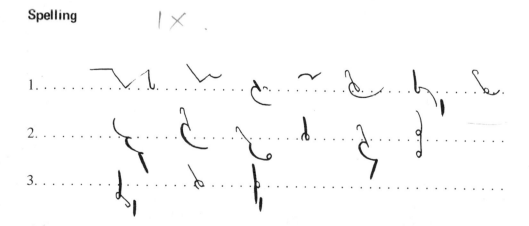

23

## Punctuation

Punctuate the following:

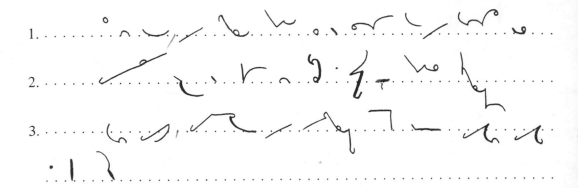

1. . . . . . . . . . . . . . . . . . . . . . . . . . . . . . . . . . . . . . . . . . . . . . . . . . . . . . . . . . . . . . . . . . . . . . . .

2. . . . . . . . . . . . . . . . . . . . . . . . . . . . . . . . . . . . . . . . . . . . . . . . . . . . . . . . . . . . . . . . . . . . . . . .

3. . . . . . . . . . . . . . . . . . . . . . . . . . . . . . . . . . . . . . . . . . . . . . . . . . . . . . . . . . . . . . . . . . . . . . . .

. . . . . . . . . . . . . . . . . . . . . . . . . . . . . . . . . . . . . . . . . . . . . . . . . . . . . . . . . . . . . . . . . . . . . . . . . .

## Transcription Tips

If you are given special instructions about the handling of a particular letter, write the instructions in your notebook.

24

# 4

## VOCABULARY BUILDING

expansion 1. 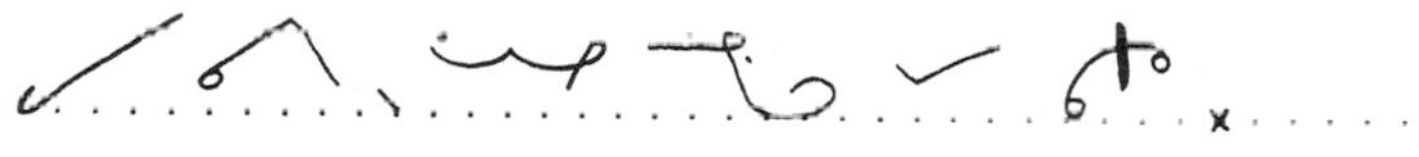

interview 2. 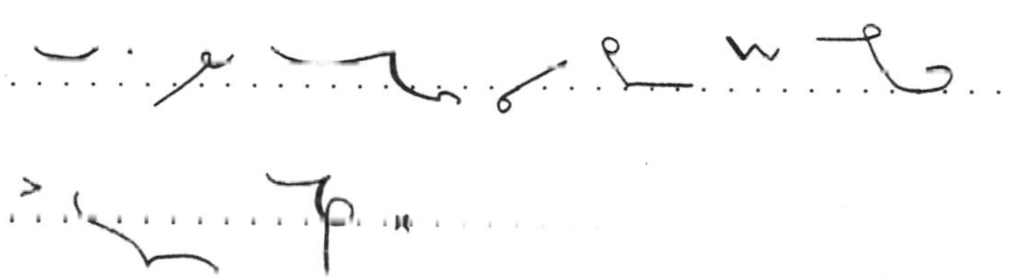

demonstration 3. 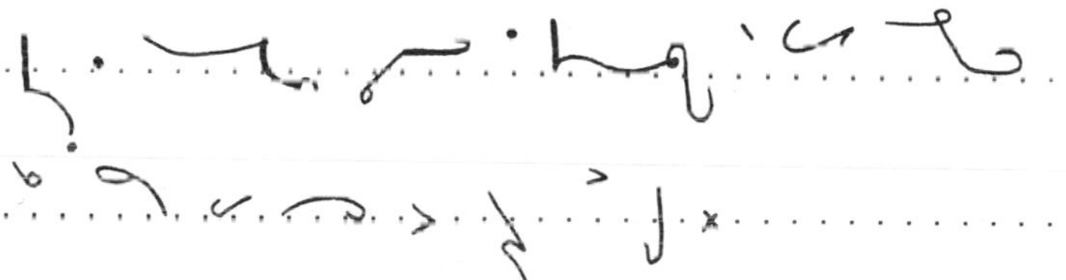

specify 4. 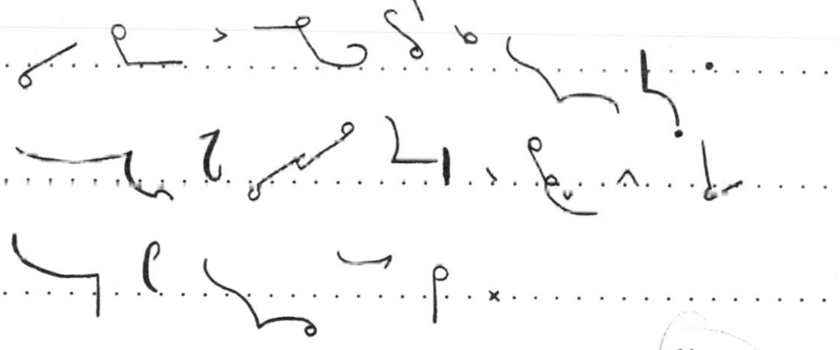

conference facilities 5. 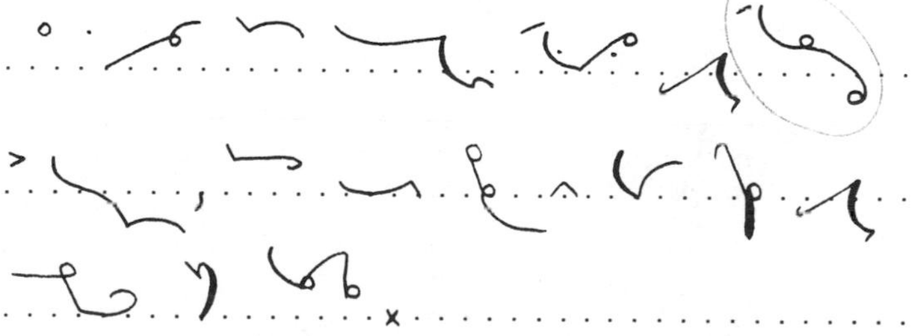

patronage 6.

signature 7.

privilege 8.

## THEORY PRACTICE

# (SPEED BUILDING PRACTICE)

# TRANSCRIPTION LETTERS

**Preview**

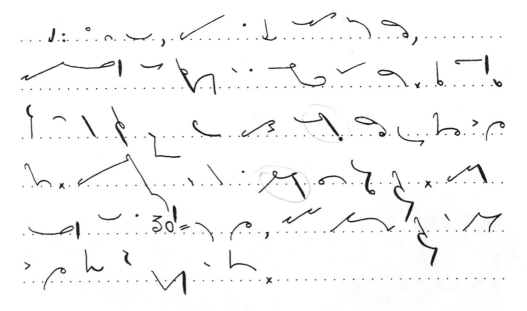

possibility      occurred      neighboring      prepared      require

renewal      period

Union Realty Company
P.O. Box 2006
Hamilton, Ontario

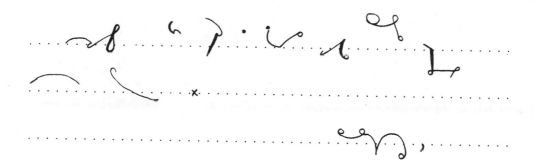

## Preview

| owners | expire | grant | forbids | acceptable |
| --- | --- | --- | --- | --- |

Madison Dry Cleaning Company
98 Sparks Street
Ottawa, Ontario

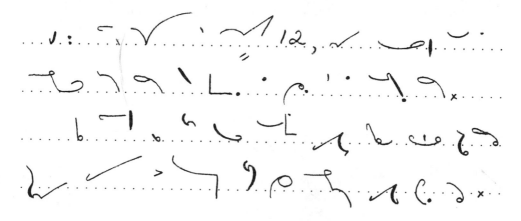

## BUSINESS UNDERSTANDING

What is meant by a "lease" and how is it used in renting a store or an apartment? What would be the value of a "privilege to renew a lease"?

## Preview

granting

Union Realty Company
P.O. Box 2006
Hamilton, Ontario

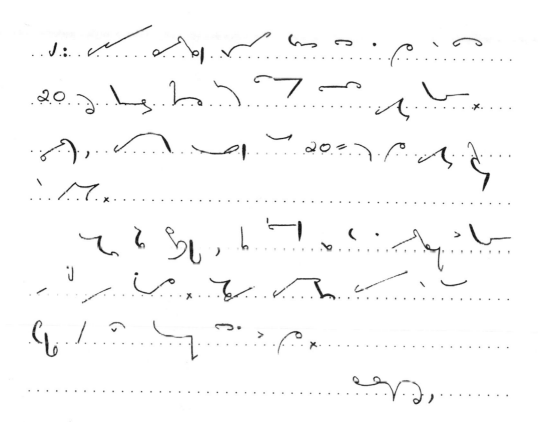

## TRANSCRIPTION SKILL DEVELOPMENT

### Spelling

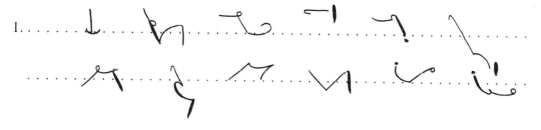

2. . . . . . .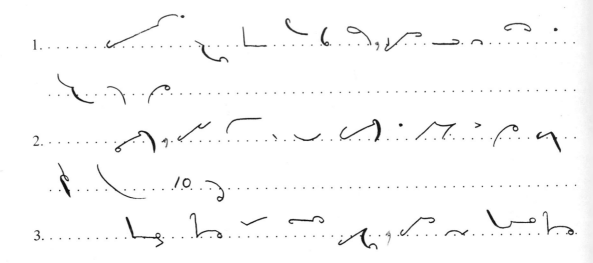

3. . . . . . .

## Punctuation

Punctuate the following:

1. . . . . . .

2. . . . . . .

3. . . . . . .

## Transcription Tips

If you take dictation from different persons, use a separate notebook for each one.

# 5

## VOCABULARY BUILDING

convinced     1.

budget
experiment     2.

employees     3.

steadily     4.

impressed     5.

private 6.

unfortunately 7.

## THEORY PRACTICE

1 + 1B.

## SPEED BUILDING PRACTICE

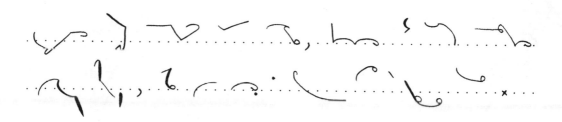

# TRANSCRIPTION LETTERS

**Preview**

obligated    husband's    provisions    sublet    province

Metropolitan Realty Corporation
504 Princess Avenue
Brandon, Manitoba

## Preview

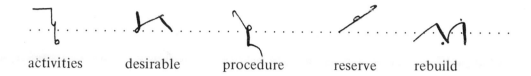

| activities | desirable | procedure | reserve | rebuild |

Mrs. Lois Hanson
36 Albert Street
Regina, Saskatchewan

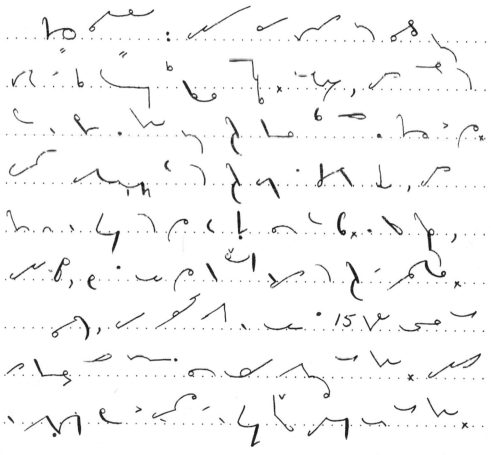

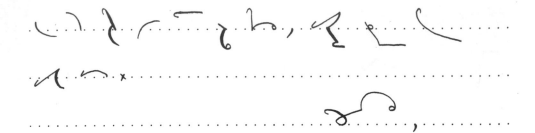

## BUSINESS UNDERSTANDING

What is meant by "subletting" an apartment? What are its advantages and disadvantages to the tenant and to the landlord?

## Preview

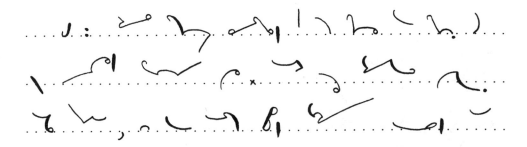

permitting    released    contact

Metropolitan Realty Corporation
504 Princess Avenue
Brandon, Manitoba

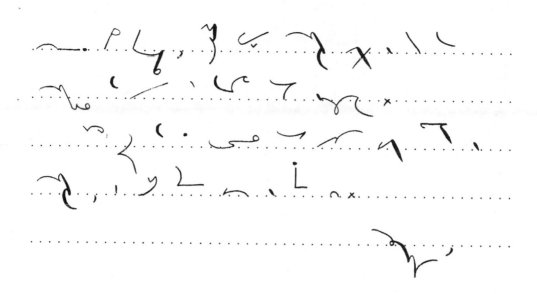

## TRANSCRIPTION SKILL DEVELOPMENT

**Spelling**

1. ................................................................

2. ................................................................

3. ................................................................

**Punctuation**

Punctuate the following:

1. ................................................................

39

2. ......................................................................................................

3. ......................................................................................................

......................................................................................................

## Transcription Tips

File all carbon copies of completed letters as soon as possible. Your employer may want a letter to which he has just dictated a reply. If it hasn't been filed, it may be difficult to find.

# 6

## VOCABULARY BUILDING

association 1. 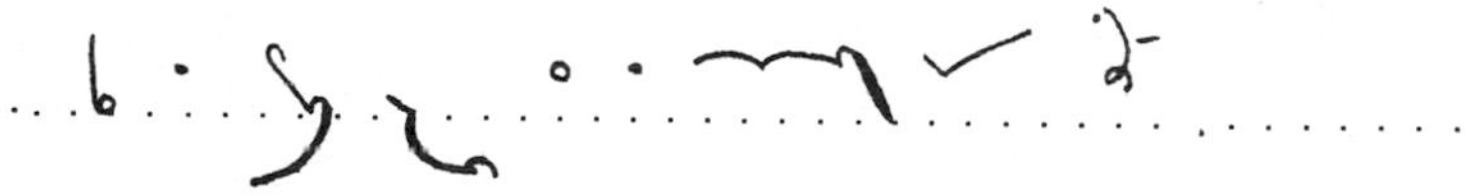

variety 2. 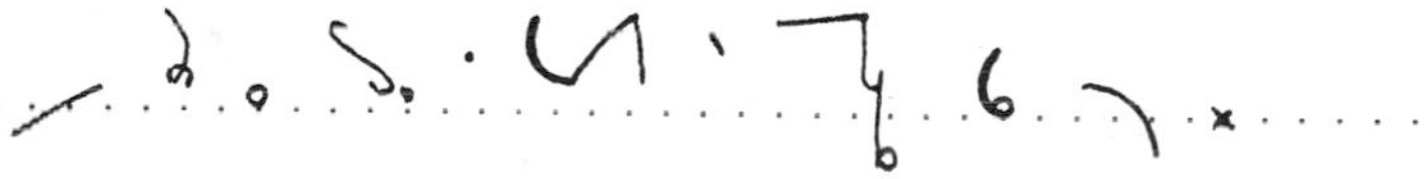

encourage functions 3. 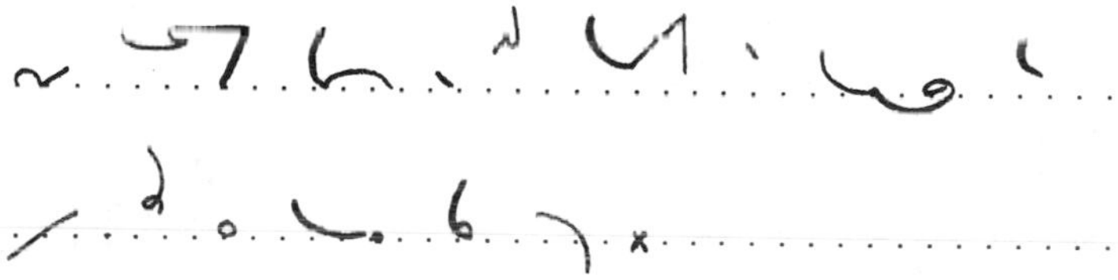

interfere 4. 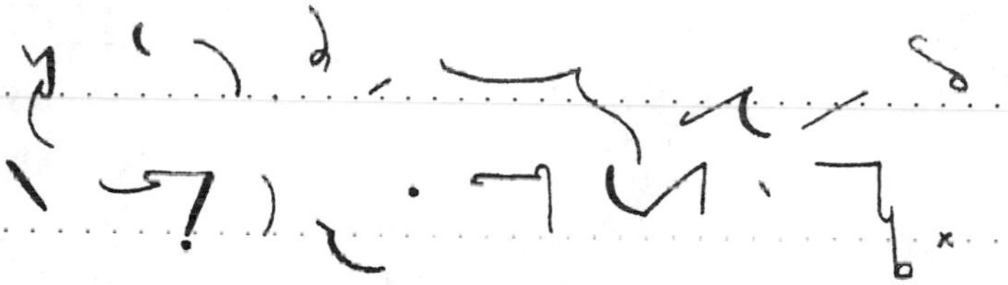

discussion 5. 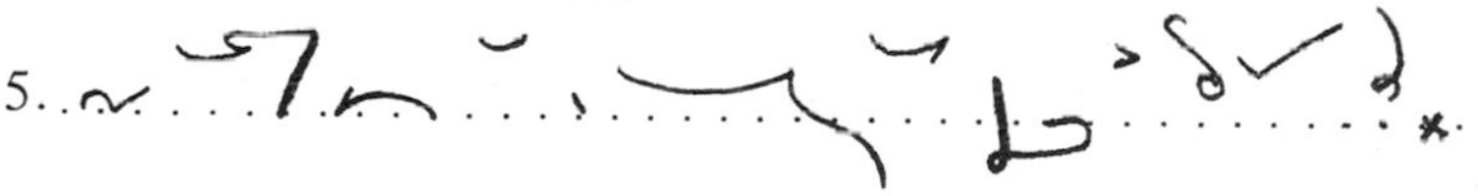

instrument 6. 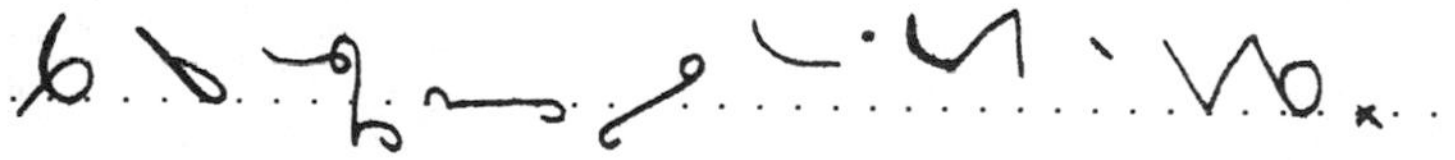

extensive 7. 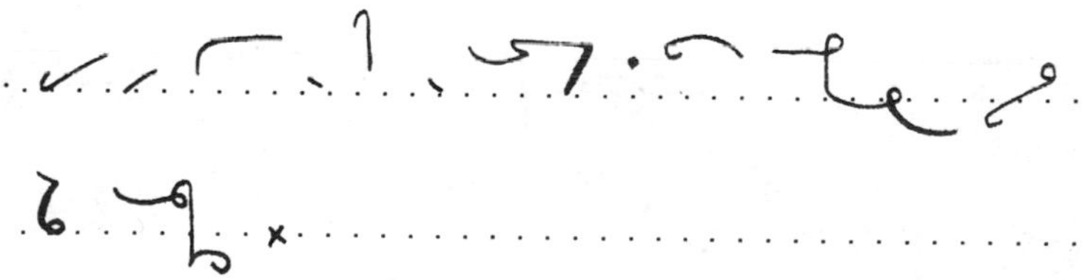

installed 8.

## THEORY PRACTICE

# SPEED BUILDING PRACTICE

## TRANSCRIPTION LETTERS

**Preview**

deposit          securities

Provincial Trust Company
160 Borden Avenue North
Fort William, Ontario

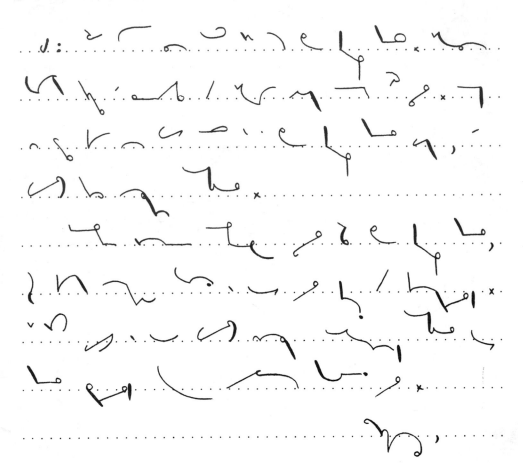

**Preview**

facilities　　slightly　　limited　　furnish　　duplicate　　permission

44

Mr. Paul B. Franklin
64 Jackson Avenue
Toronto 18, Ontario

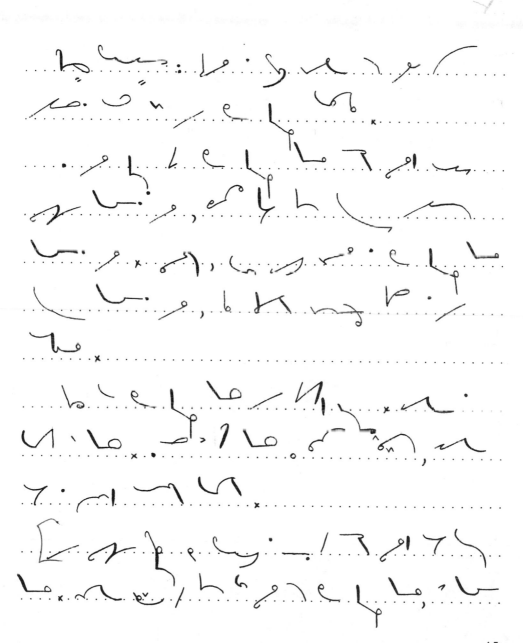

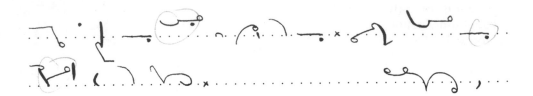

## BUSINESS UNDERSTANDING

What is a "safe deposit box" and what are its uses?

## Preview

................................................
containing

Provincial Trust Company
160 Borden Avenue North
Fort William, Ontario

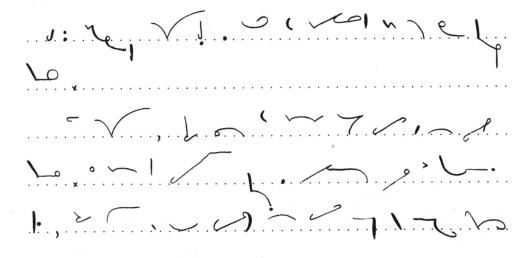

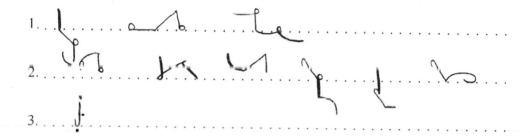

## TRANSCRIPTION SKILL DEVELOPMENT

### Spelling

1.

2.

3.

### Punctuation

Punctuate the following:

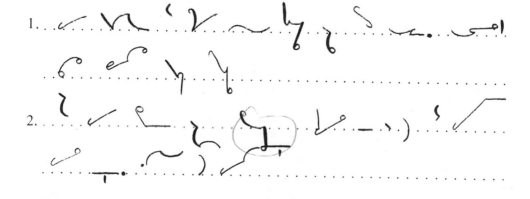

3. 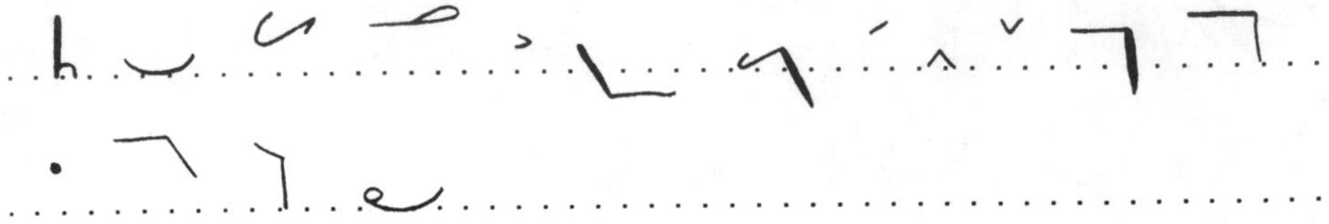 ⌐ ⌐ ⌐ ⌐ ⌐ ⌐ ⌐ ⌐ ⌐ ⌐ ⌐ ⌐

⌐ ⌐ ⌐ ⌐

## Transcription Tips

When a figure such as $25.49 is dictated to you, it should be written $25^{49}$ in your shorthand notes. It should, of course, be transcribed $25.49.

# 7

## VOCABULARY BUILDING

standard

1.

competent

2.

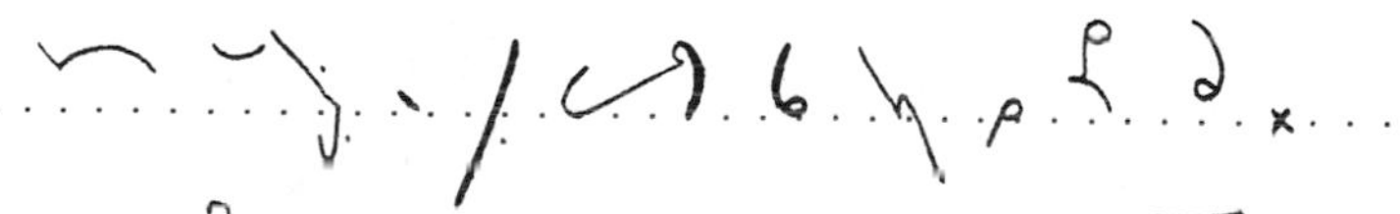

courteous

3.

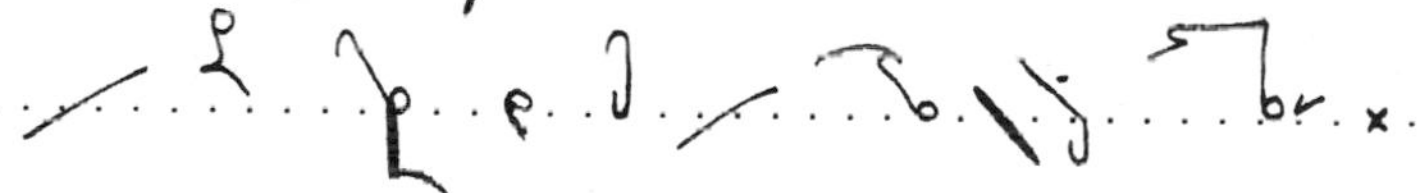

attend

4.

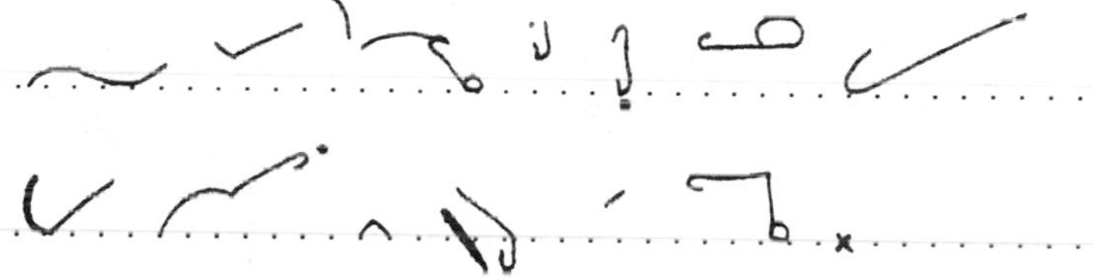

afford

5.

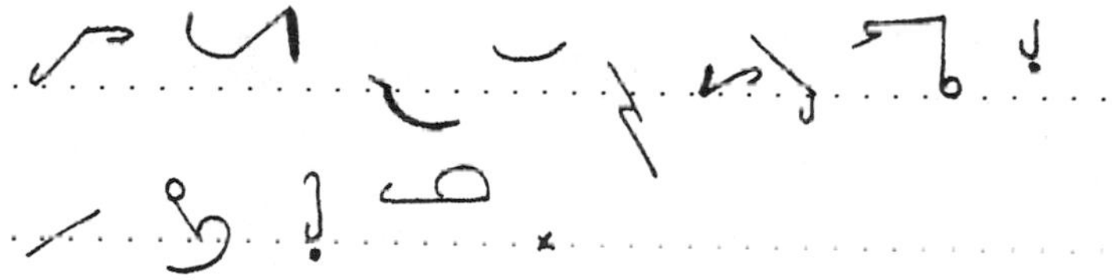

maximum

6.

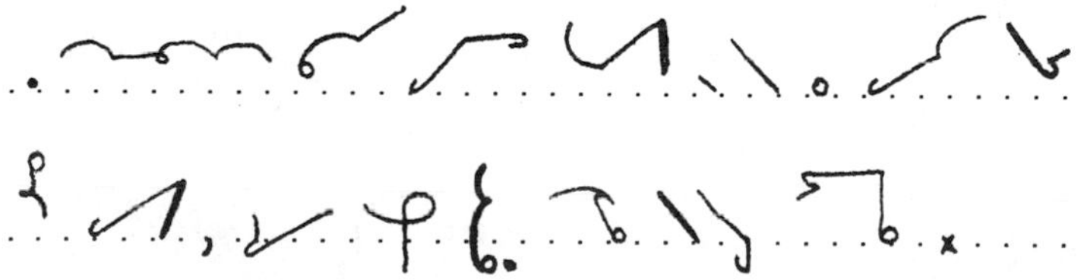

superior

7.

current        8.

## THEORY PRACTICE

# SPEED BUILDING PRACTICE

## Preview

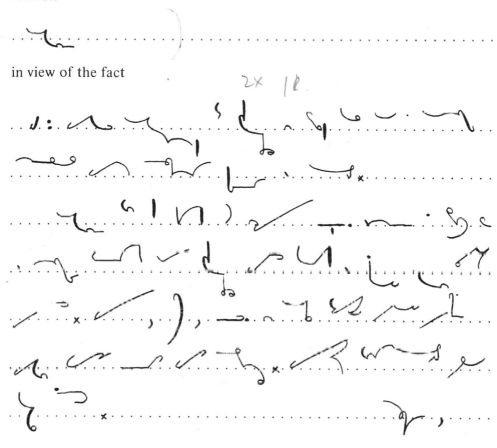

in view of the fact

## TRANSCRIPTION LETTERS

## Preview

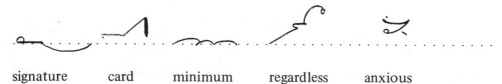

signature    card    minimum    regardless    anxious

Note the intersections

Municipal Bank and Trust Company
150 East 24th Street
New York, New York 10017

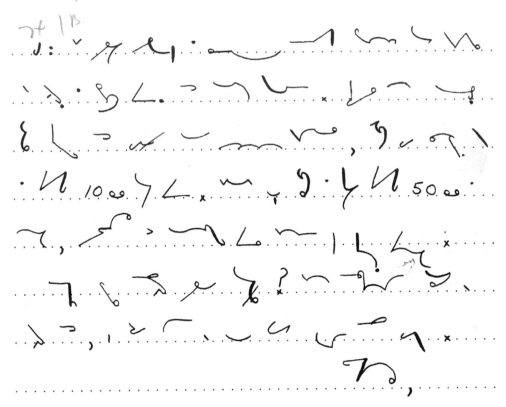

**Preview**

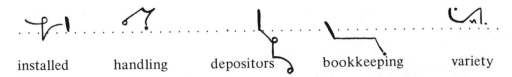

installed    handling    depositors    bookkeeping    variety

52

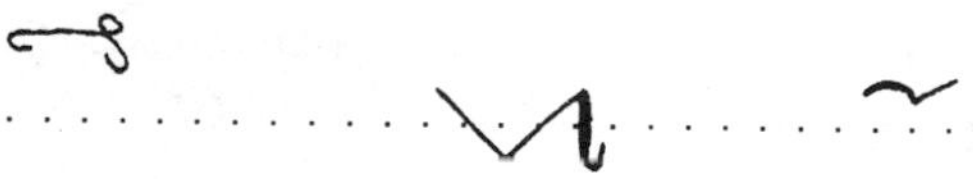

......⌐s............∿............⌒.........∿................................................
correspond        period of        moderate

Mrs. Eileen Jansen
54 Dale Avenue
Toronto 12, Ontario

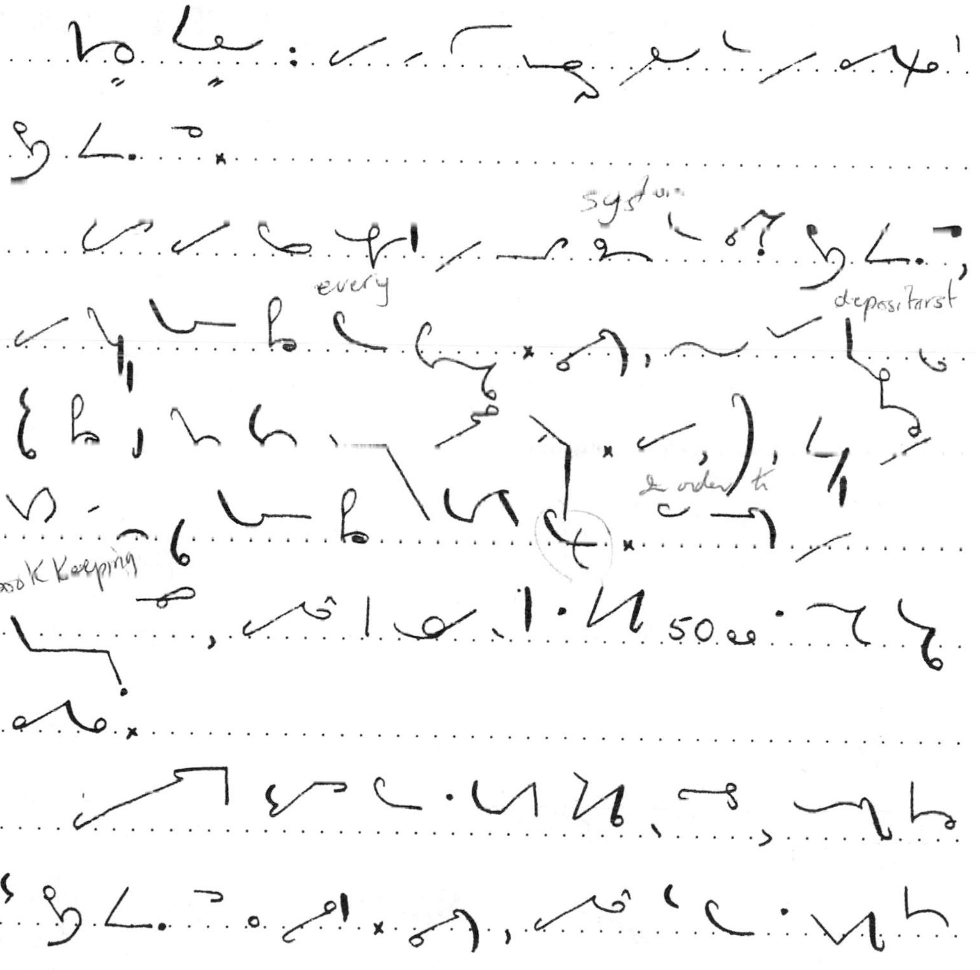

*(shorthand lines with interlinear notes)*

*system*

*every*                                                          *depositors'*

*book keeping*                                    *I order to*

50

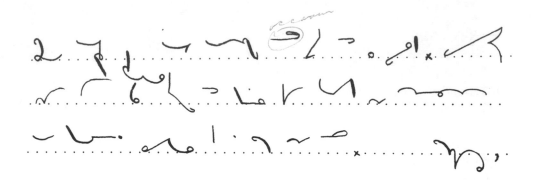

## BUSINESS UNDERSTANDING

What is meant by a "special checking account" and what are its advantages and disadvantages?

## Preview

while          appreciate

Municipal Bank and Trust Company
150 East 24th Street
New York, New York 10017

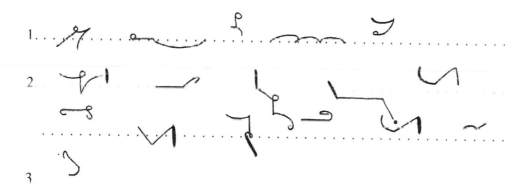

## TRANSCRIPTION SKILL DEVELOPMENT

### Spelling

1.

2.

3.

### Punctuation

Punctuate the following:

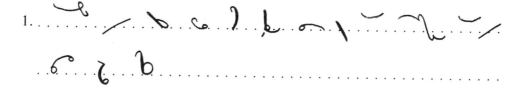

1.

2.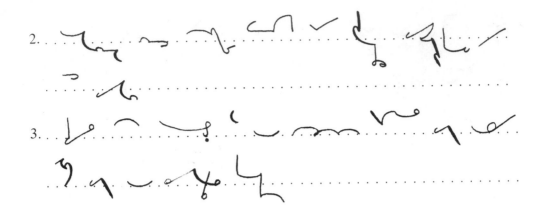

3.

## Transcription Tips

If a figure containing only dollars ($125) is dictated to you, it should be transcribed as $125 without a period or the two zeros after it.

# 8

## VOCABULARY BUILDING

display 1. [shorthand outline]

protest 2. [shorthand outline]

interior 3. [shorthand outline]

fashion 4. [shorthand outline]

expert 5. [shorthand outline]

delighted 6. [shorthand outline]

complaining    7.

competition    8.

## THEORY PRACTICE

# SPEED BUILDING PRACTICE

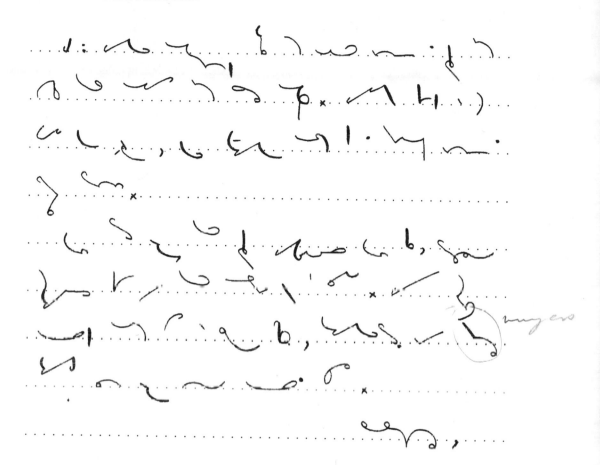

# TRANSCRIPTION LETTERS

## Preview

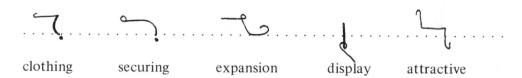

| clothing | securing | expansion | display | attractive |

transaction    involve    approximately

National Bank and Trust Company
Three Rivers
Quebec

**Preview**

incorporated    indicate    security    standard    forwarded concern    collateral    previous    branch

Fitwell Dresses Incorporated
Arvida
Quebec

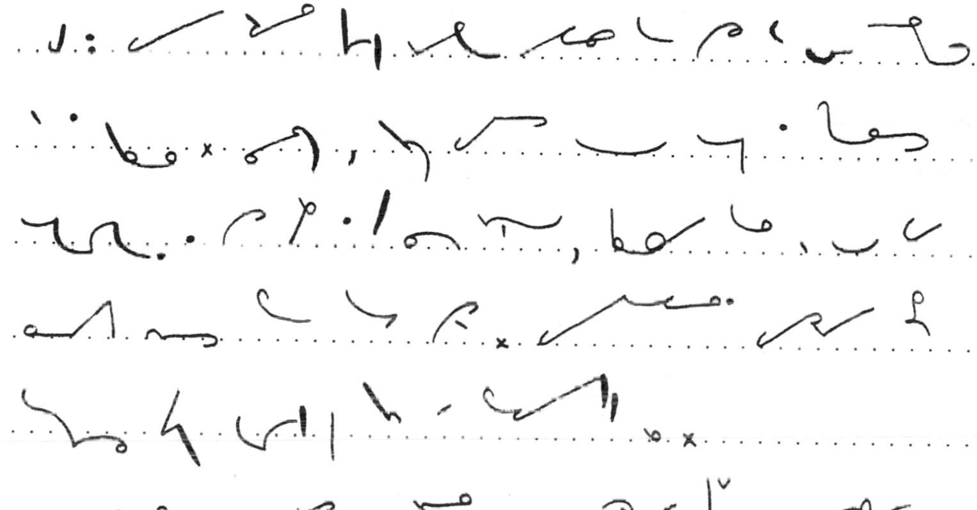

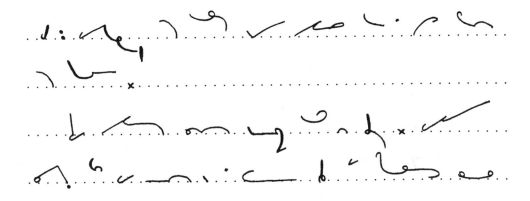

## BUSINESS UNDERSTANDING

What is meant by "collateral" and why is it used in obtaining a loan?

**Preview**

some time     quick     decision     mentioned

National Bank and Trust Company
Three Rivers
Quebec

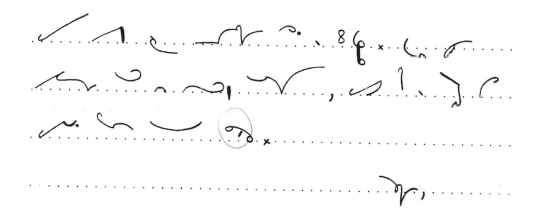

## TRANSCRIPTION SKILL DEVELOPMENT

### Spelling

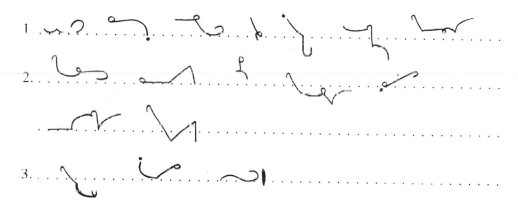

### Punctuation

Punctuate the following:

1.

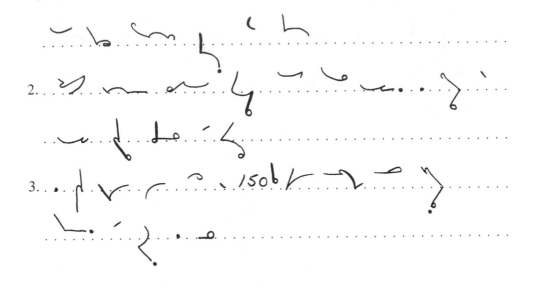

2.

3. 150

## Transcription Tips

When transcribing, type out in full all numbers one to ten. Always spell out numbers at the beginning of a sentence.

# 9

## VOCABULARY BUILDING

economy       1.

distinctive
printed       2.

identification       3.

omit       4.

security       5.

enlarging
capacity       6.

65

# THEORY PRACTICE

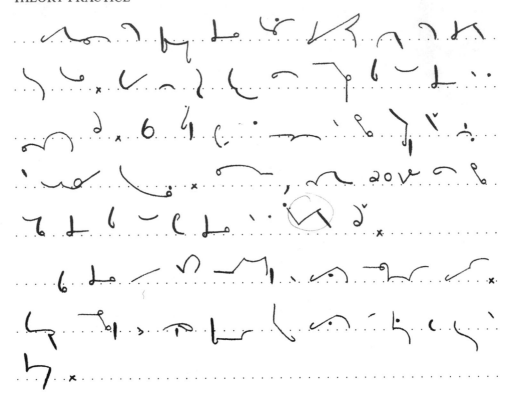

# SPEED BUILDING PRACTICE

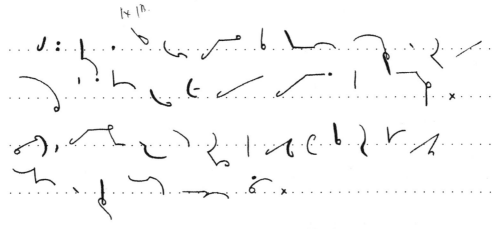

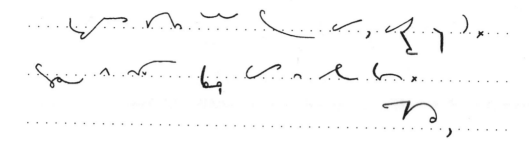

## TRANSCRIPTION LETTERS

**Preview**

figure    disagrees    error    intended    explanation

Central Bank and Trust Company $2 \times 13$.
Greenwood Shopping Plaza
Ottawa, Ontario

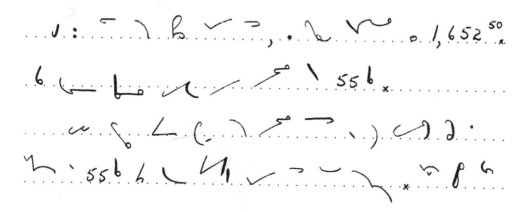

## Preview

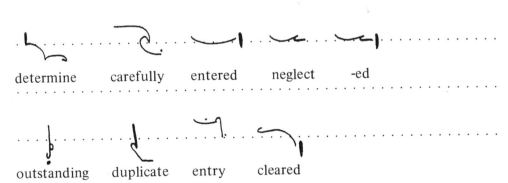

determine    carefully    entered    neglect    -ed

outstanding    duplicate    entry    cleared

James Borden and Brothers Incorporated
P.O. Box 22
Pembroke, Ontario

## BUSINESS UNDERSTANDING

What is a "bank statement"? What is meant by an "outstanding" cheque? How do outstanding cheques affect your bank balance?

**Preview**

followed       suggestion

Central Bank and Trust Company
Greenwood Shopping Plaza
Ottawa, Ontario

# TRANSCRIPTION SKILL DEVELOPMENT

## Spelling

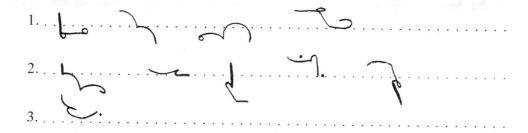

## Punctuation

Punctuate the following:

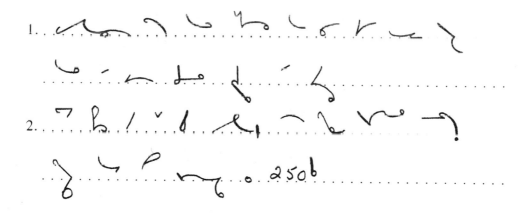

## Transcription Tips

When typing dates always use the full spelling of the month. The letters "st", "rd", "nd", or "th" should not be used after the day of the month.

# 10

## VOCABULARY BUILDING

ambitious
faithful

1. 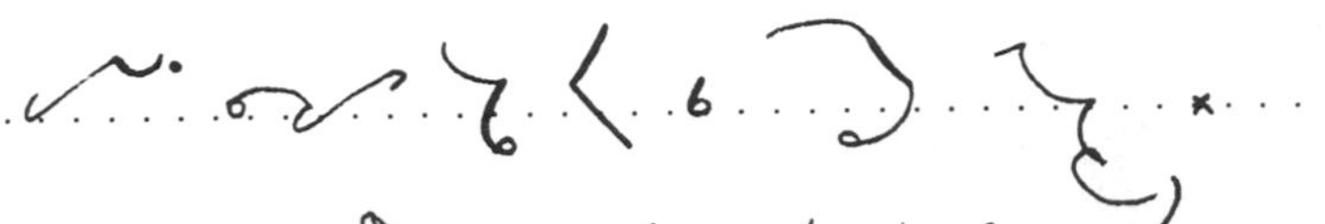

supplementary

2. 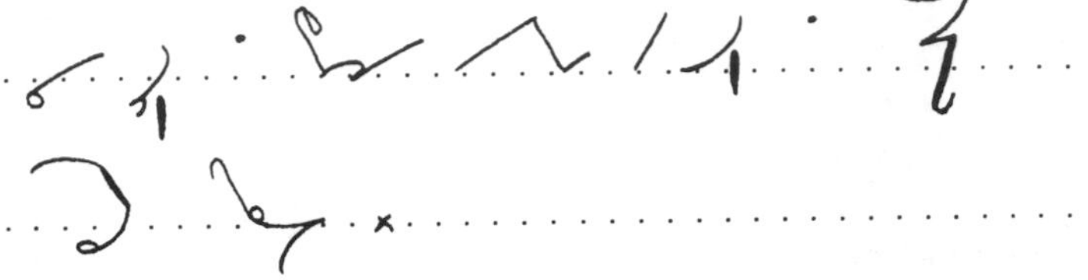

highlights

3. 

assignment

4. 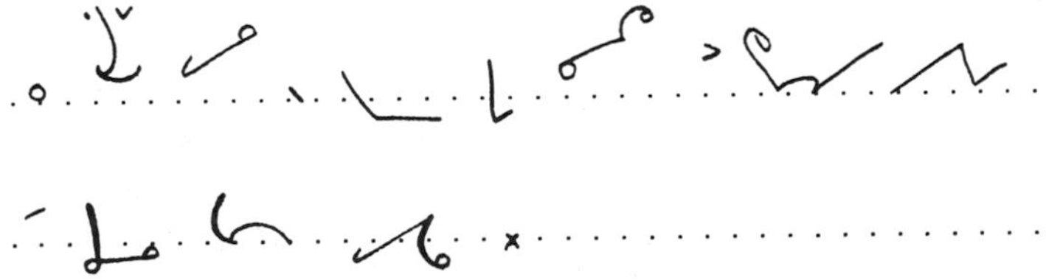

ascertain

5. 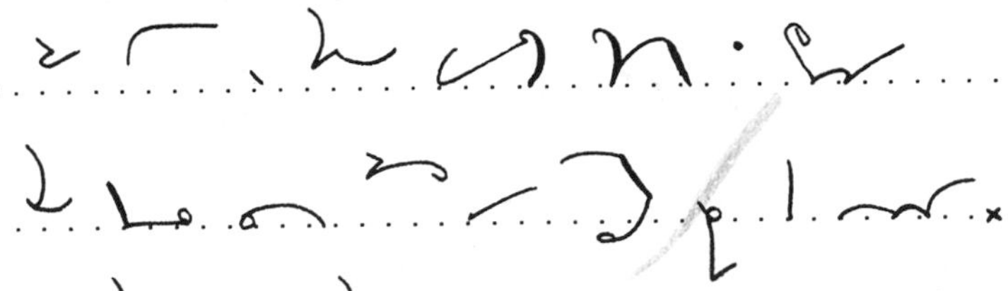

surrounding

6. 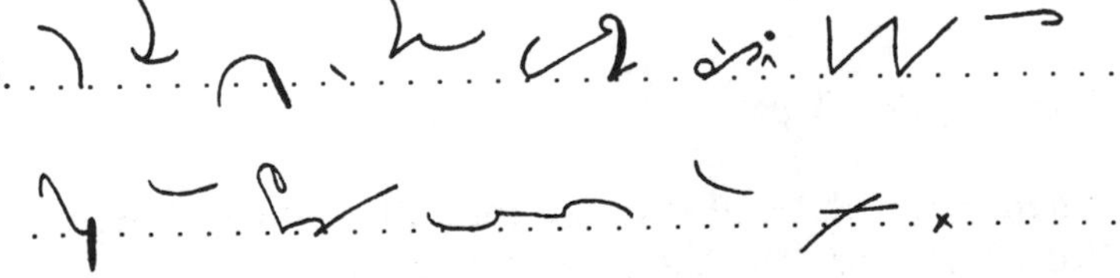

circulation 7.

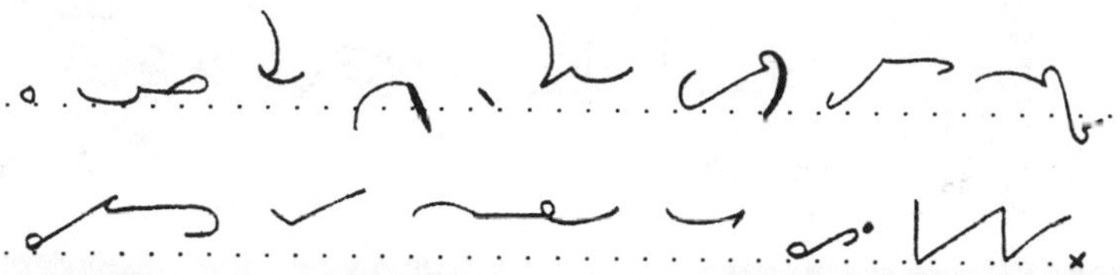

*(shorthand outlines)*

## THEORY PRACTICE

*(shorthand outlines)*

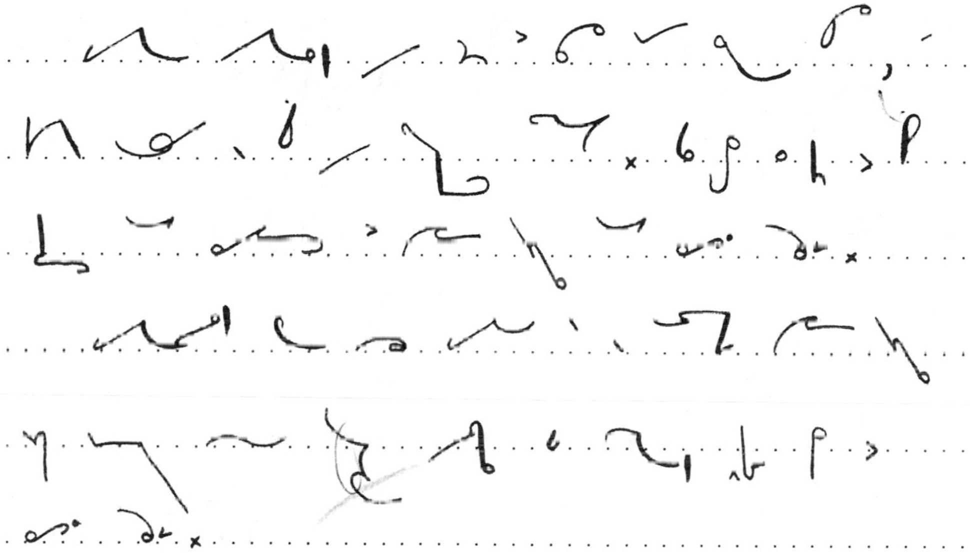

## SPEED BUILDING PRACTICE

**Preview**

*(shorthand outlines)*

as a result

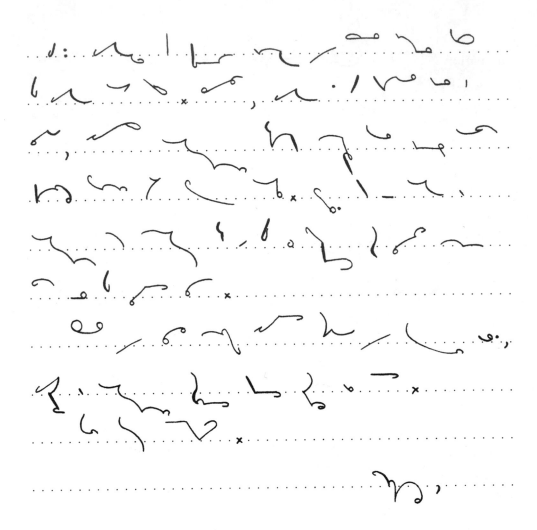

## TRANSCRIPTION LETTERS

**Preview**

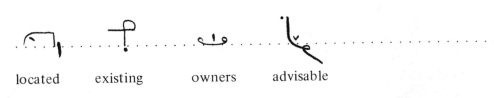

located     existing     owners     advisable

Kingston Savings Bank
102 Main Street
Kingston, Ontario

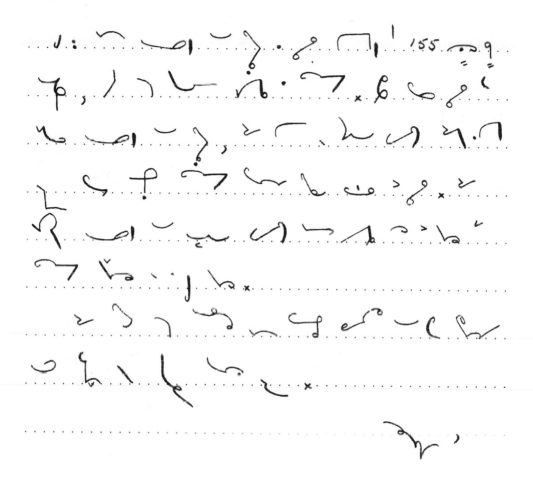

**Preview**

assist    easily    efficient    -ly    -cy    completely

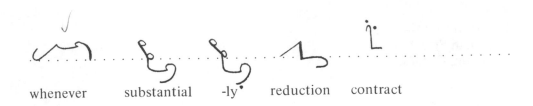

| whenever | substantial | -ly | reduction | contract |

Mr. Lawrence J. Thompson
24 Douglas Street
Woodstock, Ontario

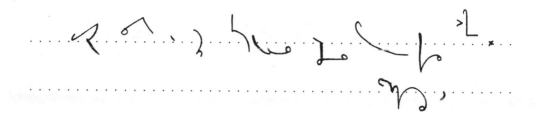

## BUSINESS UNDERSTANDING

What effect would the size of a "down payment" on a house have on the number and size of the monthly payments?

## Preview

prefer      reconsider

Kingston Savings Bank
102 Main Street
Kingston, Ontario

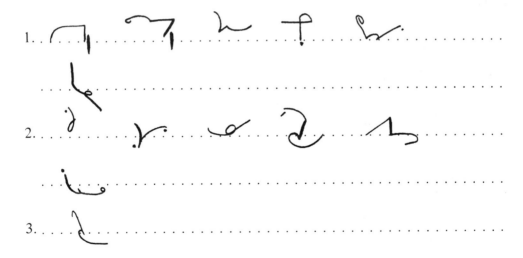

## TRANSCRIPTION SKILL DEVELOPMENT

**Spelling**

1.

2.

3.

**Punctuation**

Punctuate the following:

1.

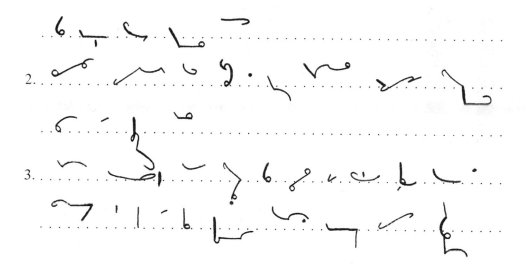

## Transcription Tips

If a number above twenty is dictated to you, write it in longhand numbers in your notes. Large numbers are generally typed in figures rather than spelled out.

# 11

## VOCABULARY BUILDING

frankly
disappointed

1. 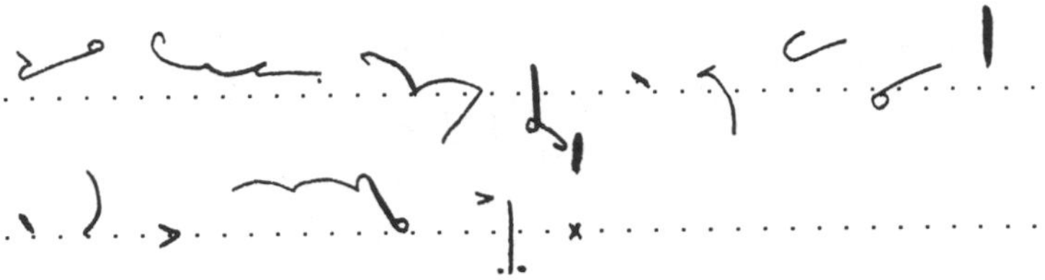 [shorthand]

√ situated

2. 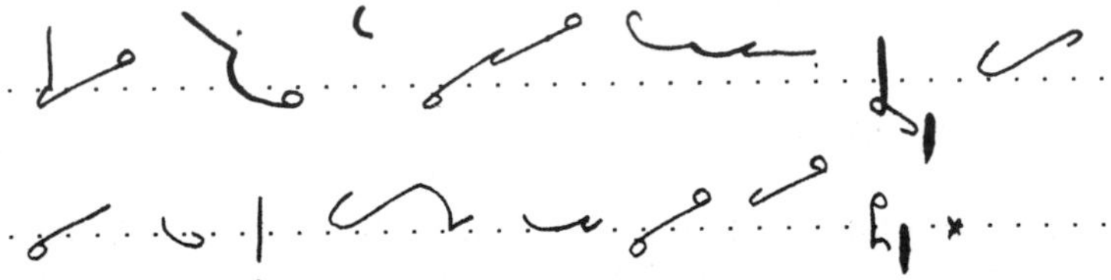 [shorthand]

furnishing

3. 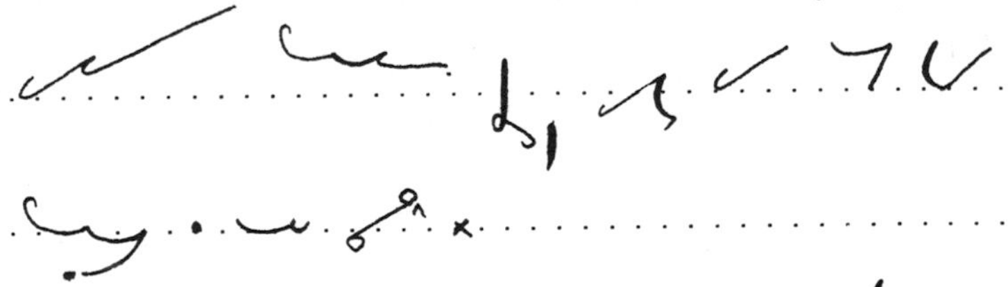 [shorthand]

desirable

4. 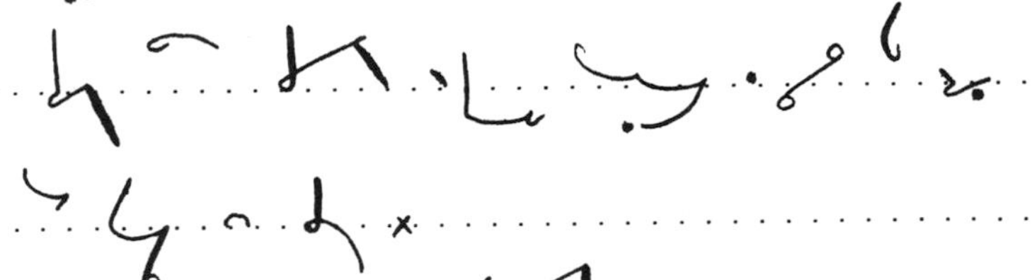 [shorthand]

consulted

5. 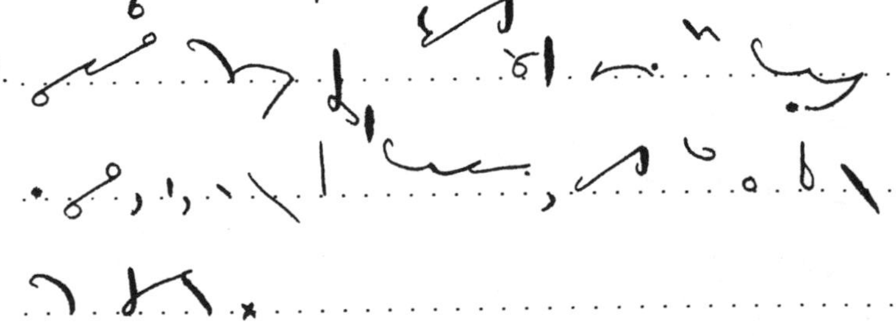 [shorthand]

80

reduction     6.

authorize     7.

**THEORY PRACTICE**     2× 1B

SPEED BUILDING PRACTICE

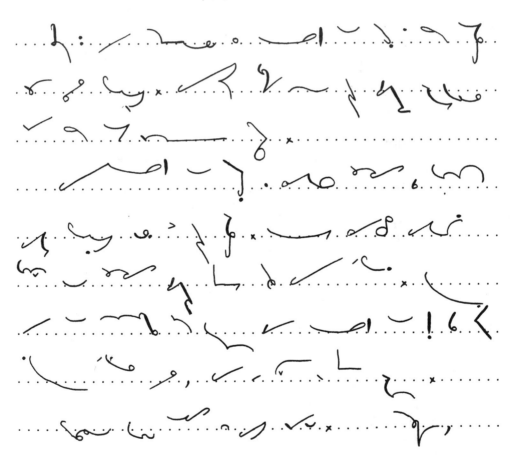

# TRANSCRIPTION LETTERS

## Preview

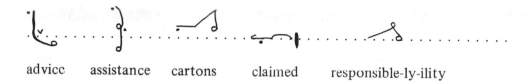

advice    assistance    cartons    claimed    responsible-ly-ility

Mr. Arnold Black
Black and Berman
Sunnyside
Trinity Bay, Newfoundland

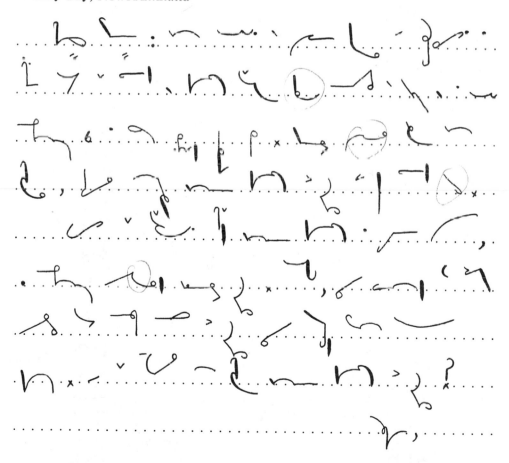

**Preview**

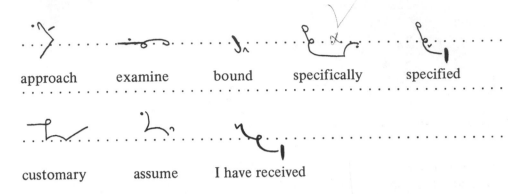

approach    examine    bound    specifically    specified

customary    assume    I have received

Mr. Frank Jacobs
Uptown Paper Company
161 John Street
Hamilton, Ontario

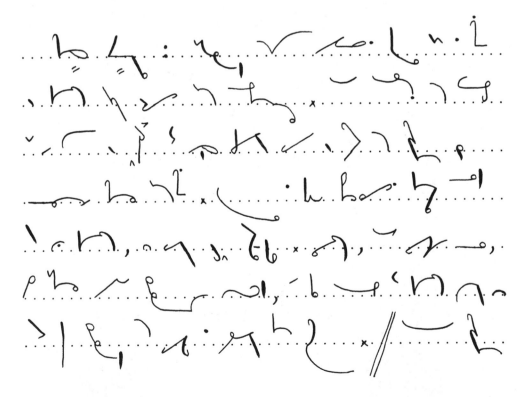

84

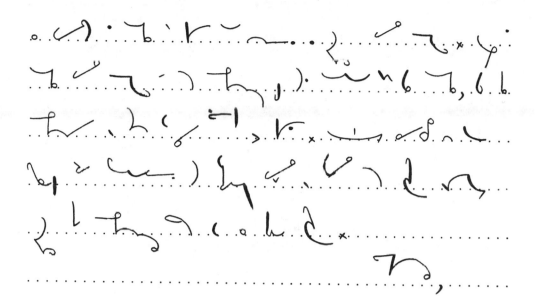

## BUSINESS UNDERSTANDING

Can a lawyer take information furnished to him by a client and use it against the client or for his own purposes? Why?

**Preview**

recover

Mr. Arnold Black
Black and Berman
Sunnyside
Trinity Bay, Newfoundland

## TRANSCRIPTION SKILL DEVELOPMENT

**Spelling**

1.

2.

3.

## Punctuation

Punctuate the following:

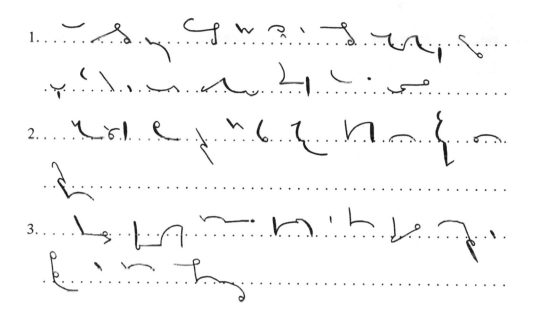

## Transcription Tips

Some fractions, such as three-fourths, are generally spelled in full.

# 12

VOCABULARY BUILDING

essential

1.

excellent

2.

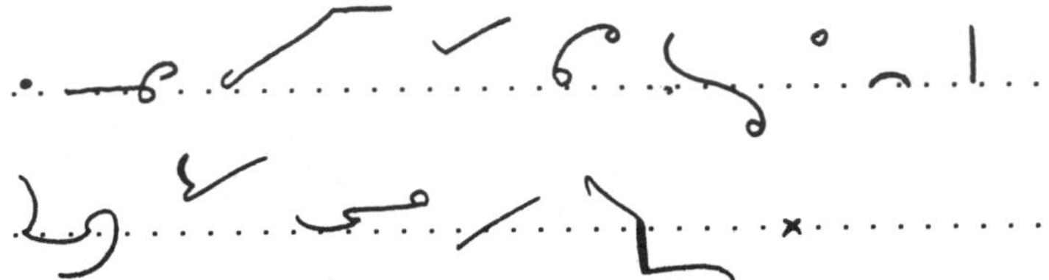

project

3.

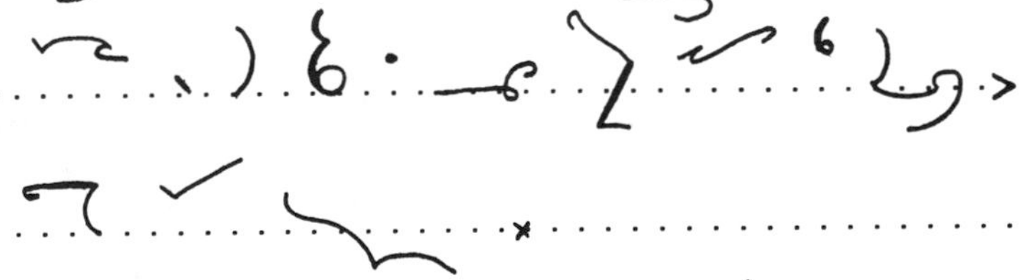

undoubtedly

4.

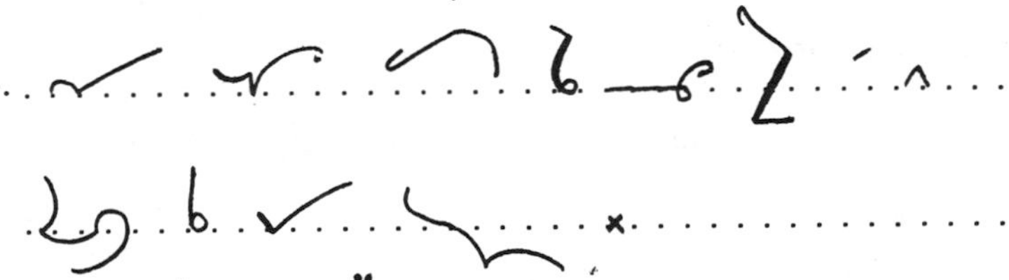

adjacent

5.

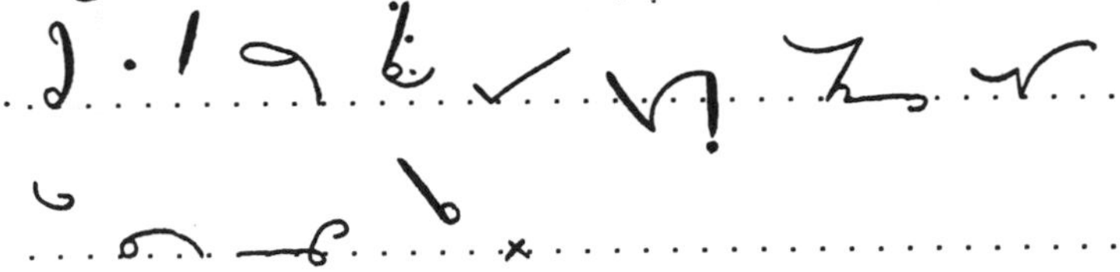

designed

6.

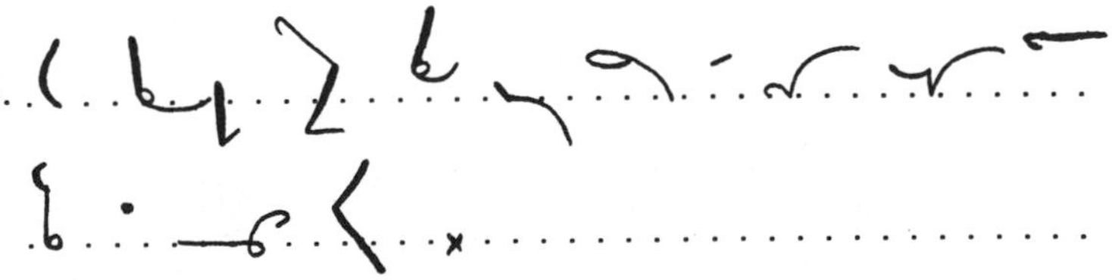

88

inspected     7. (shorthand outline)

architect     8. (shorthand outline)

## THEORY PRACTICE

(shorthand outlines)

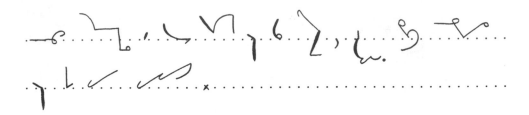

## SPEED BUILDING PRACTICE

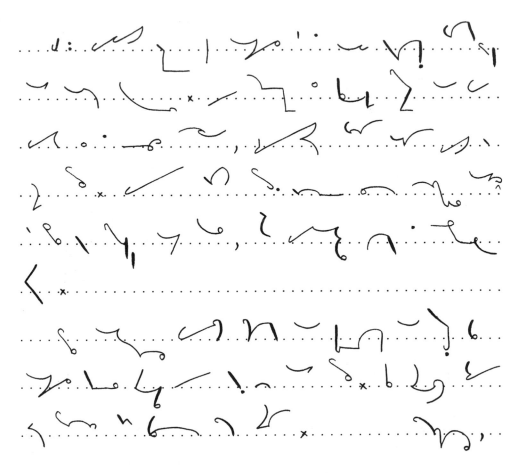

## TRANSCRIPTION LETTERS

### Preview

attorney        collection        suffered        defects        existed

excuse        owe

Messrs. Harwell and Cross
748 Webster Drive
London, Ontario

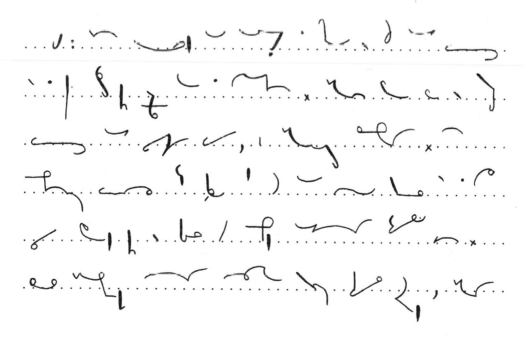

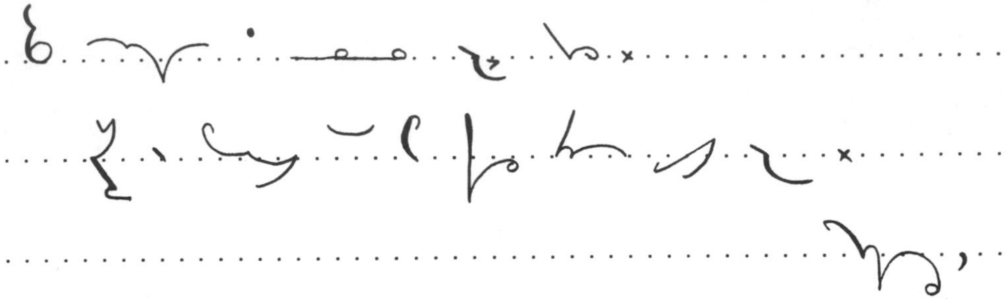

[shorthand outlines]

**Preview**

[shorthand outlines]

| incorporated | utmost | recovery | presentation | data |

[shorthand outlines]

| amicable | correspondence | you have |

Mr. Martin Randolph
Randolph and Miller Incorporated
95 Columbia Road
London, Ontario

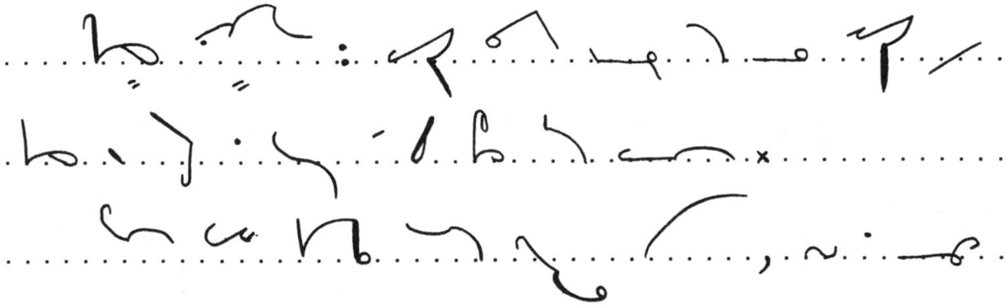

[shorthand outlines]

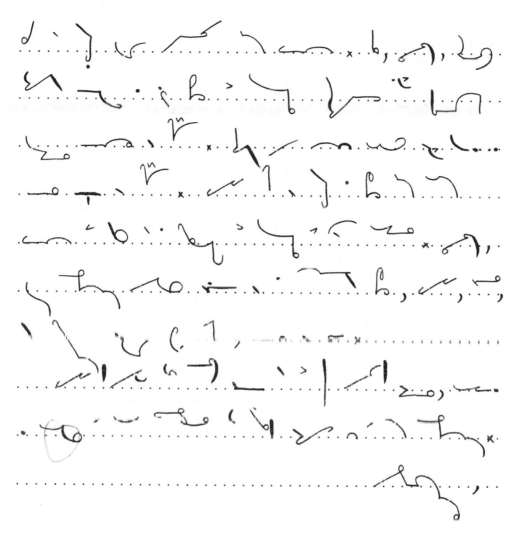

## BUSINESS UNDERSTANDING

When would it be desirable for a lawyer to try to settle a case out of court?

**Preview**

damages      collecting      grounds      entire

Messrs. Harwell and Cross
748 Webster Drive
London, Ontario

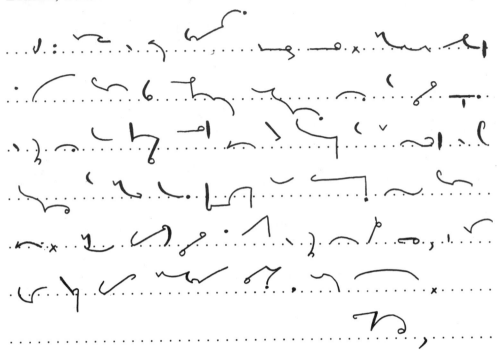

## TRANSCRIPTION SKILL DEVELOPMENT

**Spelling**

3.

## Punctuation

Punctuate the following:

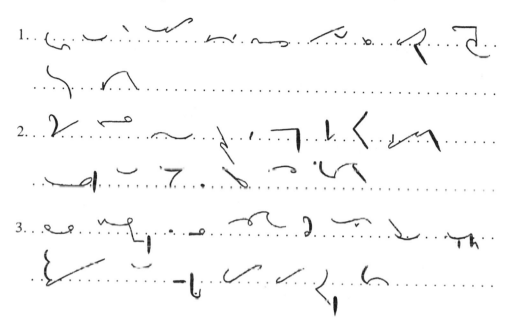

## Transcription Tips

In taking dictation use only those phrases that can be readily understood when transcribing.

# 13

## VOCABULARY BUILDING

annual

1. 

exceptional
display

2. 

gathering

3. 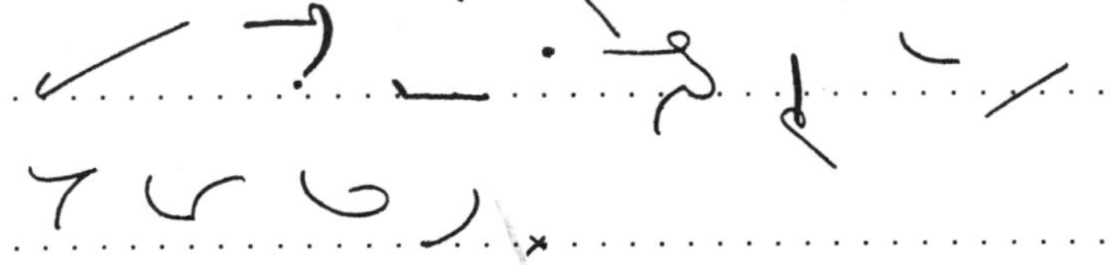

congratulate

4. 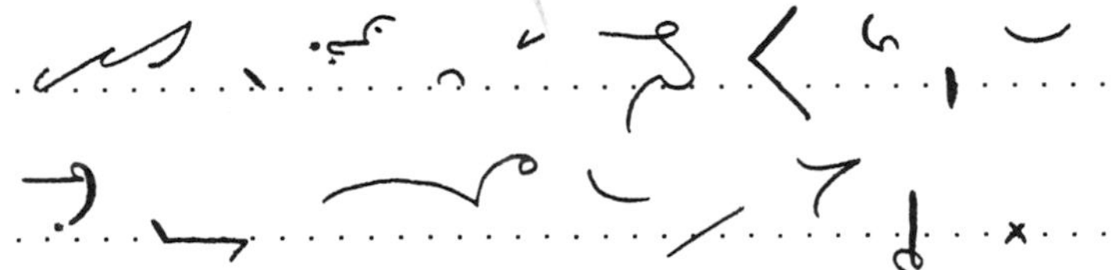

outstanding

5. 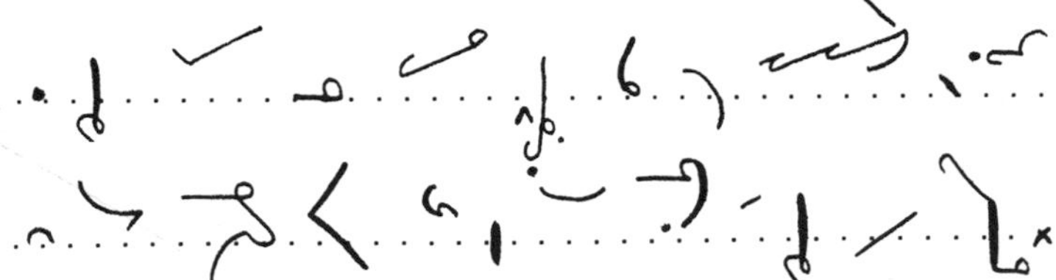

achievement

6. 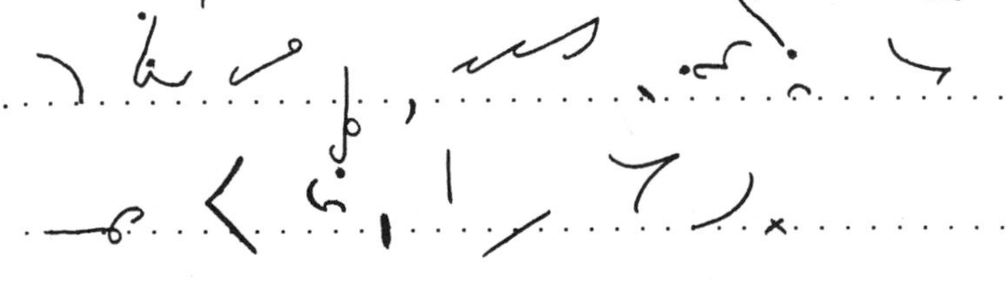

reputation 7.

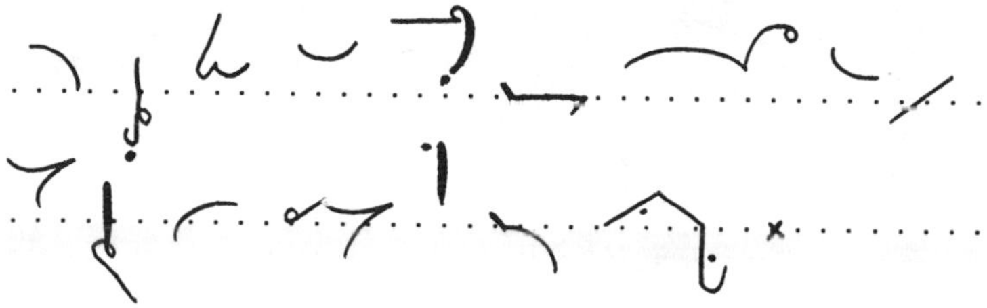

THEORY PRACTICE

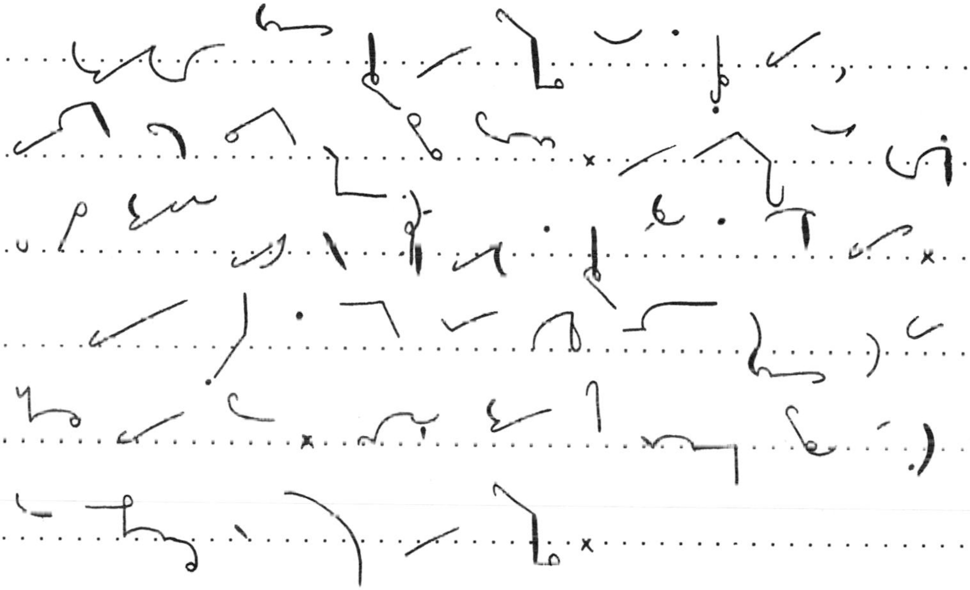

SPEED BUILDING PRACTICE

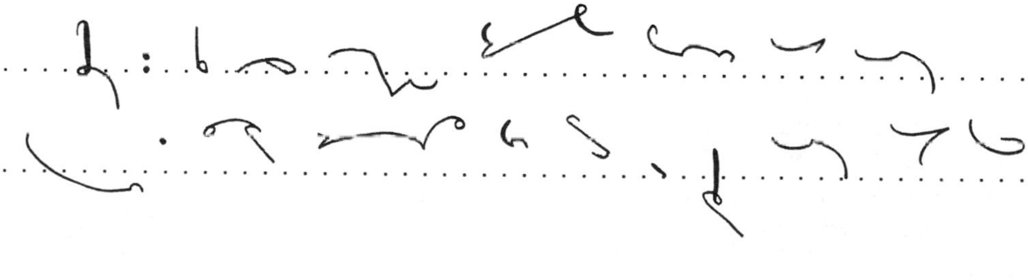

97

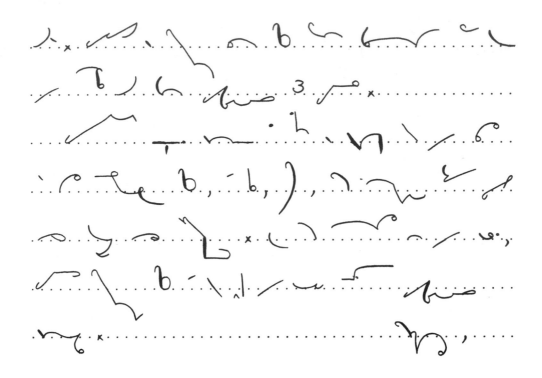

## TRANSCRIPTION LETTERS

**Preview**

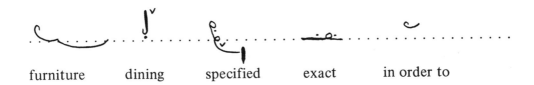

| furniture | dining | specified | exact | in order to |
|-----------|--------|-----------|-------|-------------|

Messrs. Jordan and Harrison
Greystone Building
156 West Street
Woodstock, Ontario

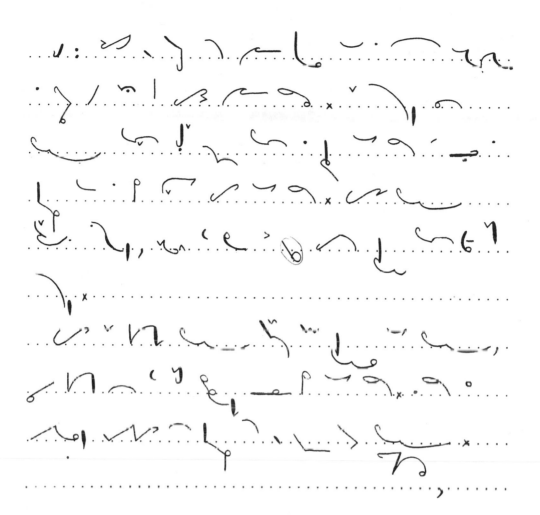

## Preview

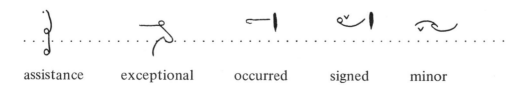

assistance    exceptional    occurred    signed    minor

Mrs. Rita Samuels
288 Nelson Road
Woodstock, Ontario

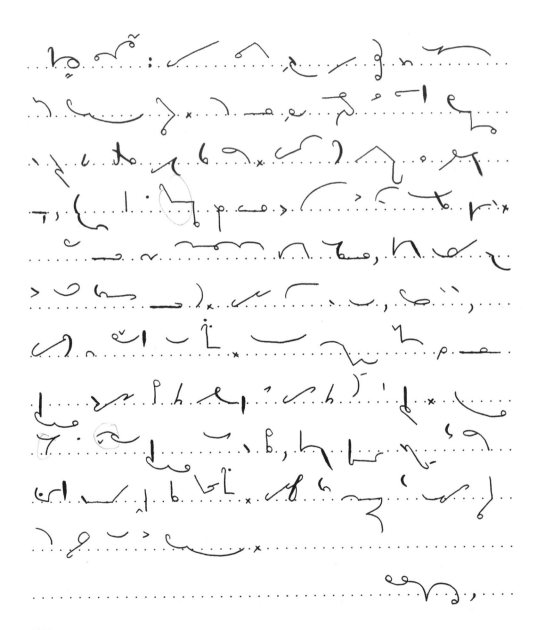

# BUSINESS UNDERSTANDING

What is meant by the expression "letter of the law"?

## Preview

encouraging      definite

Messrs. Jordan and Harrison
Greystone Building
156 West Street
Woodstock, Ontario

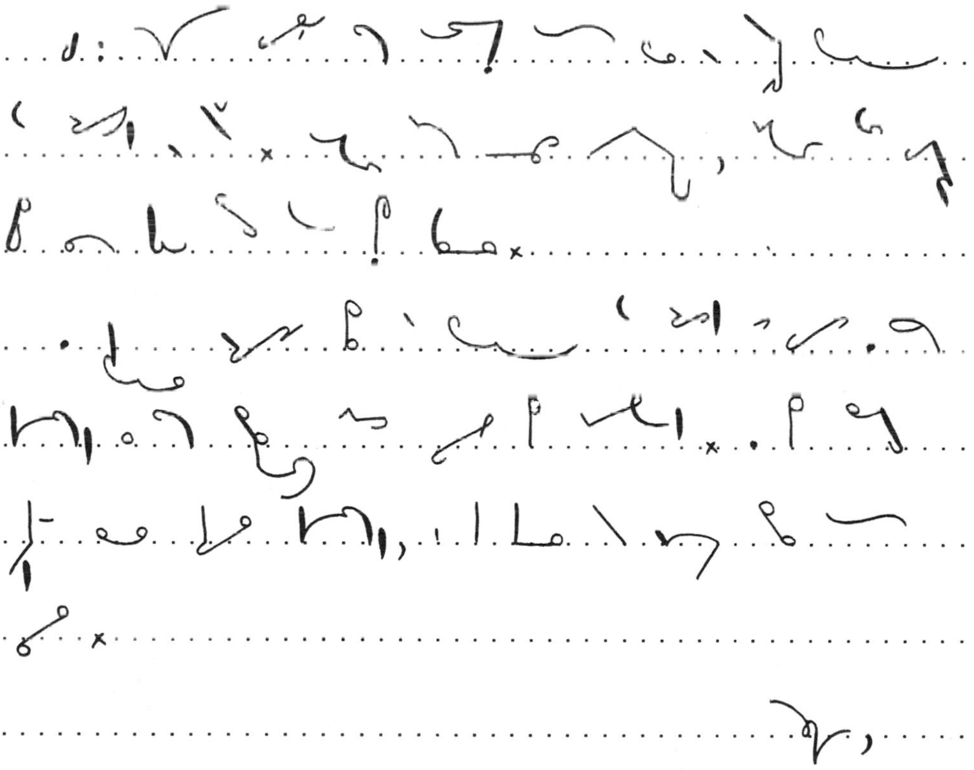

# TRANSCRIPTION SKILL DEVELOPMENT

## Spelling

1. ............................................................

2. ............................................................

3. ............................................................

## Punctuation

Punctuate the following:

1. ............................................................

............................................................

2. ............................................................

............................................................

3. ............................................................

............................................................

## Transcription Tips

When reading back your notes, be especially careful about simple words. Reading a short word incorrectly may throw your reading off completely.

# 14

## VOCABULARY BUILDING

commendable
decorated

1.

competent
combination

2.

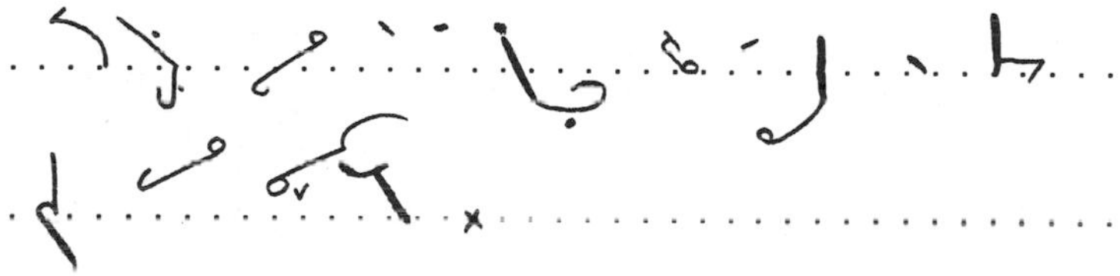

anticipate

3.

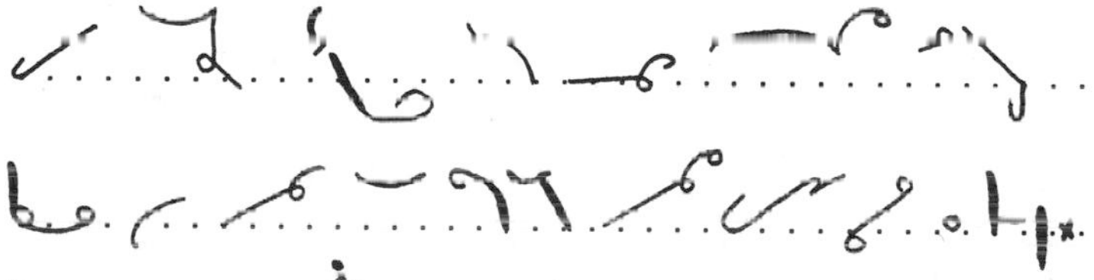

expiration

4.

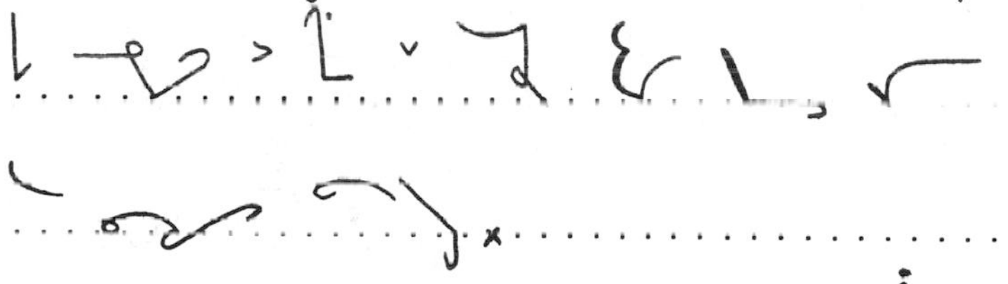

proposed

5.

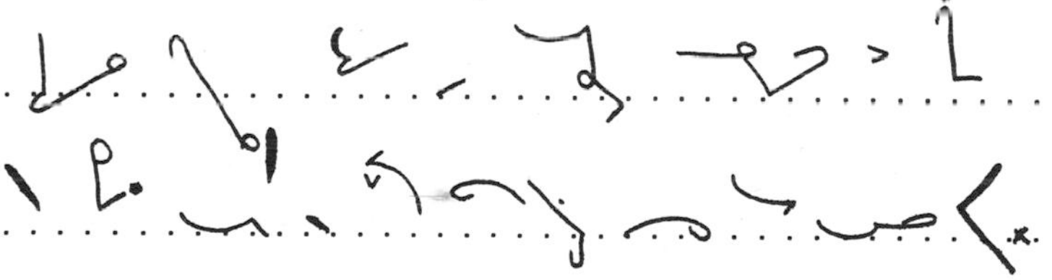

uppermost

6.

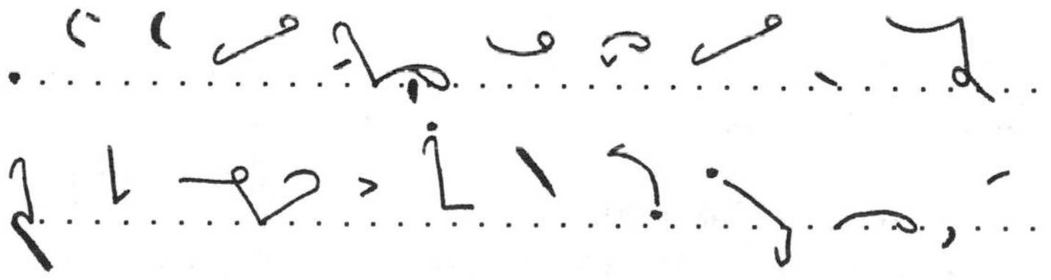

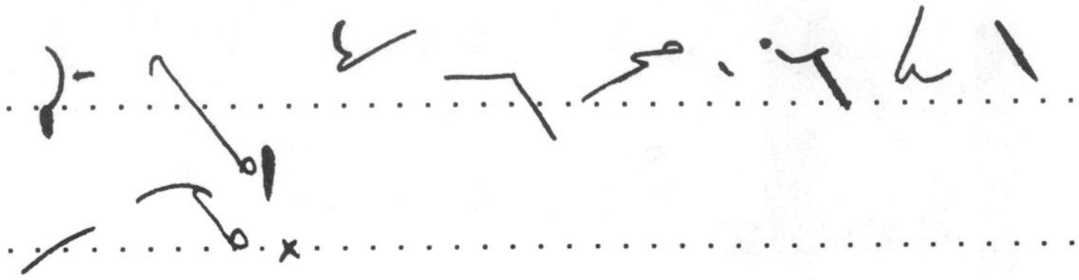

## THEORY PRACTICE

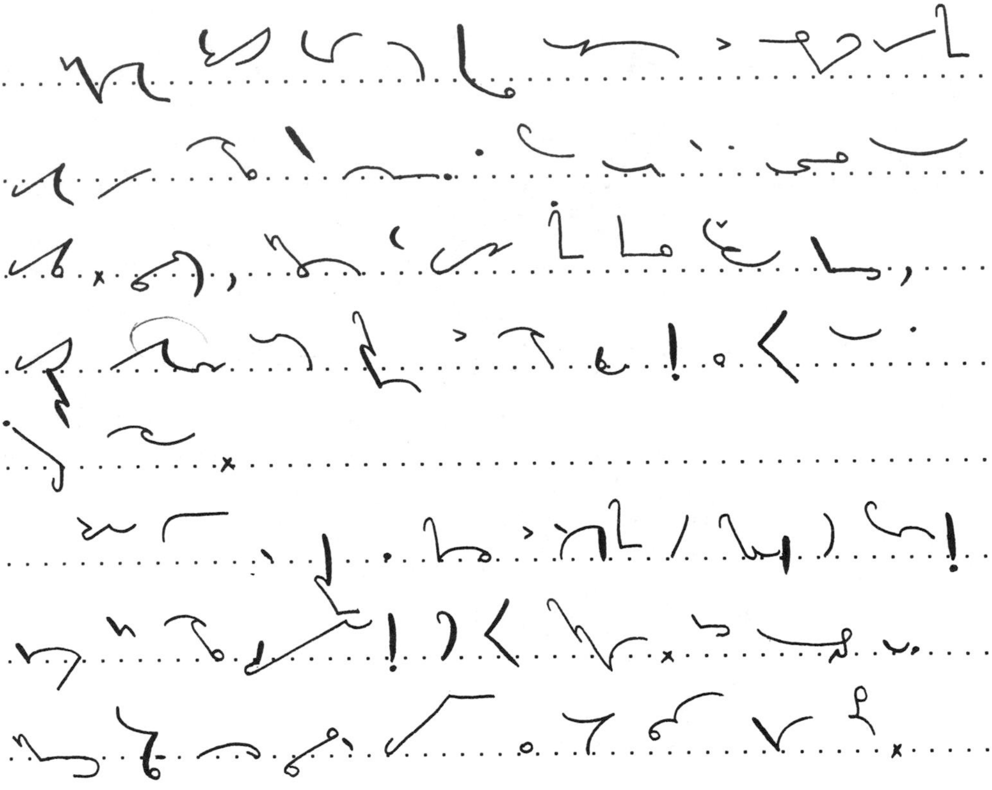

## SPEED BUILDING PRACTICE

**Preview**

percent

**TRANSCRIPTION LETTERS**

**Preview**

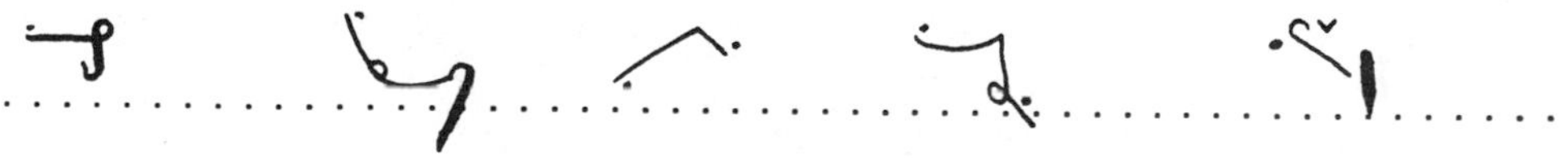

accident      passenger      rapid      anticipate      applied

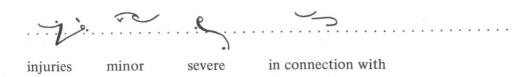

injuries    minor    severe    in connection with

Messrs. Wilson, Greenwald and Thurston
102 Madison Avenue
Toronto 5, Ontario

**Preview**

negligence    indicated    witnesses    specifically

testify    actually    behind

Mrs. Arlene Simmons
946 South Street
Toronto 5, Ontario

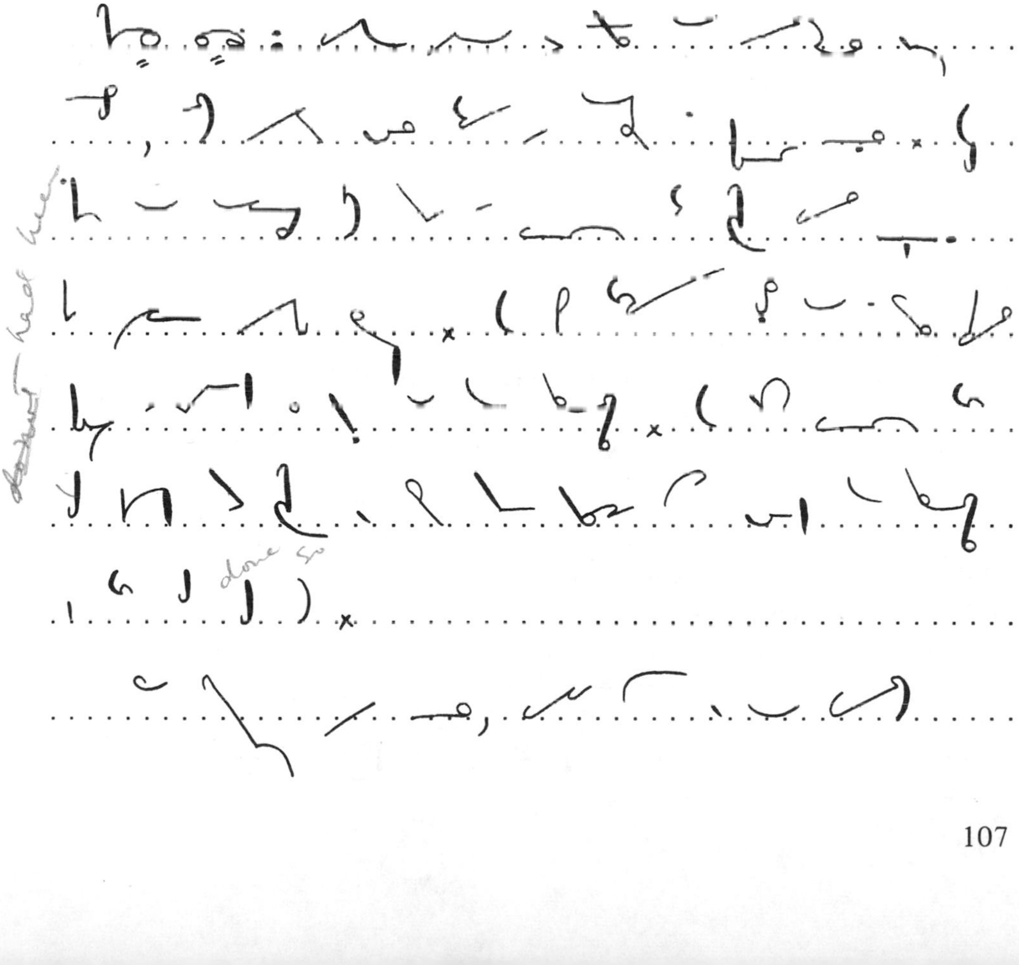

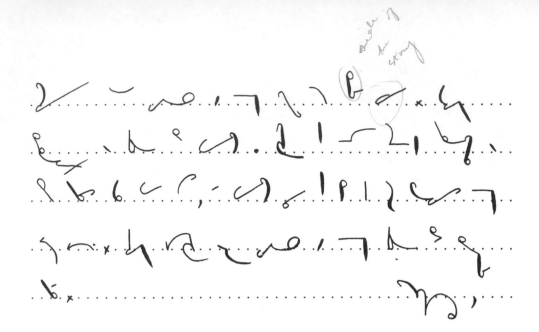

## BUSINESS UNDERSTANDING

Is a passenger held responsible for reading and following all notices about regulations governing the operation of a bus or subway?

## Preview

particularly     recall     commented     friend

Messrs. Wilson, Greenwald and Thurston
102 Madison Avenue
Toronto 5, Ontario

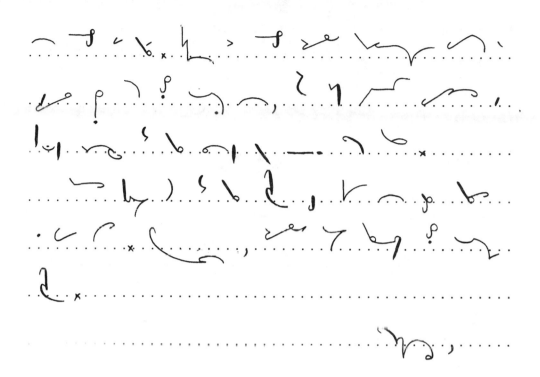

## TRANSCRIPTION SKILL DEVELOPMENT

**Spelling**

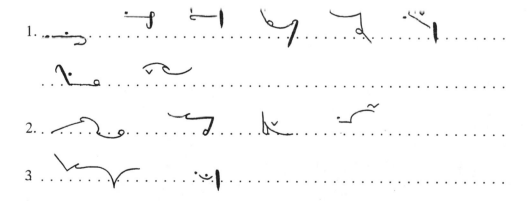

1.

2.

3.

## Punctuation

Punctuate the following:

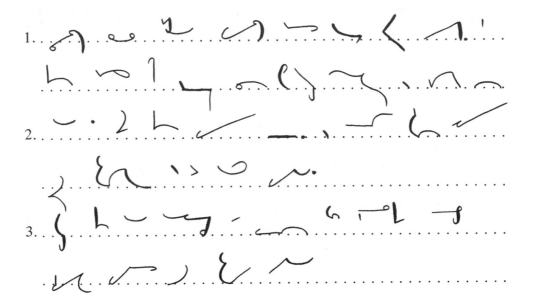

1.

2.

3.

## Transcription Tips

If you cannot read an outline in your notes, read beyond this word to pick up the meaning of the sentence and then go back to the troublesome word.

# 15

VOCABULARY BUILDING

delightful
pamphlet     1.

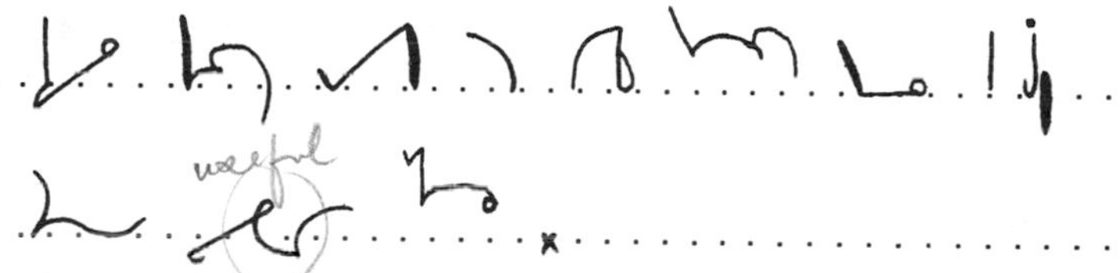

literature     2.

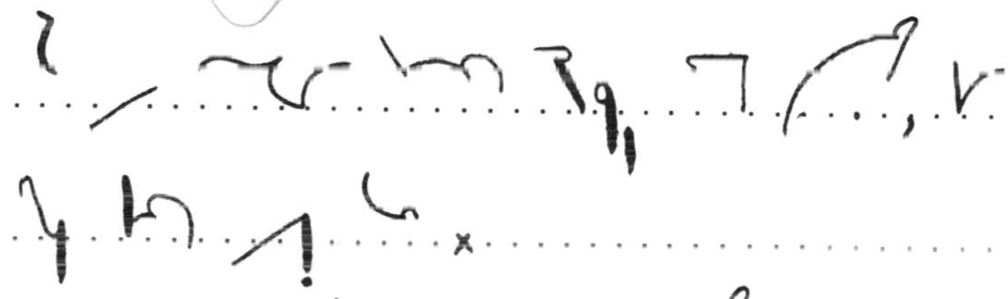

vacation     3.

experienced     4.

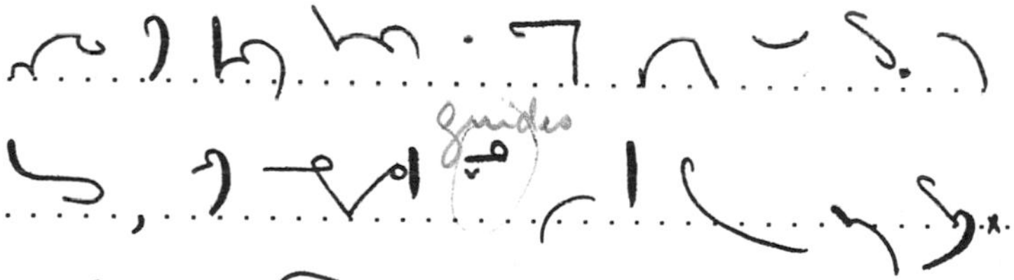

accommodations     5.

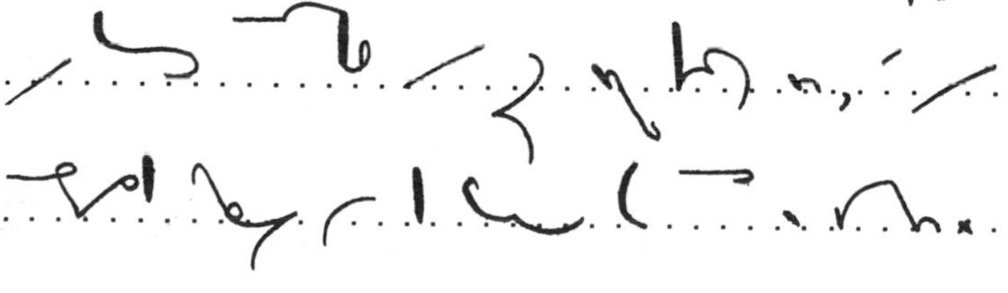

111

agency     6.

client     7.

**THEORY PRACTICE**

# SPEED BUILDING PRACTICE

## Preview

longer          whether

**Preview**

real estate     expire     renewed     remodel     granted

occupancy     acquiring

Mr. Walter Franklin
371 Maple Street
Owen Sound, Ontario

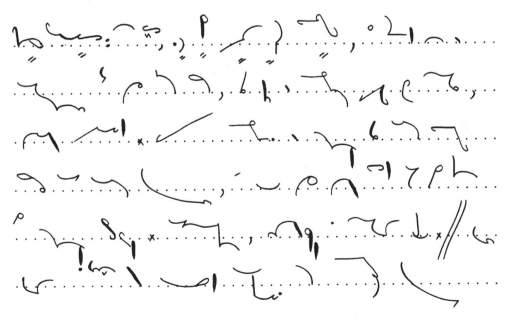

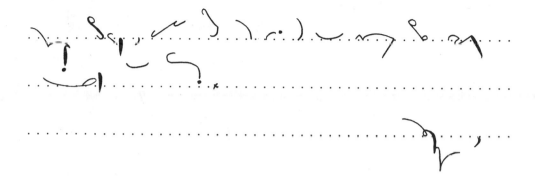

**Preview**

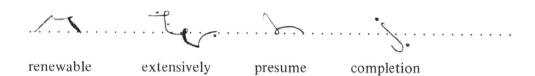

renewable     extensively     presume     completion

Messrs. Hilton and Reade
229 East Street
Owen Sound, Ontario

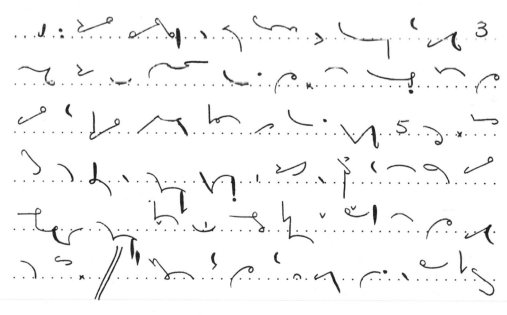

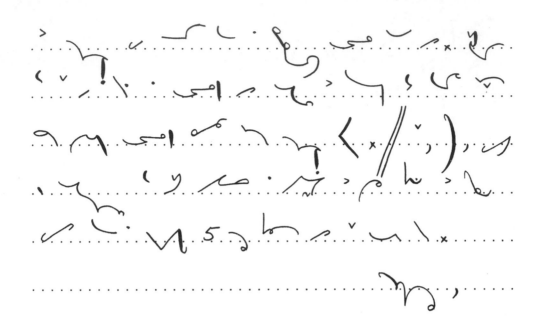

## BUSINESS UNDERSTANDING

What is the difference between paying rent under a lease and paying as a monthly tenant?

## Preview

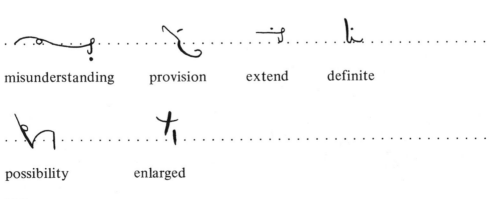

misunderstanding     provision     extend     definite

possibility     enlarged

Mr. Walter Franklin
371 Maple Street
Owen Sound, Ontario

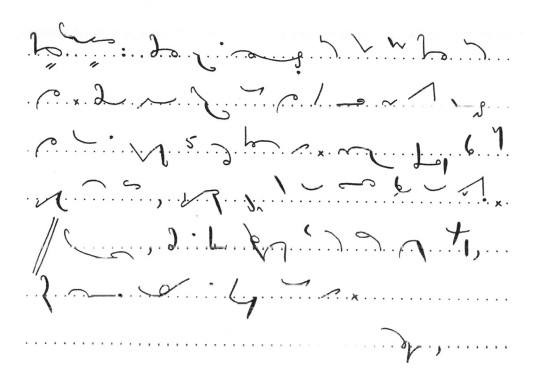

TRANSCRIPTION SKILL DEVELOPMENT

**Spelling**

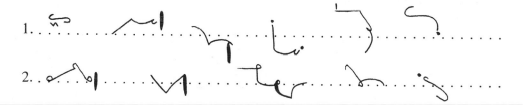

3.

## Punctuation

Punctuate the following:

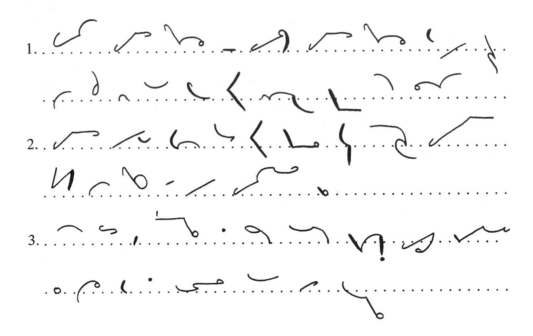

## Transcription Tips

Better transcriptions of specialized business dictation will result from the use of specialized phrases and contractions.

# 16

VOCABULARY BUILDING

expires
compact

1.

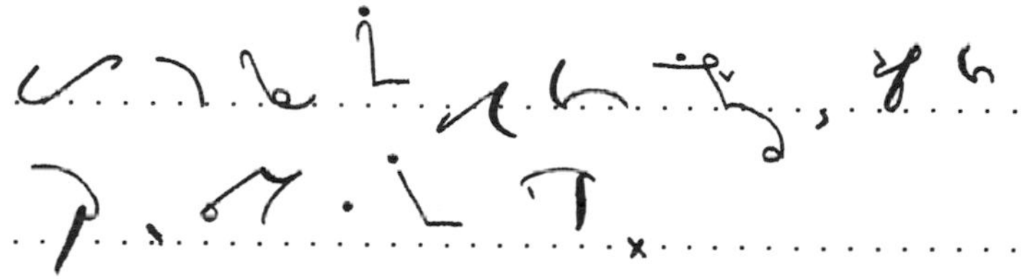

obliged

2.

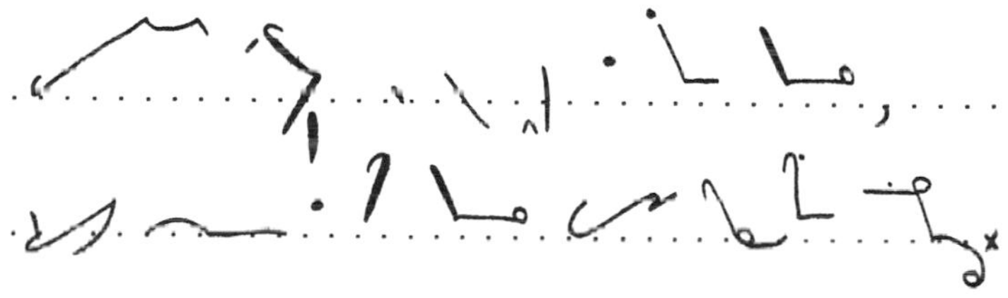

determine

3.

thoroughly
carton

4.

transit

5.

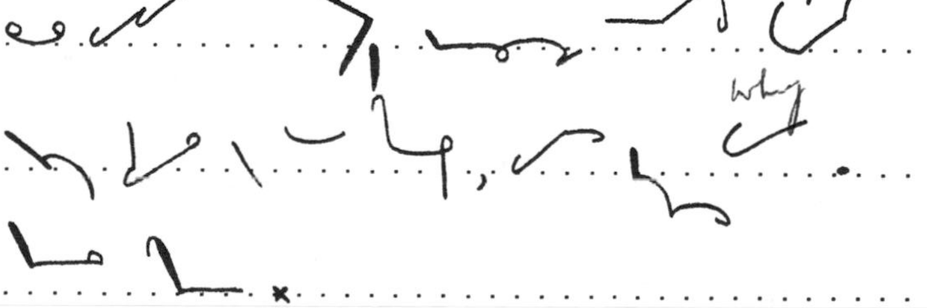

*why*

119

assured    6.

## THEORY PRACTICE

SPEED BUILDING PRACTICE

**Preview**

as a matter of fact          wonderful

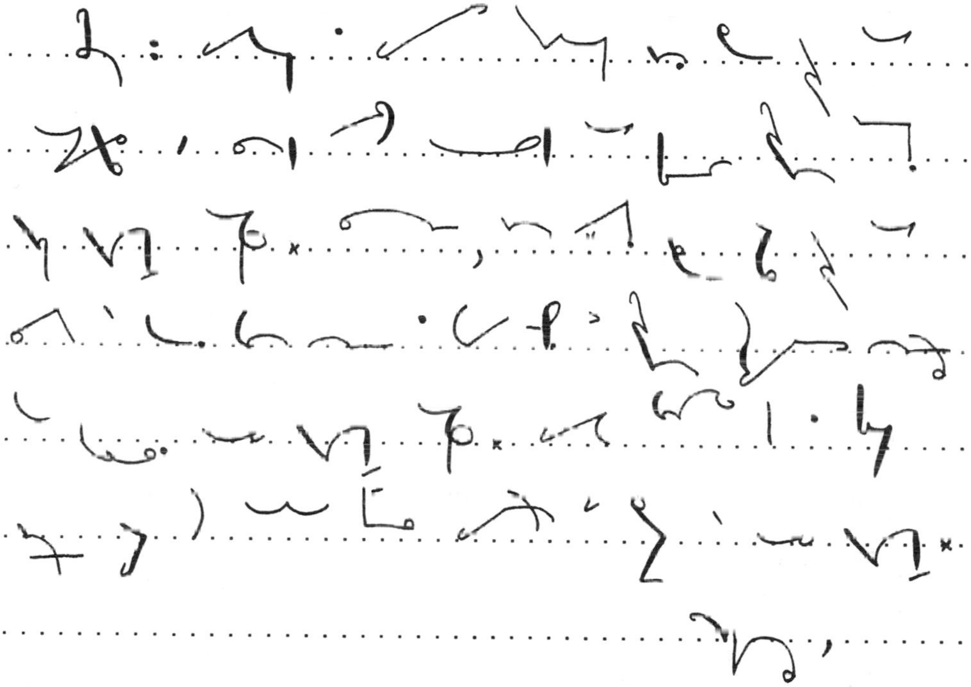

TRANSCRIPTION LETTERS

**Preview**

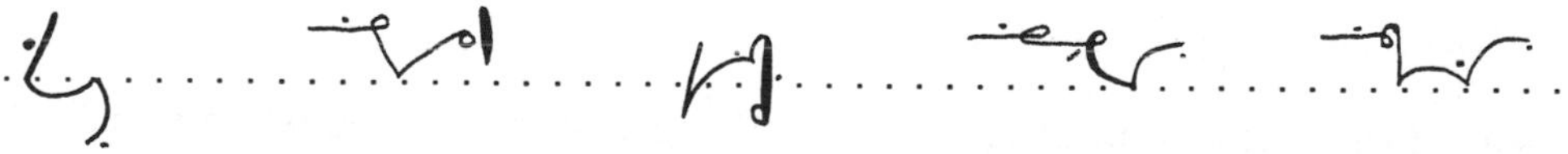

agency     experienced     children's     exclusively     extremely favorable        commission        designed        parents

Mr. George Hamilton
Southwest Merchandising Company
291 Abbott Street
Windsor, Ontario

*[shorthand outlines]*

## BUSINESS UNDERSTANDING

Why do business firms attach importance to your references when you apply for a job? What type of references are most desirable?

**Preview**

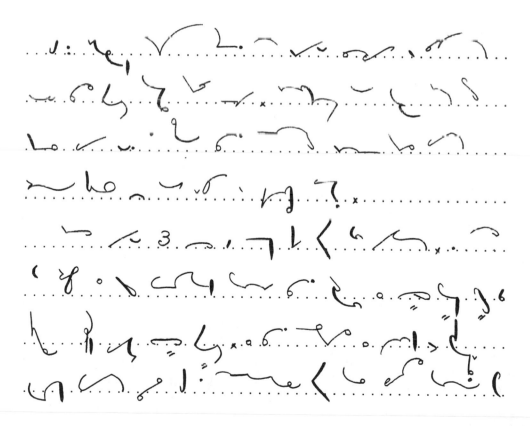

campaign     advances     qualified     associated     limited

magnificent     familiar     production

Junior Clothes Incorporated
447 Regent Street
Hamilton, Ontario

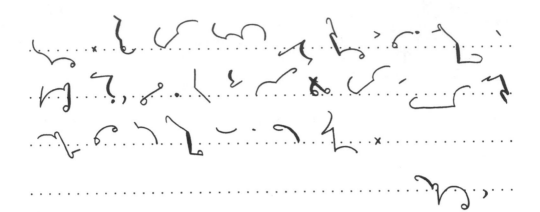

**Preview**

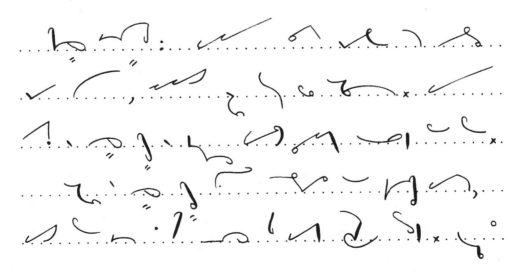

response    efforts    presentation

Mr. George Hamilton
Southwest Merchandising Company
291 Abbott Street
Windsor, Ontario

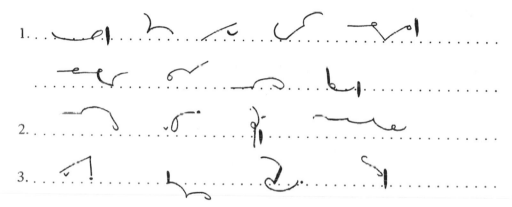

## TRANSCRIPTION SKILL DEVELOPMENT

### Spelling

1.

2.

3.

### Punctuation

Punctuate the following:

1.

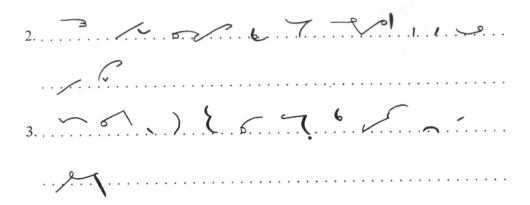

2. ......

3. ......

**Transcription Tips**

If your employer dictates a name that has several possible spellings, such as "Reid", check your files for previous correspondence with this man before you ask your employer to verify the spelling.

126

# 17

## VOCABULARY BUILDING

urge
initial

1.

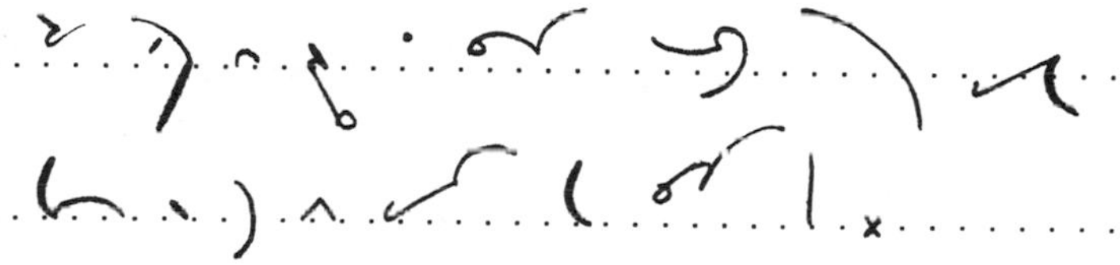

confidence

2.

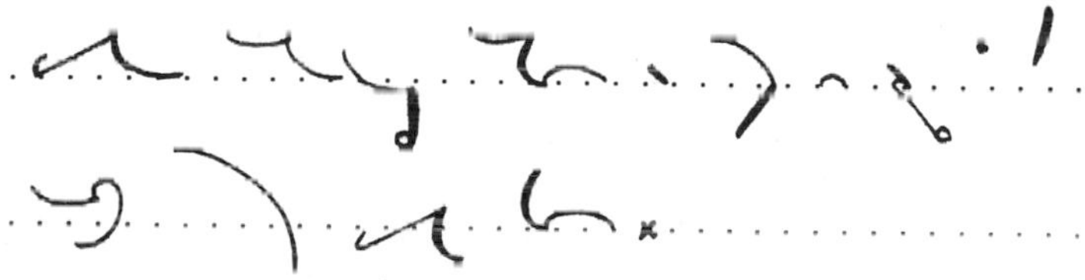

assigned

3.

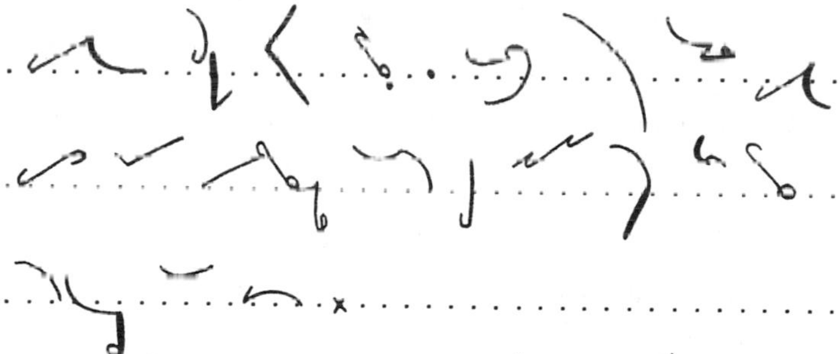

technical

4.

fortunate     5.

favorite     6.

gratifying     7.

THEORY PRACTICE

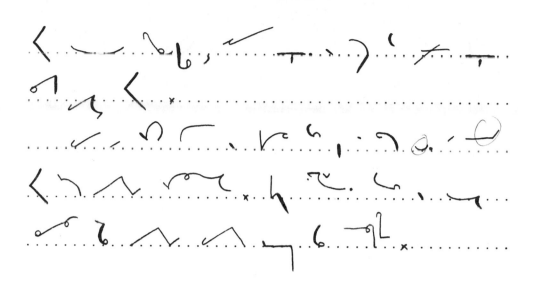

SPEED BUILDING PRACTICE 1※

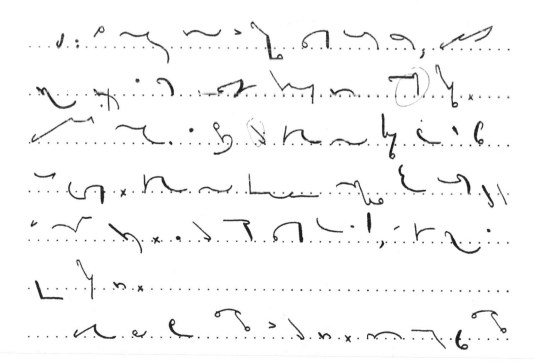

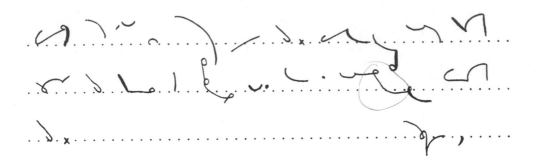

## TRANSCRIPTION LETTERS

**Preview**

colonial     campaign     allowance     conduct     telephone

neighborhood

Colonial Automobile Corporation
595 Westwood Avenue
Brockville, Ontario

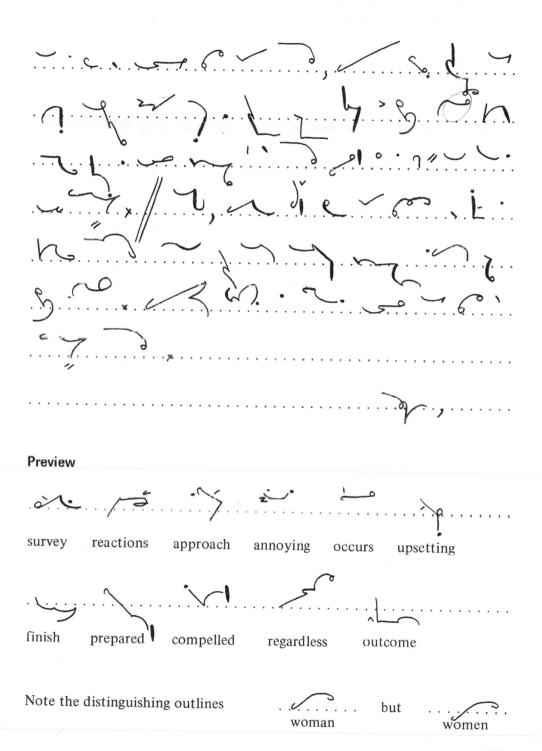

**Preview**

survey  reactions  approach  annoying  occurs  upsetting

finish  prepared  compelled  regardless  outcome

Note the distinguishing outlines

woman  but  women

131

Colonial Motors Incorporated
650 Forest Hill Drive
Brockville, Ontario

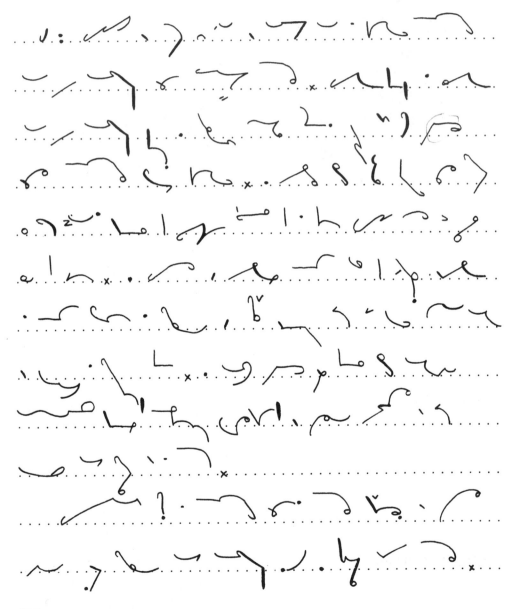

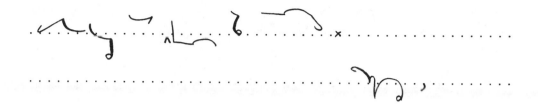

## BUSINESS UNDERSTANDING

In the fields of advertising and selling, the expressions "hard sell" and "soft sell" are used. Explain what these terms mean and give illustrations of industries that use each one.

## Preview

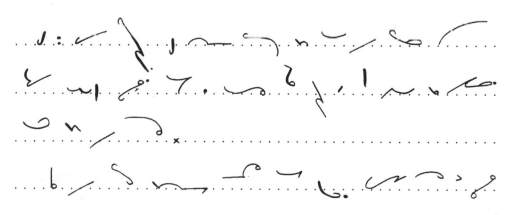

requesting      prospective      pressure      efforts

Colonial Automobile Corporation
595 Westwood Avenue
Brockville, Ontario

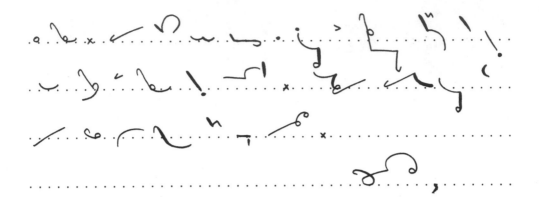

## TRANSCRIPTION SKILL DEVELOPMENT

### Spelling

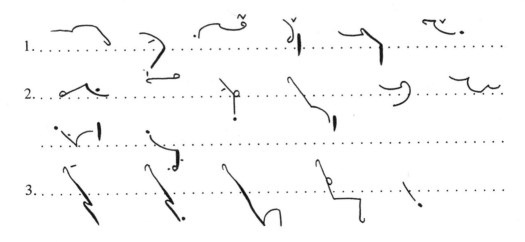

1. . . . . . . . . . . . . . . . . . . . . . . . . . . . . . . . . . . . . . . . . . . .

2. . . . . . . . . . . . . . . . . . . . . . . . . . . . . . . . . . . . . . . . . . . .

. . . . . . . . . . . . . . . . . . . . . . . . . . . . . . . . . . . . . . . . . . . .

3. . . . . . . . . . . . . . . . . . . . . . . . . . . . . . . . . . . . . . . . . . . .

### Punctuation

Punctuate the following:

1. . . . . . . . . . . . . . . . . . . . . . . . . . . . . . . . . . . . . . . . . . . .

134

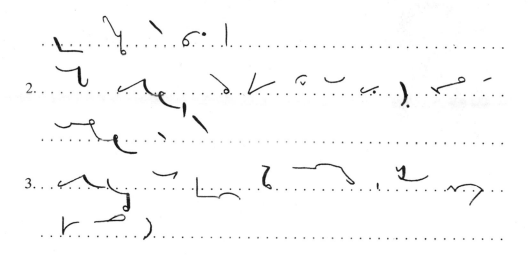

## Transcription Tips

To calculate the number of words in the body of a letter from your shorthand notes, add the number of words in two of the lines, divide the result by two, and then multiply this figure by the total number of lines of notes.

# 18

## VOCABULARY BUILDING

contribution     1.

storage     2.

hazard     3.

protection     4.

garment     5.

coverage     6.

respond     7.

136

appearance     8.

## THEORY PRACTICE

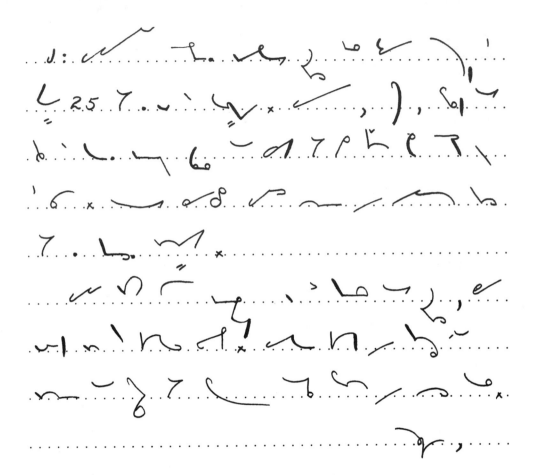

## TRANSCRIPTION LETTERS

**Preview**

welcomed    container    guaranteed    protection    damaged insect   chemical   destroy   display   introducing

Maxwell Trading Company
298 Princess Street
Kingston, Ontario

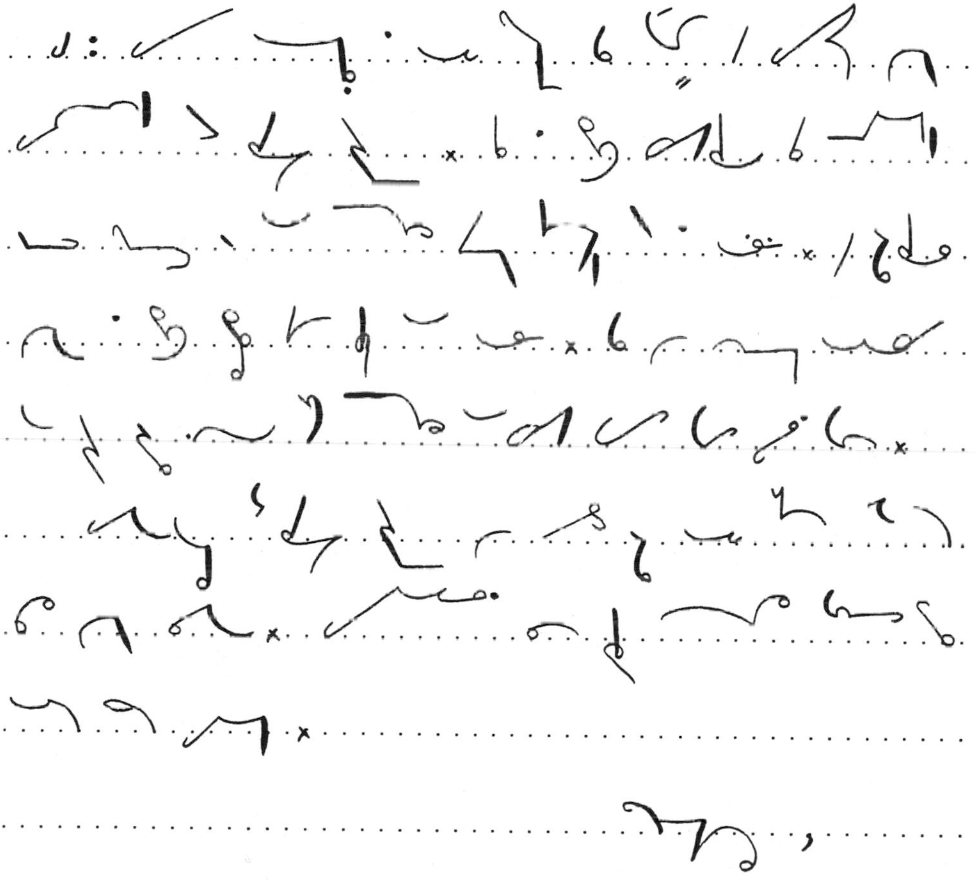

**Preview**

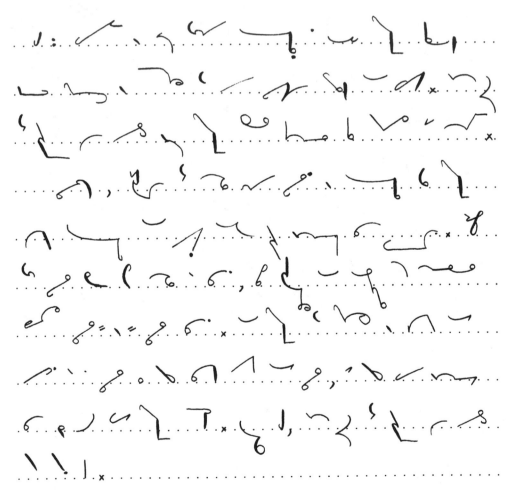

designed     effective     running

Sanitary Manufacturing Company
452 Taylor Avenue
Montreal, Quebec

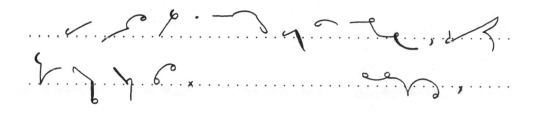

## BUSINESS UNDERSTANDING

What are the advantages and disadvantages of a "house-to-house" selling campaign? What products are frequently sold in this way?

## Preview

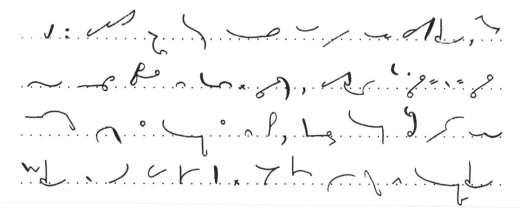

excellent     suggestions     really     extensive     publicity

Maxwell Trading Company
298 Princess Street
Kingston, Ontario

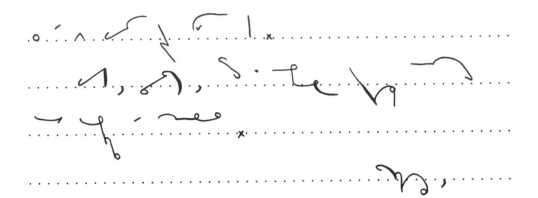

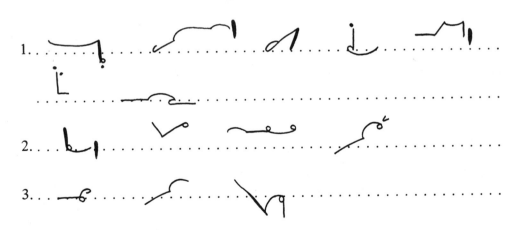

## TRANSCRIPTION SKILL DEVELOPMENT

### Spelling

1. .......... .......... .......... .......... ..........

2. .......... .......... .......... .......... ..........

3. .......... .......... .......... ..........

### Punctuation

Punctuate the following:

1.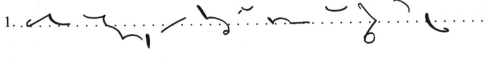

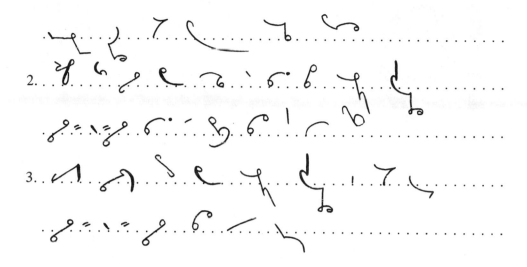

2.

3.

## Transcription Tips

If your employer tends to make frequent changes or corrections while dictating a letter, use only the left side of your notebook for the dictation and the right side for corrections.

# 19

VOCABULARY BUILDING

endeavor
workmanship

1.

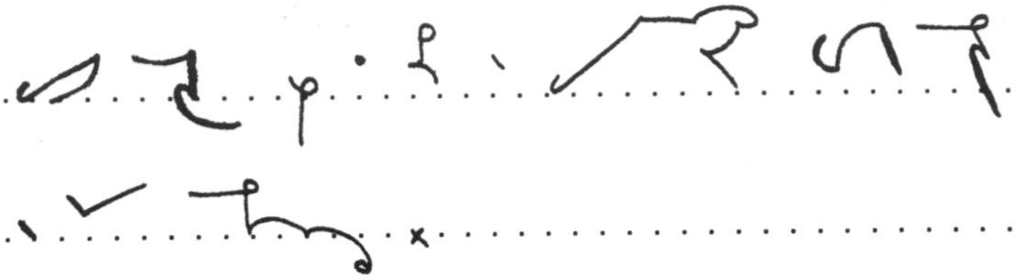

economic

2.

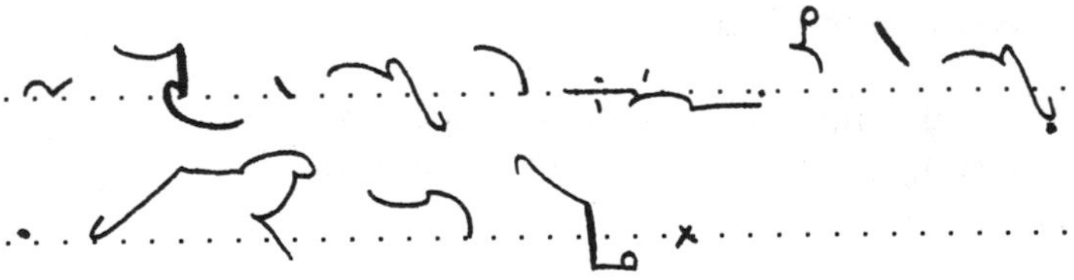

progressive

3.

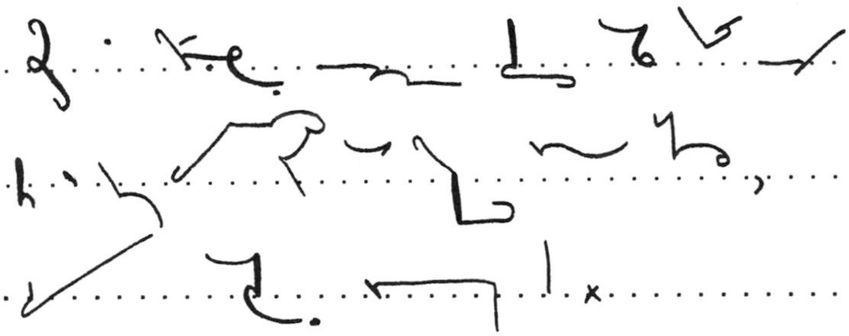

proudly

4.

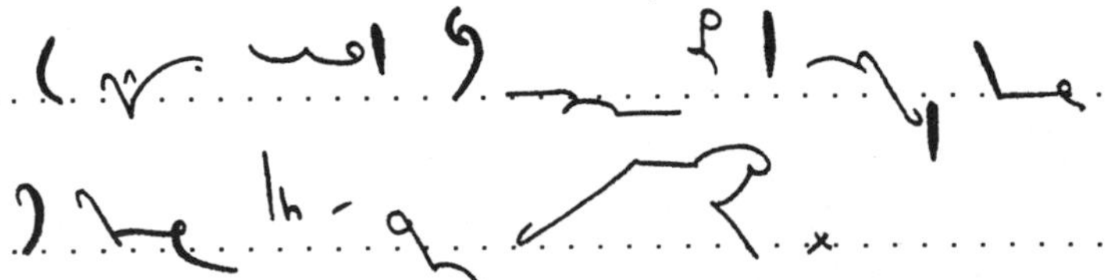

cordial

5.

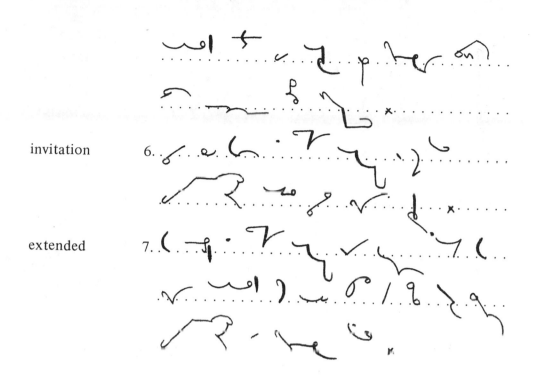

invitation 6.

extended 7.

## THEORY PRACTICE

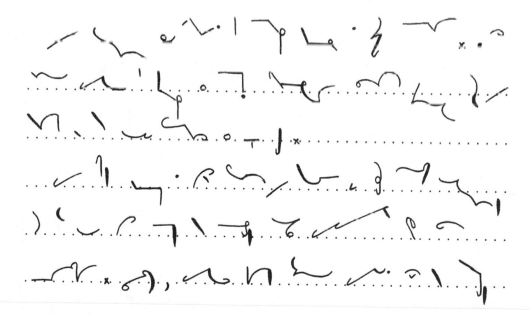

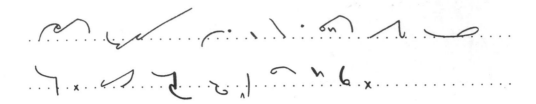

## SPEED BUILDING PRACTICE

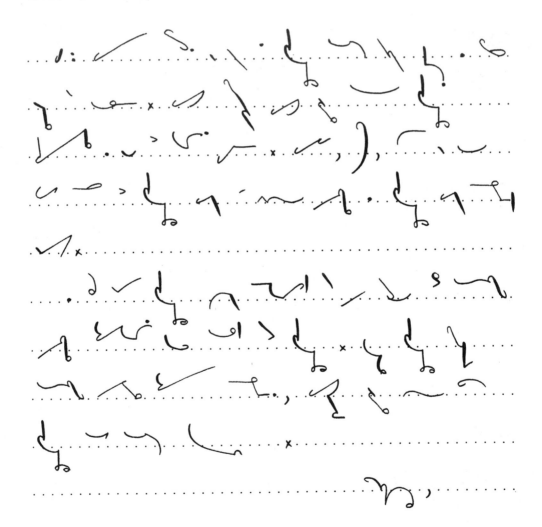

# TRANSCRIPTION LETTERS

**Preview**

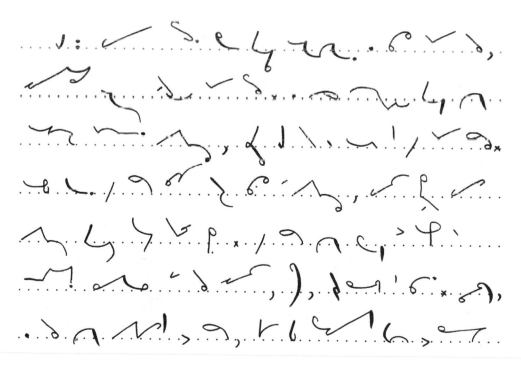

involving    agency    freed    necessity    guaranteeing

concentrate    central    fullest

Marshall Stationery Store
1246 Sherwood Avenue
Belleville, Ontario

[shorthand outlines spanning four lines]

**Preview**

[shorthand outline]   [shorthand outline]   [shorthand outline]   [shorthand outline]   [shorthand outline]

appreciate    cordial    centers    specializing    superior

[shorthand outline]   [shorthand outline]   [shorthand outline]

quality    concerned    assured

Superior Pen Company
501 Bay Street
Toronto 2, Ontario

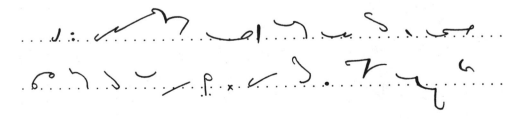

## BUSINESS UNDERSTANDING

Is it wise for a firm to guarantee free repairs of its product for a period of time? What are the advantages and disadvantages of offering free repair service?

**Preview**

comments    welcome    major    actually    complaint

Marshall Stationery Store
1246 Sherwood Avenue
Belleville, Ontario

# TRANSCRIPTION SKILL DEVELOPMENT

## Spelling

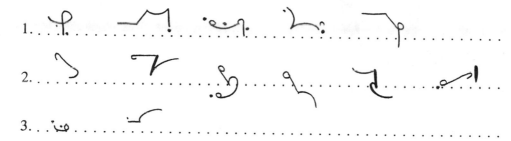

## Punctuation

Punctuate the following:

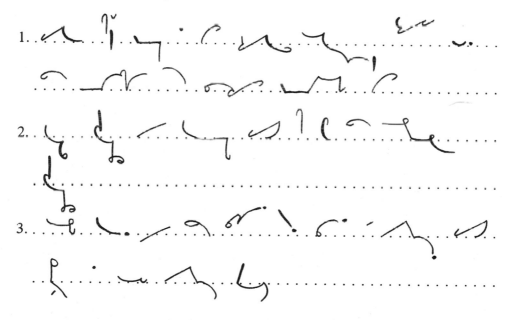

## Transcription Tips

Draw a line through the shorthand notes of a letter as soon as it is transcribed.

# 20

VOCABULARY BUILDING

amazed

1.  ⟨shorthand outline⟩

device

2. 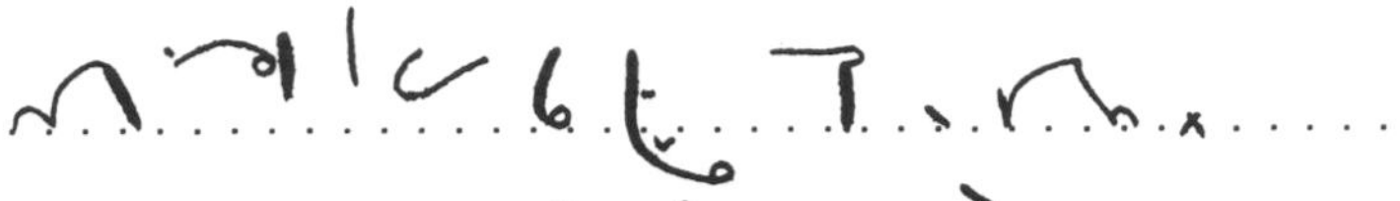 ⟨shorthand outline⟩

accurate

3. 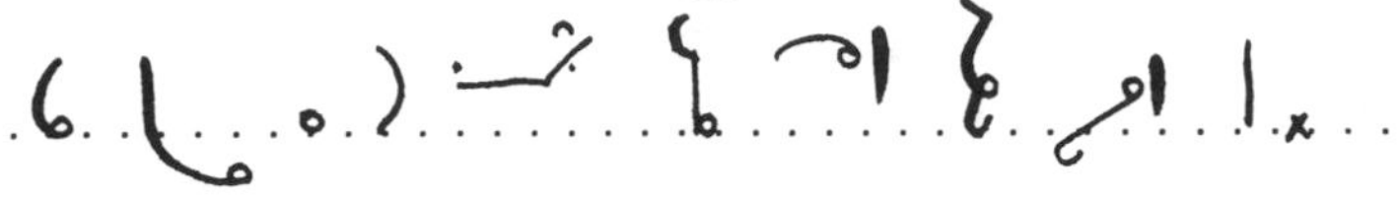 ⟨shorthand outline⟩

generous

4. 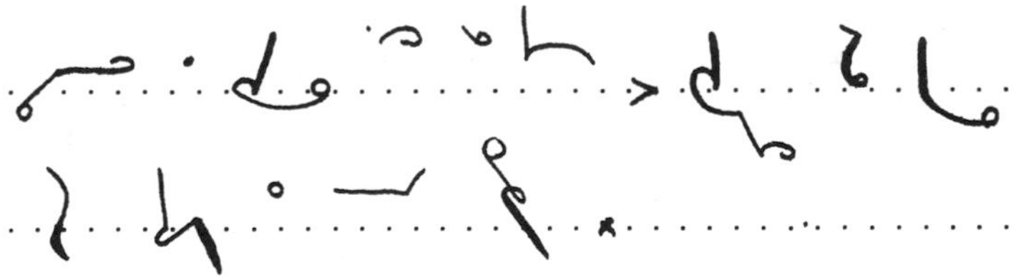 ⟨shorthand outline⟩

courteous

5. 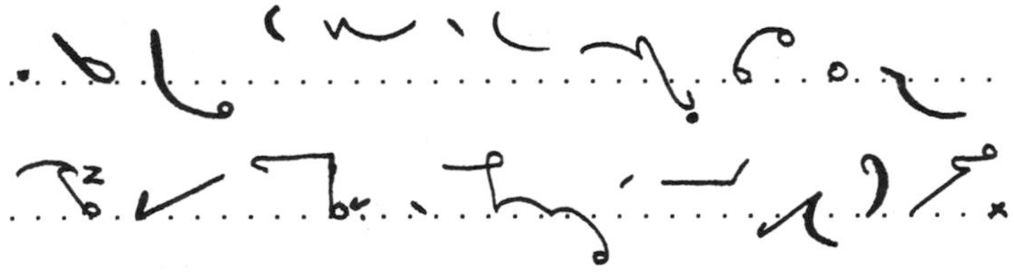 ⟨shorthand outline⟩

dependable

6. 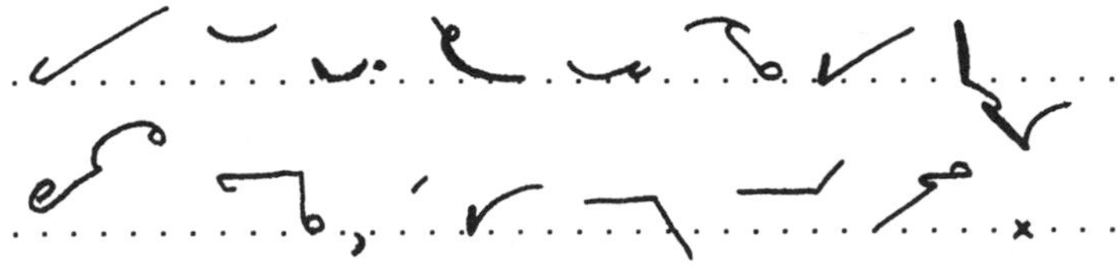 ⟨shorthand outline⟩

various

7. 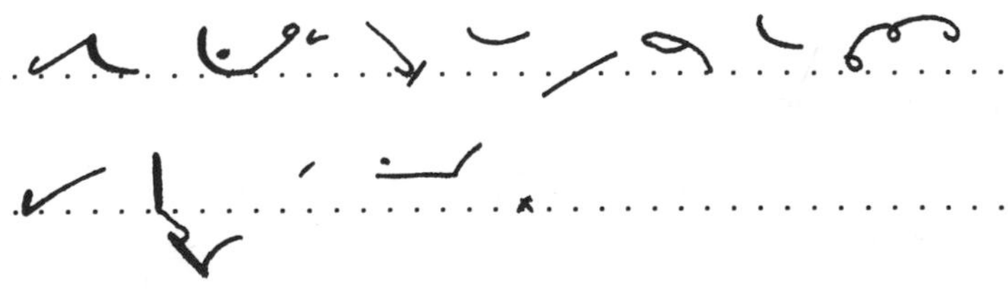 ⟨shorthand outline⟩

152

installments 8.

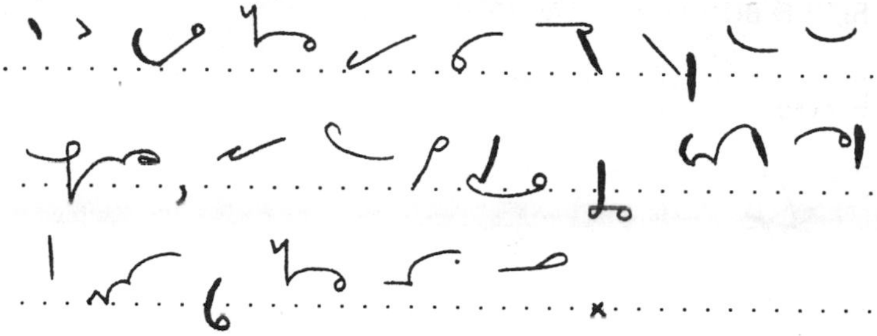

THEORY PRACTICE

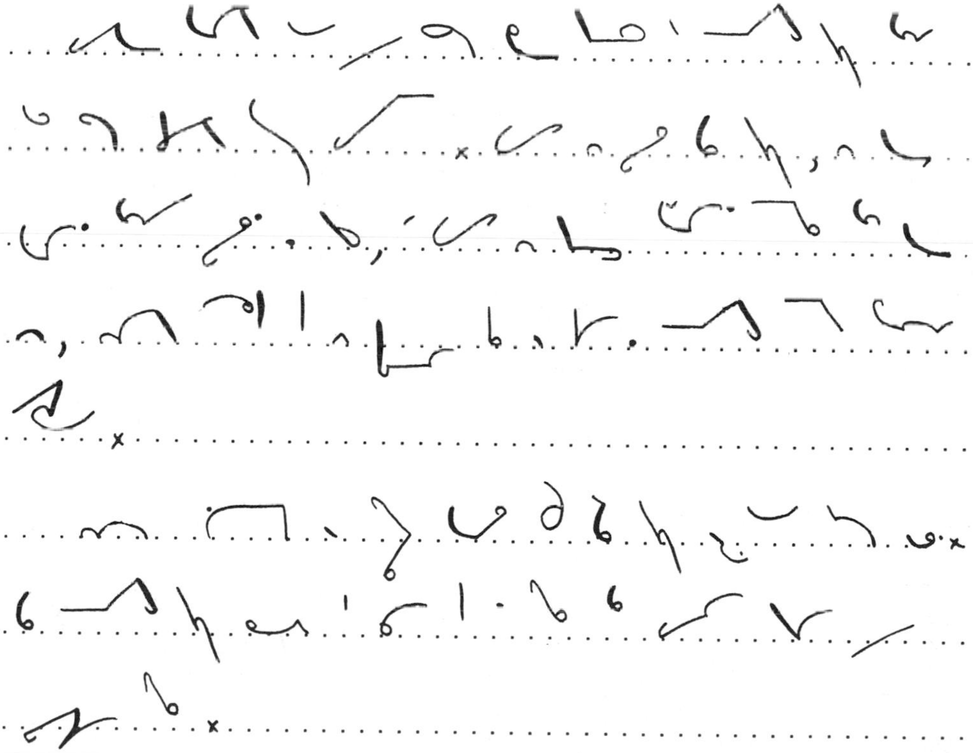

153

## SPEED BUILDING PRACTICE

**Preview**

in general

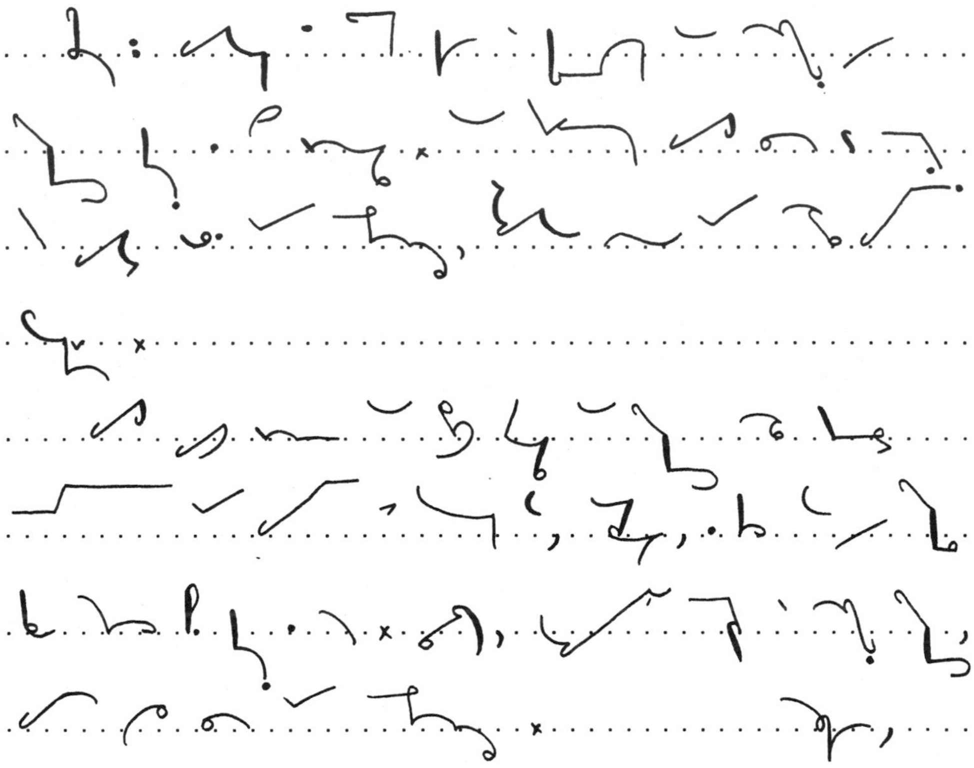

## TRANSCRIPTION LETTERS

**Preview**

decline           served

Butler Machine Shops, Incorporated
884 St. George Street
Barrie, Ontario

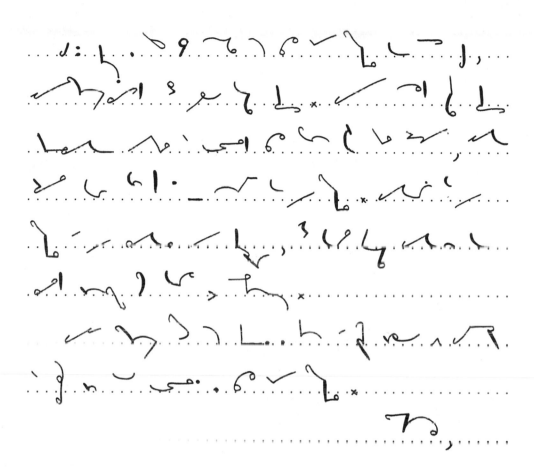

**Preview**

| complained | exact | unusual | -ly | prevent |

reputation      finally

General Machine Manufacturing Company
421 Hillcrest Avenue
Toronto, Ontario

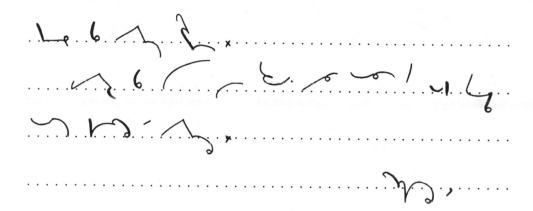

## BUSINESS UNDERSTANDING

Why should a firm that sells its product all over Canada be concerned about poor sales in only one part of the country?

**Preview**

| admit | proud | delayed | shortages |

Butler Machine Shops, Incorporated
884 St. George Street
Barrie, Ontario

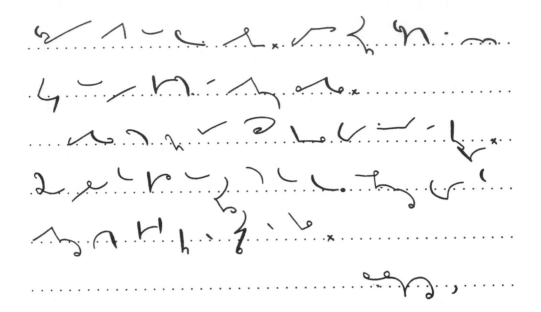

## TRANSCRIPTION SKILL DEVELOPMENT

**Spelling**

1. . . . . . . . . . . . . . . . . . . . . . . . . . . . . . . . . . . . . . . . . . . . . . . . .

2. . . . . . . . . . . . . . . . . . . . . . . . . . . . . . . . . . . . . . . . . . . . . . . . .

3. . . . . . . . . . . . . . . . . . . . . . . . . . . . . . . . . . . . . . . . . . . . . . . . .

**Punctuation**

Punctuate the following:

1. . . . . . . . . . . . . . . . . . . . . . . . . . . . . . . . . . . . . . . . . . . . . . . . .

158

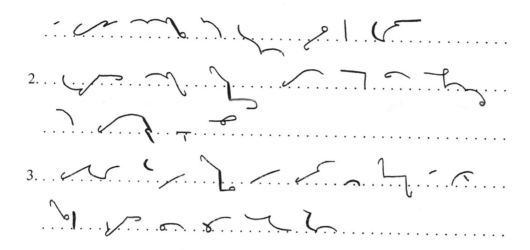

## Transcription Tips

If your employer makes an obvious error during his dictation, don't make a major correction unless you have informed him of it.

# 21

VOCABULARY BUILDING

creditors    1.

decline    2.

accomplish    3.

export    4.

adopted    5.

eventually     6.

ambitious     7.

fault     8.

## THEORY PRACTICE

SPEED BUILDING PRACTICE

# TRANSCRIPTION LETTERS

## Preview

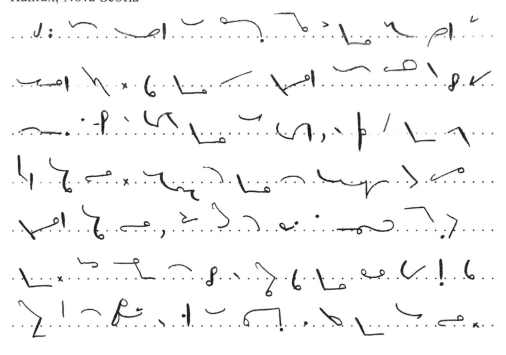

securing      listed      examination     projected   -ed

Very sincerely yours     in view of the fact

Adams Publishing Company
106 Cumberland Road
Halifax, Nova Scotia

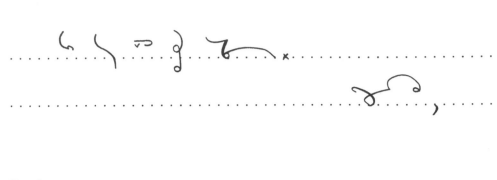

## Preview

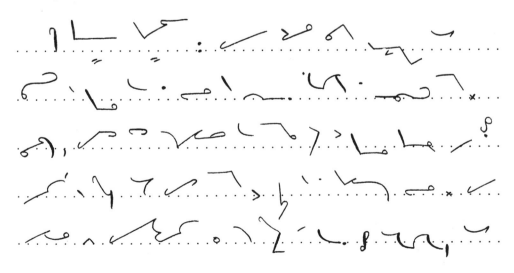

cooperate    grant    recognize    library    librarian

formal    textbooks

Dr. Charles Parker
Maritime College
490 Oakland Street
Truro, Nova Scotia

BUSINESS UNDERSTANDING

What is an "examination copy" and when and why does a publisher make it available?

**Preview**

indicating    approval    project    -ed    whatever

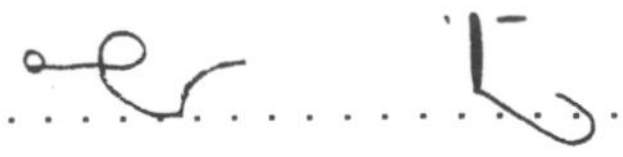

*(shorthand outlines)*

successful      adoption

Adams Publishing Company
106 Cumberland Road
Halifax, Nova Scotia

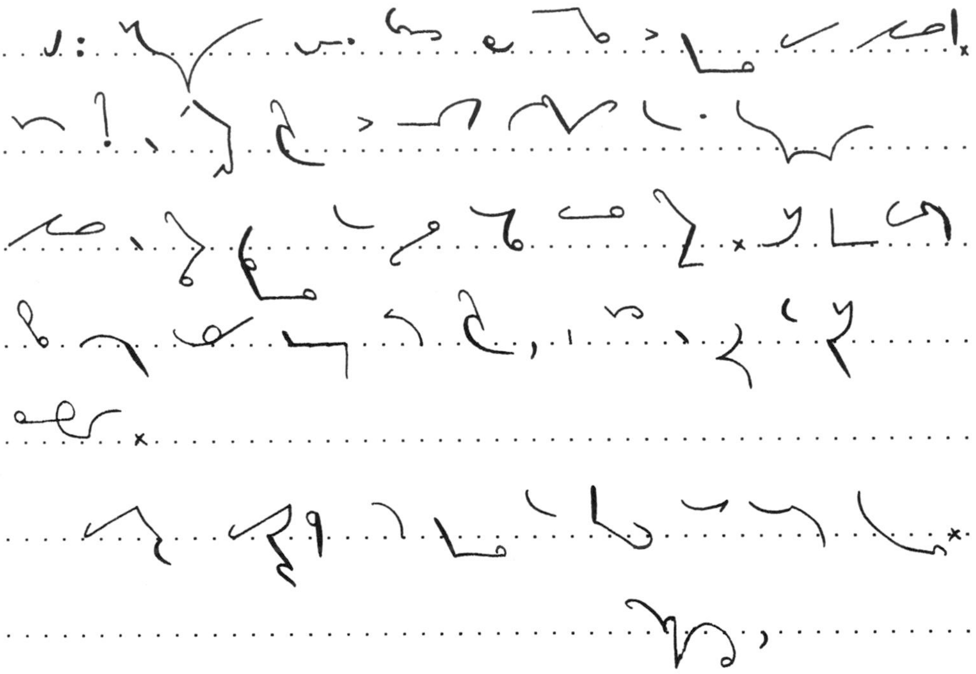

*(shorthand outlines)*

## TRANSCRIPTION SKILL DEVELOPMENT

**Spelling**

1. 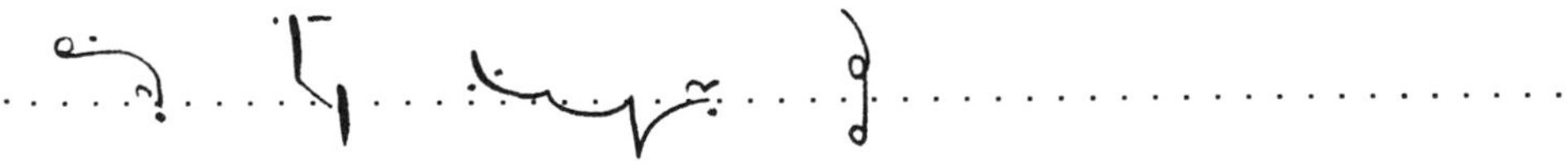 *(shorthand outlines)*

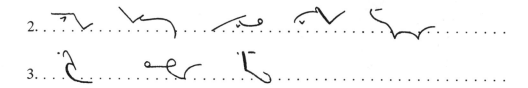

## Punctuation

Punctuate the following:

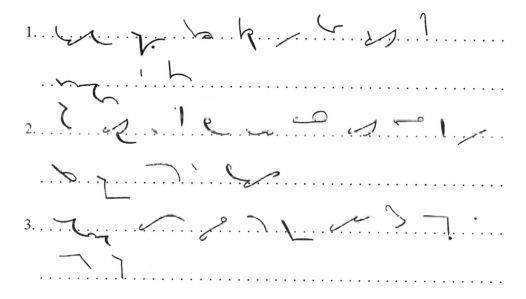

## Transcription Tips

If dates, times, or amounts are dictated to you, check your transcript with your shorthand notes or with the original correspondence.

# 22

## VOCABULARY BUILDING

accurate
excessive

1. 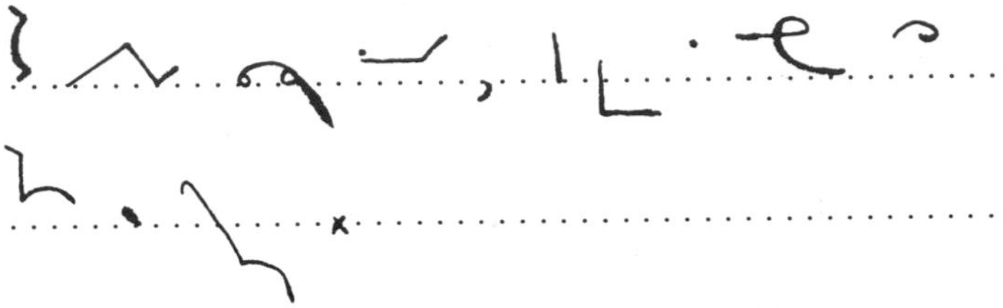

bookkeeping

2. 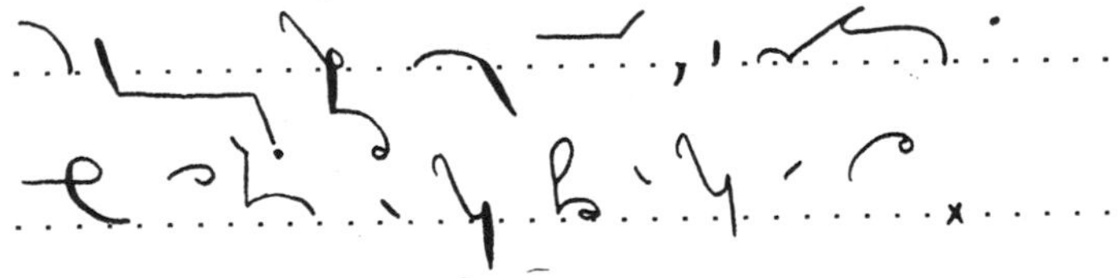

analysis

3. 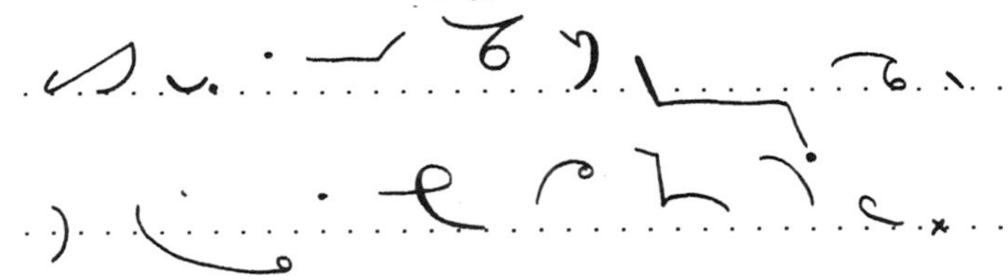

injustice

4. 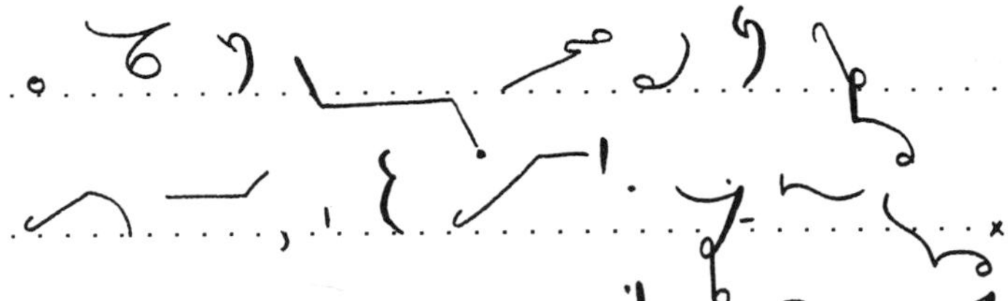

margin

5. 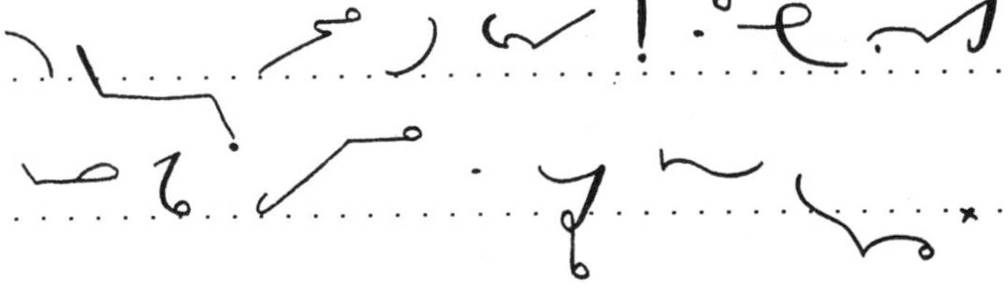

appropriate 6.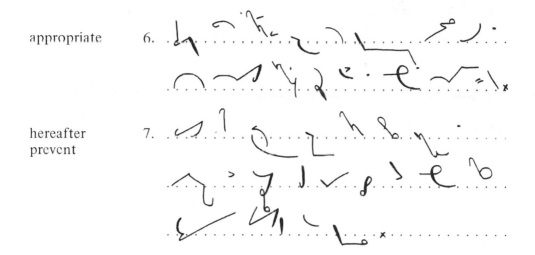

hereafter
prevent 7.

## THEORY PRACTICE

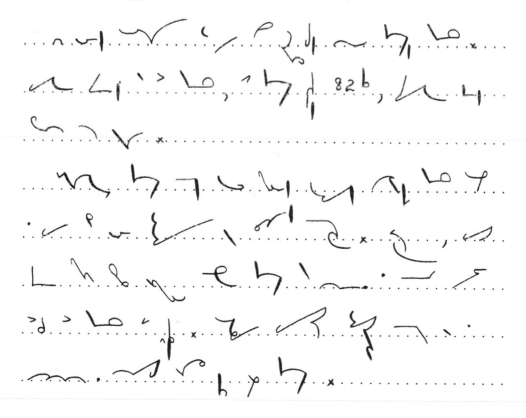

SPEED BUILDING PRACTICE

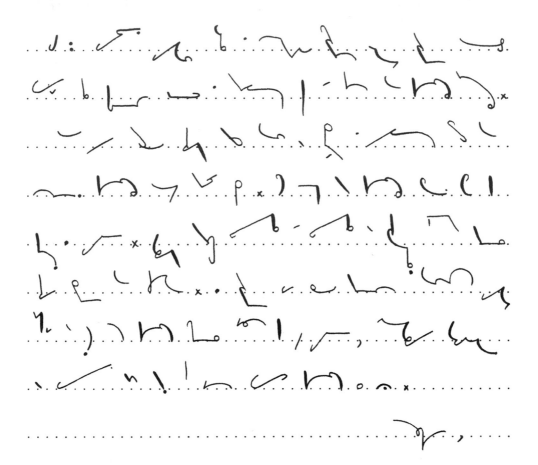

TRANSCRIPTION LETTERS

**Preview**

subscriptions     encourage     subscribe     -ed     billed

Mrs. Pearl Anderson
52 Belmont Avenue
Hull, Quebec

**Preview**

| friends | subject | -ed | annoyance | subscriber | ample |

171

sufficient    -ly    -cy     convince     source     frequently

Russell Publishing Company
St. Catharine Street
Montreal 3, Quebec

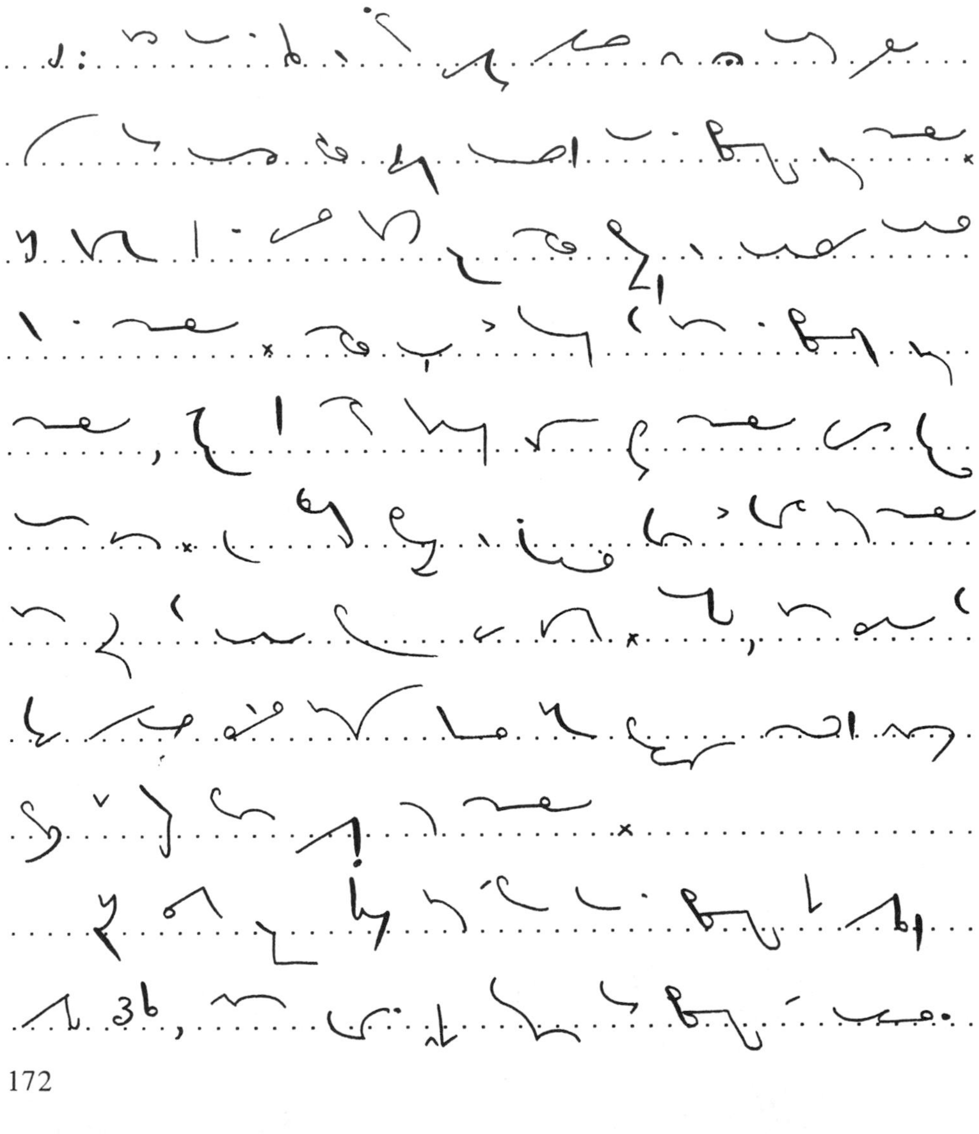

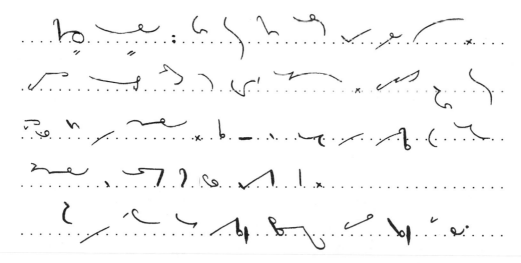

## BUSINESS UNDERSTANDING

Why does a publishing firm offer reduced rates to new subscribers? Do these new rates apply to old subscriptions? Why?

**Preview**

comments        prospective

Mrs. Pearl Anderson
52 Belmont Avenue
Hull, Quebec

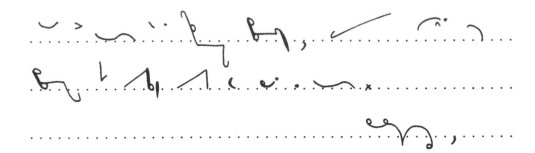

## TRANSCRIPTION SKILL DEVELOPMENT

### Spelling

1.

2.

3.

### Punctuation

Punctuate the following:

1.

174

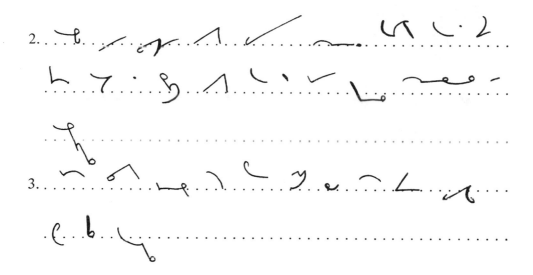

## Transcription Tips

If you have just obtained a job and your employer dictates a little too rapidly for you, you may ask him to slow down temporarily until you have built up your shorthand speed through home or evening-school practice.

# 23

## VOCABULARY BUILDING

obvious
popular

1. 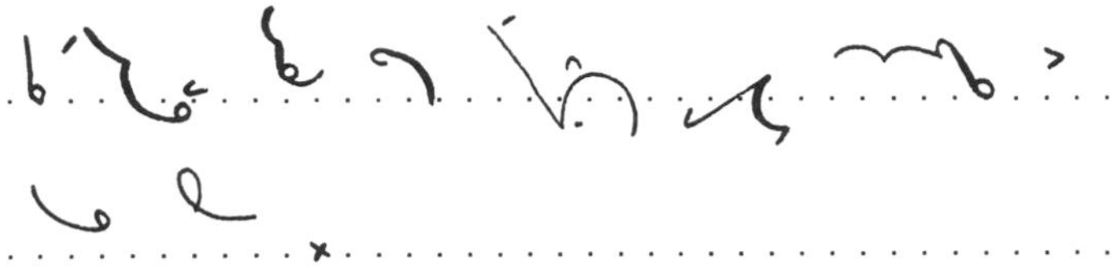 [shorthand outlines]

majority

2. 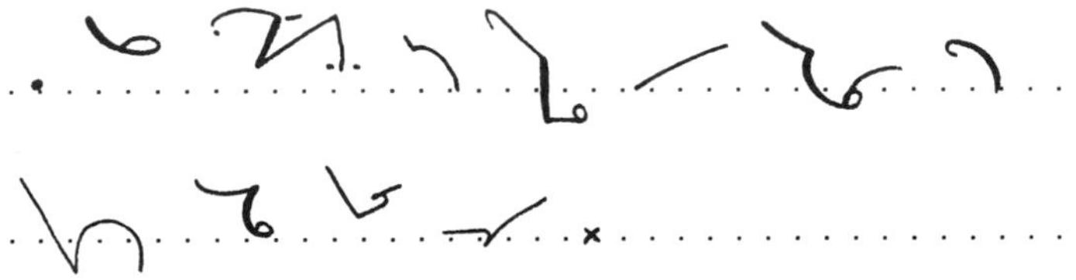 [shorthand outlines]

qualified

3. 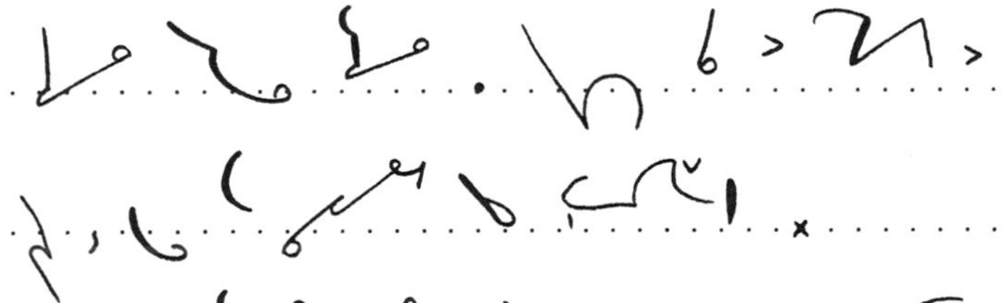 [shorthand outlines]

reliable

4. 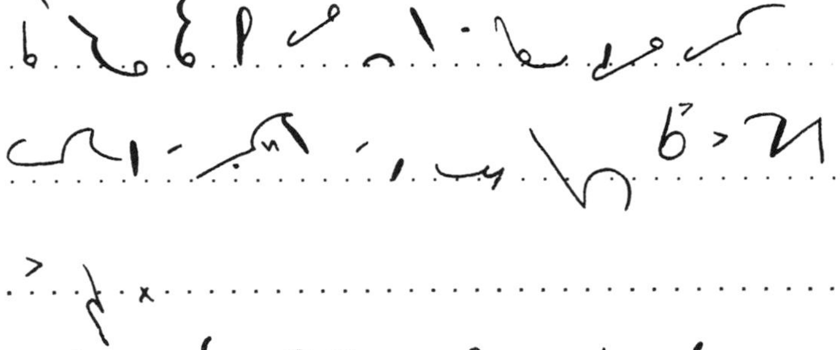 [shorthand outlines]

folly

5. 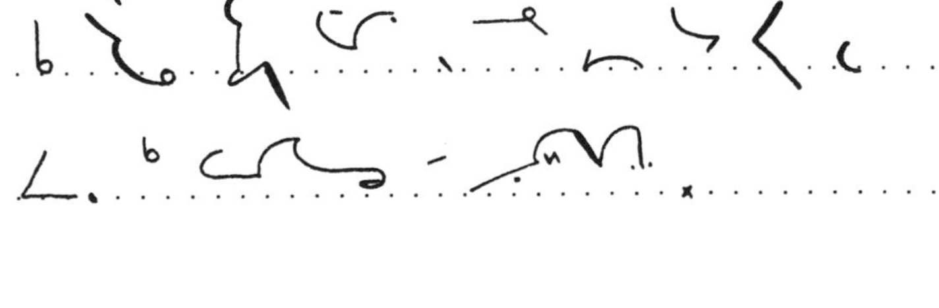 [shorthand outlines]

seemingly 6.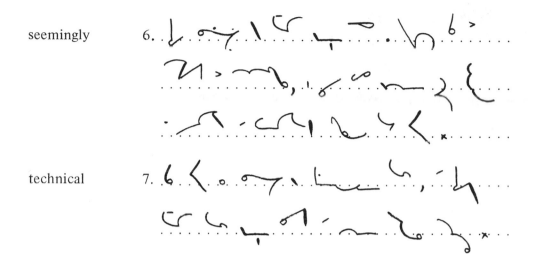

technical 7.

## THEORY PRACTICE

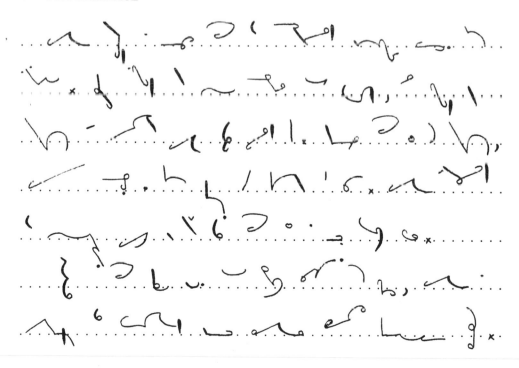

177

# SPEED BUILDING PRACTICE

**Preview**

any information

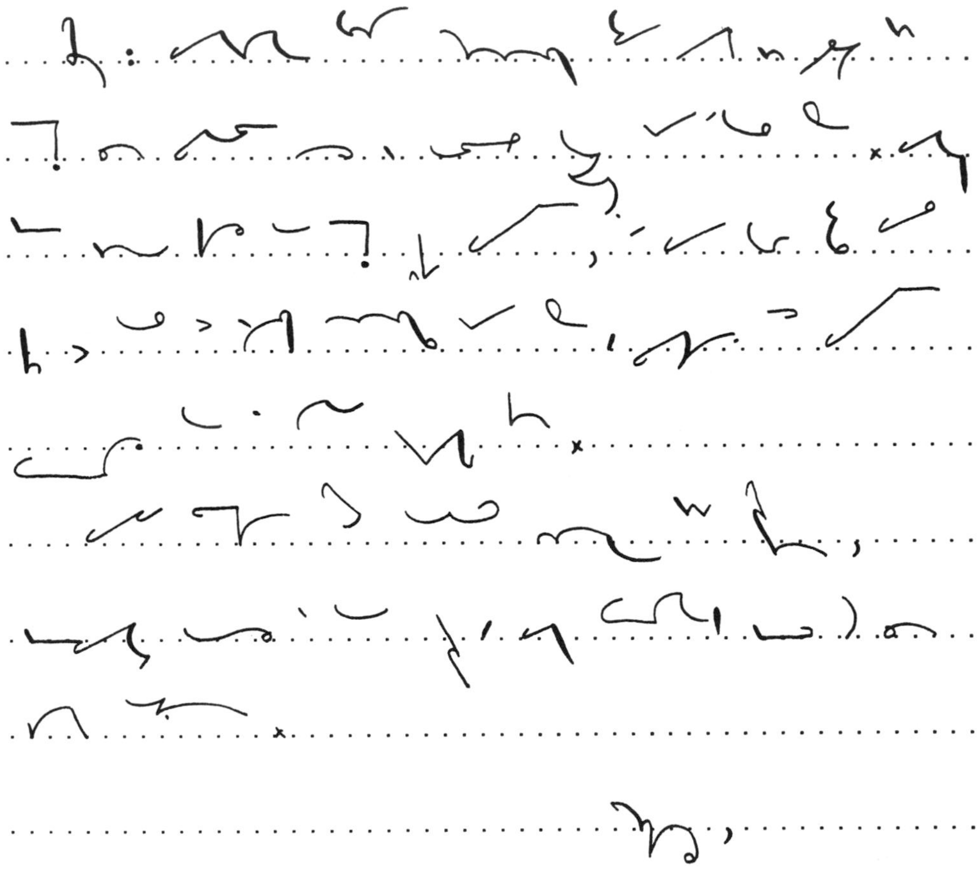

## TRANSCRIPTION LETTERS

### Preview

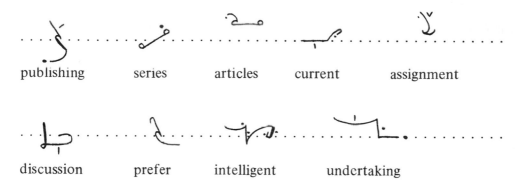

publishing     series     articles     current     assignment

discussion     prefer     intelligent     undertaking

Mr. James Dailey
342 Beverly Place
Regina, Saskatchewan

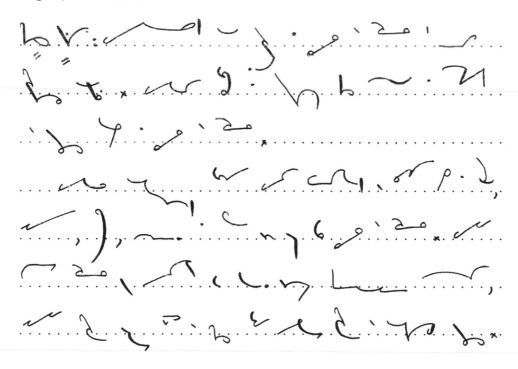

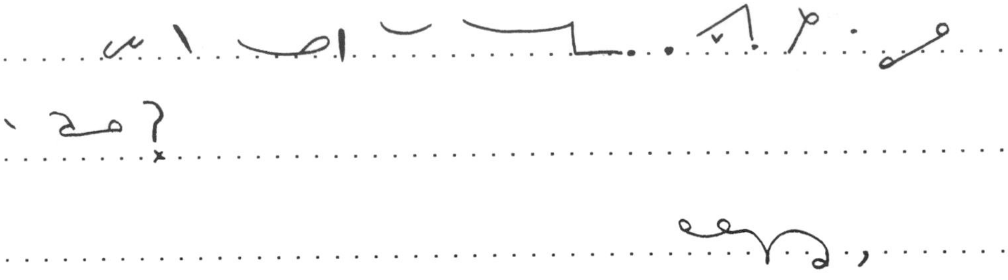

[shorthand outlines]

**Preview**

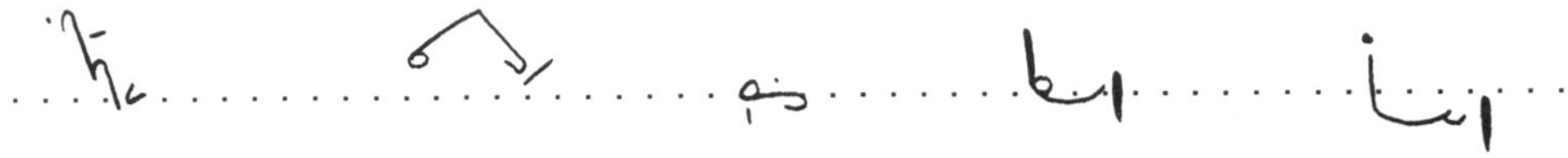

[shorthand] [shorthand] [shorthand] [shorthand] [shorthand]

appropriate    happenings    second    designed    continued

[shorthand]    [shorthand]

agreement    whenever

Spencer Publishing Company
196 Gardner Street
Winnipeg, Manitoba

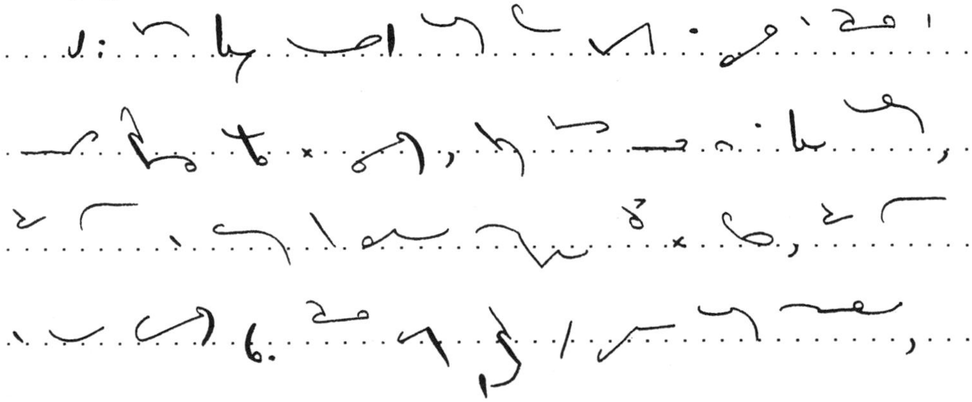

[shorthand outlines]

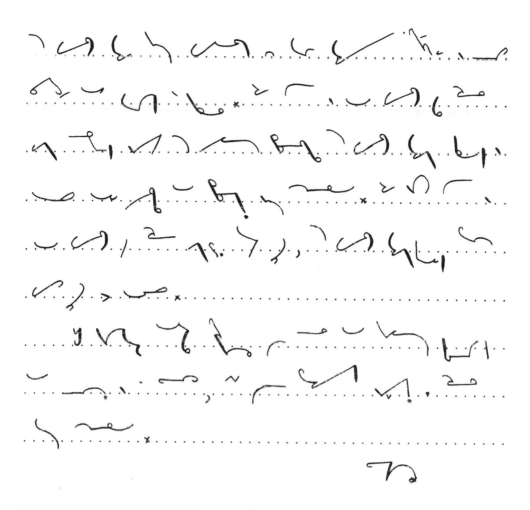

## BUSINESS UNDERSTANDING

What are some of the techniques that a magazine publisher can use to encourage new subscriptions to his magazine?

**Preview**

topics        sufficient        publicity

Mr. James Bailey
342 Beverly Place
Regina, Saskatchewan

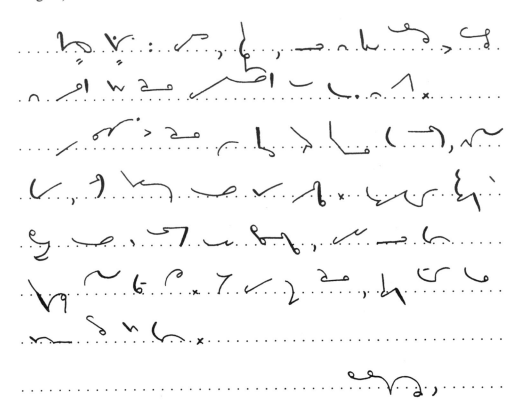

## TRANSCRIPTION SKILL DEVELOPMENT

### Spelling

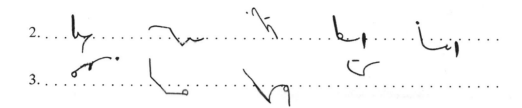

## Punctuation

Punctuate the following:

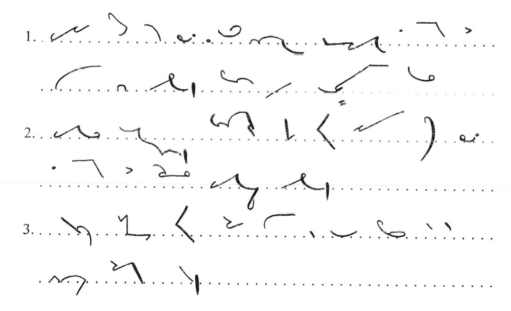

## Transcription Tips

Prepare special shorthand phrases for routine beginnings and endings of the letters you take. Most employers tend to use a similar approach or ending in their dictation.

# 24

## VOCABULARY BUILDING

endeavor
delinquent

1.  [shorthand outline]

discretion

2.  [shorthand outline]

indebtedness

3. 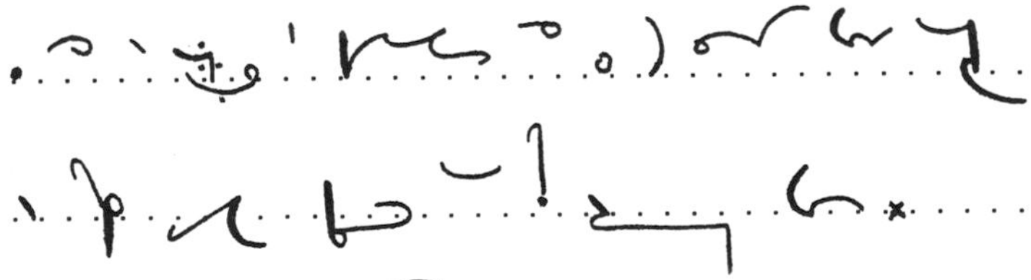 [shorthand outline]

describe

4. 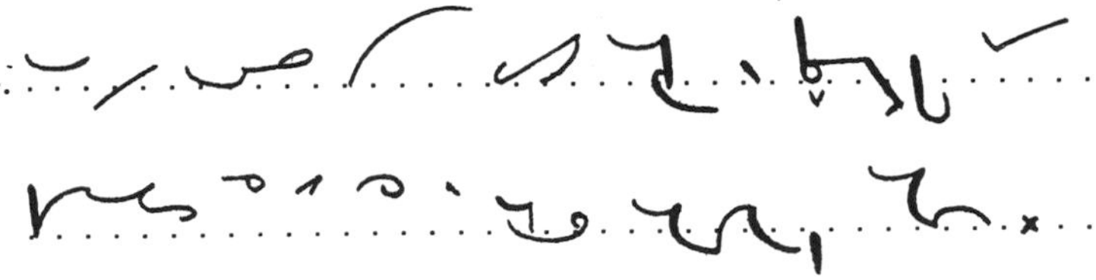 [shorthand outline]

disposition

5. 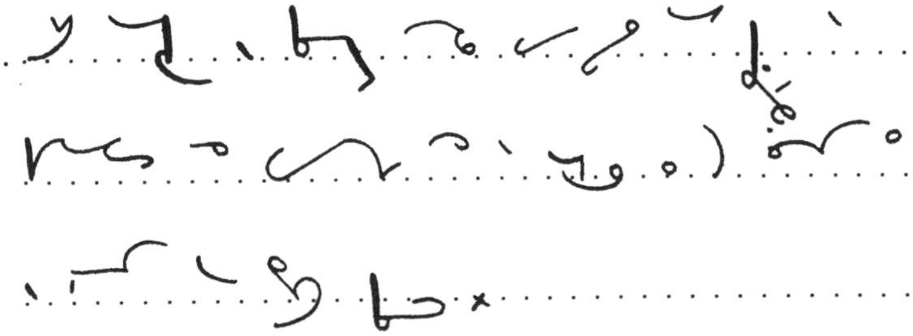 [shorthand outline]

inclined 6.

persuade 7.

## THEORY PRACTICE

# SPEED BUILDING PRACTICE

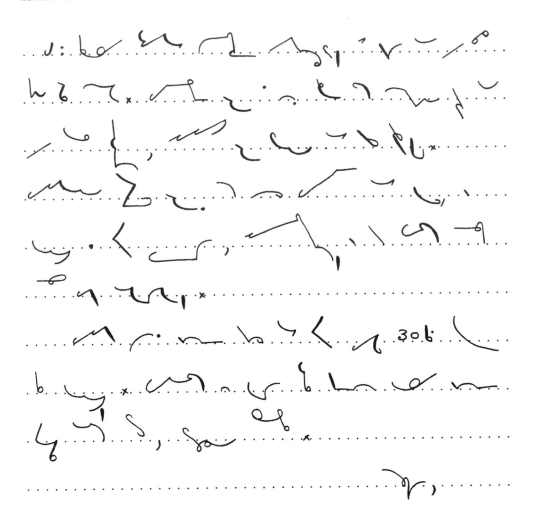

## TRANSCRIPTION LETTERS

**Preview**

subscriber      renewed      subscription      reliable

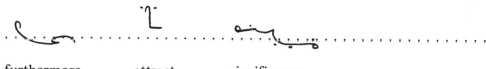

furthermore      attract      significance

Ingram Publications Incorporated
444 Jasper Avenue
Edmonton, Alberta

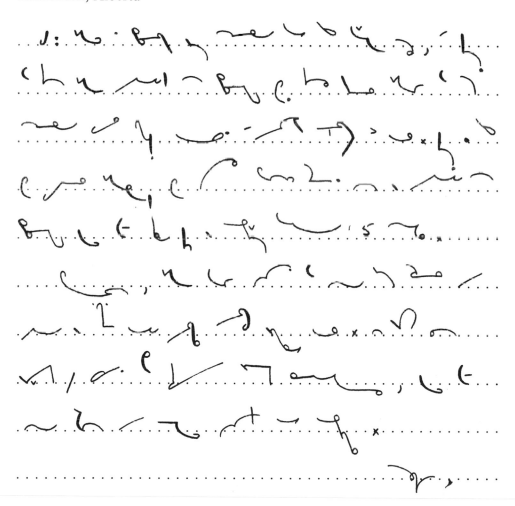

**Preview**

frank        honest   apologies   reminding  renewed

merely

Mr. Lester Hopkins
47 West 15th Street
Calgary, Alberta

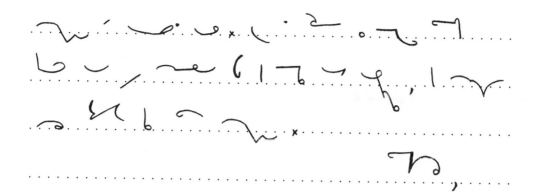

## BUSINESS UNDERSTANDING

Should a magazine publish the news it thinks is important, or should it publish principally the news items it thinks its readers want?

**Preview**

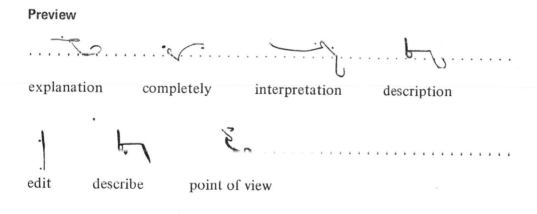

explanation      completely      interpretation      description

edit      describe      point of view

Ingram Publications Incorporated
444 Jasper Avenue
Edmonton, Alberta

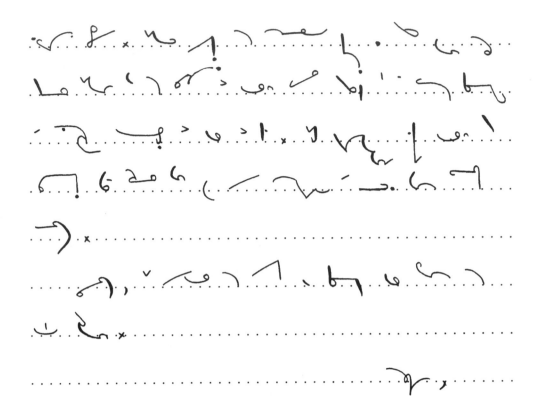

## TRANSCRIPTION SKILL DEVELOPMENT

### Spelling

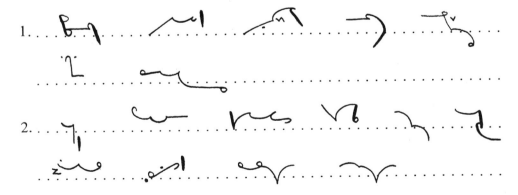

3.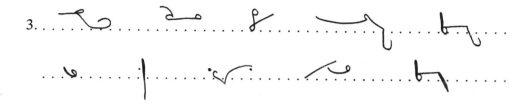

## Punctuation

Punctuate the following:

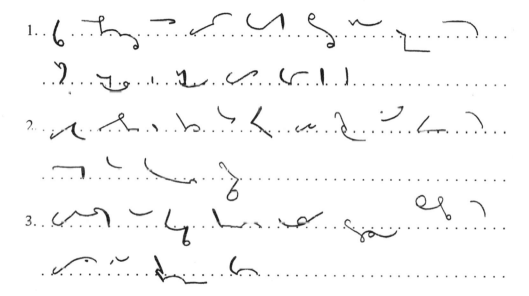

## Transcription Tips

If you cannot read an outline, try to substitute words that would make sense in the context of the sentence. If your employer does not object, you may occasionally substitute a word for one you cannot read.

# 25

VOCABULARY BUILDING

renewal
routine

1.  ...

document

2. 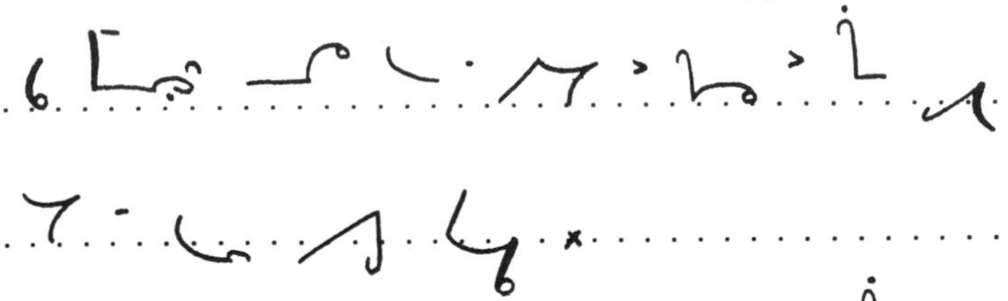 ...

signature

3. 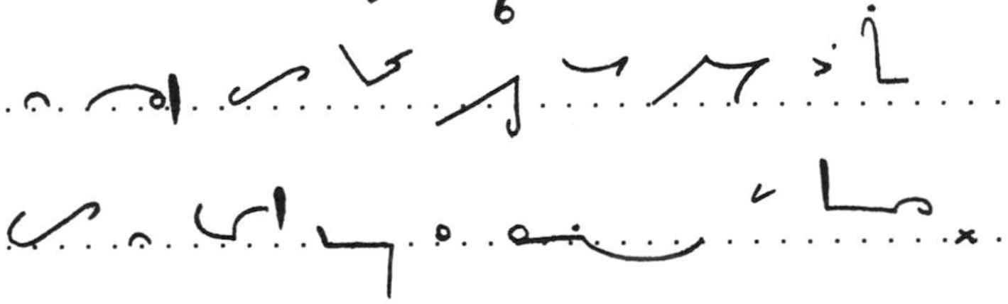 ...

devote
some time

4. 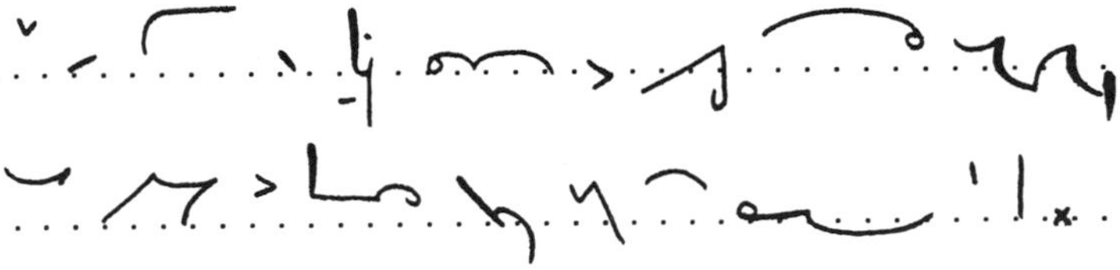 ...

survey

5. 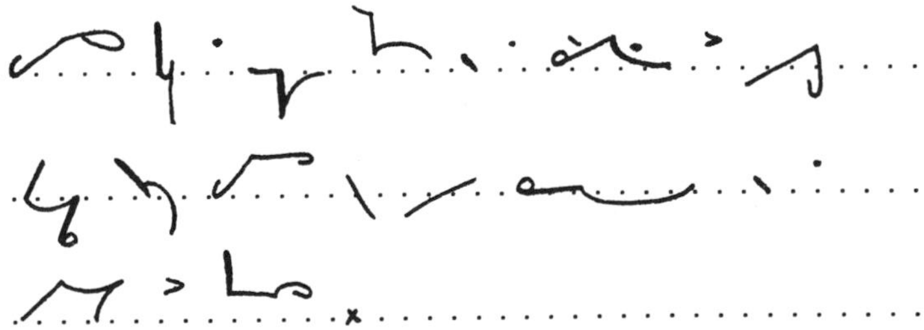 ...

eliminating   6.

elaborate   7.

## THEORY PRACTICE

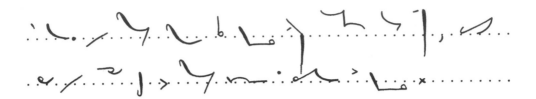

## SPEED BUILDING PRACTICE

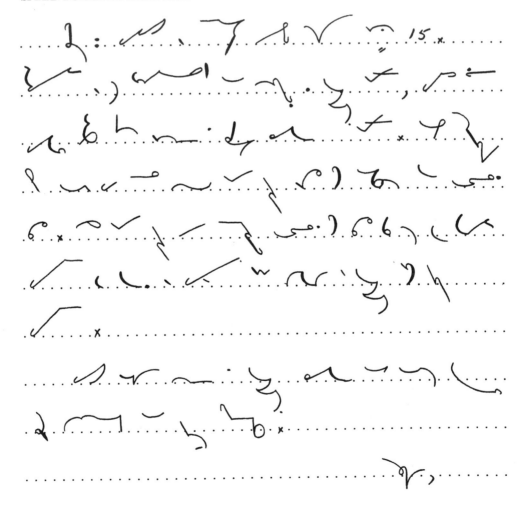

# TRANSCRIPTION LETTERS

**Preview**

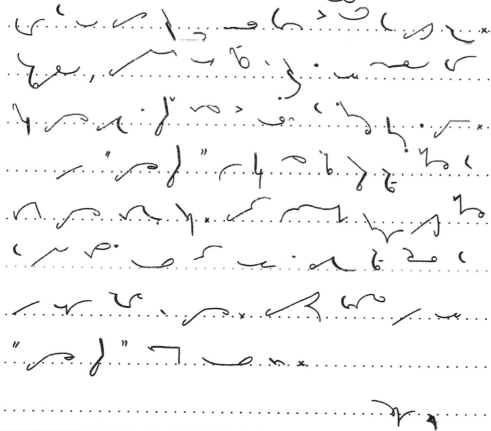

| publication | process | digest | devote | purely |

Mrs. Alberta Chase
49 Oxford Road
Swift Current, Saskatchewan

**Preview**

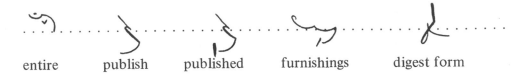

entire     publish     published     furnishings     digest form

Rogers Publishing Company
281 Dexter Boulevard
Vancouver, British Columbia

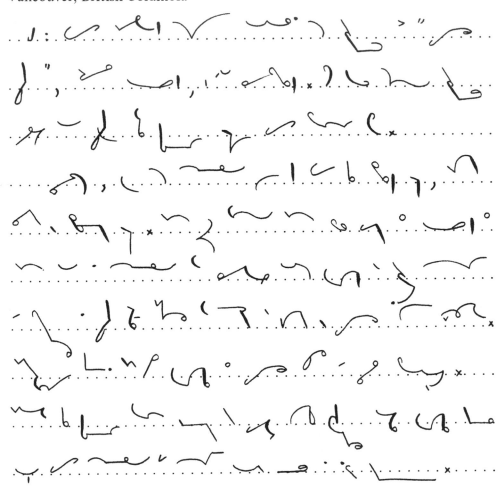

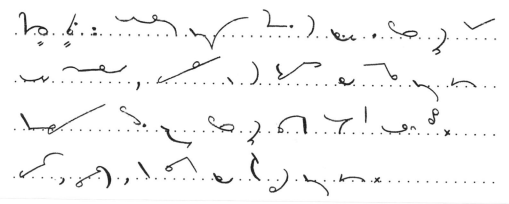

## BUSINESS UNDERSTANDING

What is meant by a "digest" type of magazine and why is it so popular today?

### Preview

stands                    issues

Mrs. Alberta Chase
49 Oxford Road
Swift Current, Saskatchewan

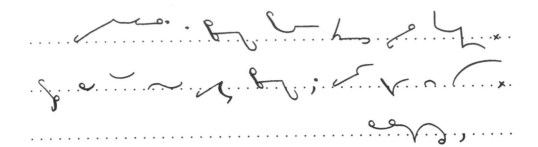

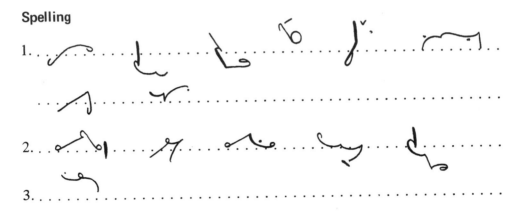

TRANSCRIPTION SKILL DEVELOPMENT

**Spelling**

1.

2.

3.

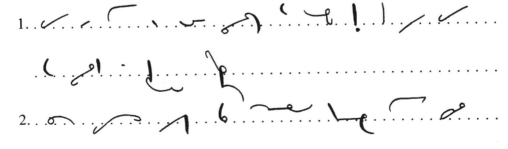

**Punctuation**

Punctuate the following:

1.

2.

198

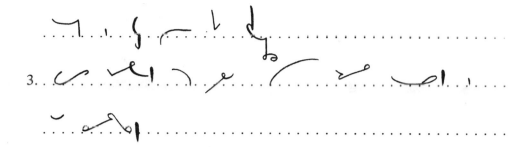

3.

## Transcription Tips

If your job requires you to take dictation from several men, use a code to identify each man and put the code in your shorthand notes next to each letter dictated by that man.

# 26

VOCABULARY BUILDING

annoyance    1.

expression   2.

anxiety      3.

management   4.

compiled     5.

postpone     6.

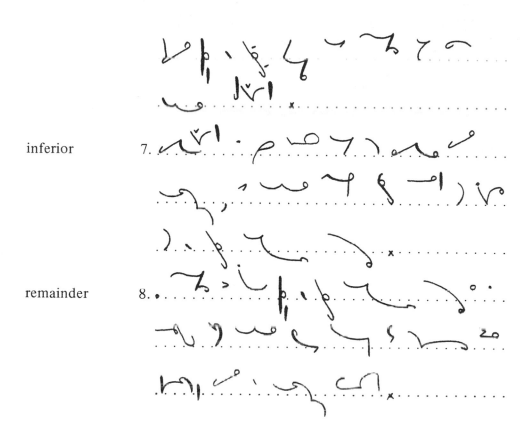

inferior

remainder

## THEORY PRACTICE

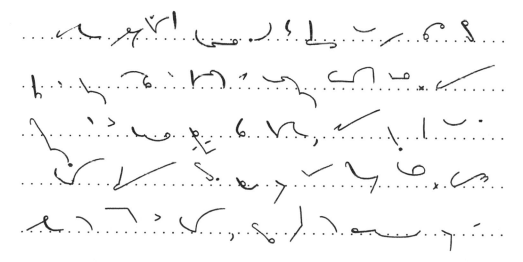

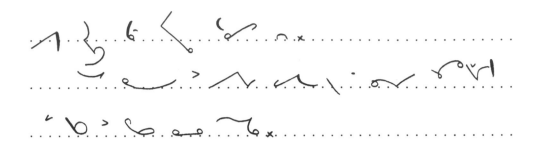

SPEED BUILDING PRACTICE

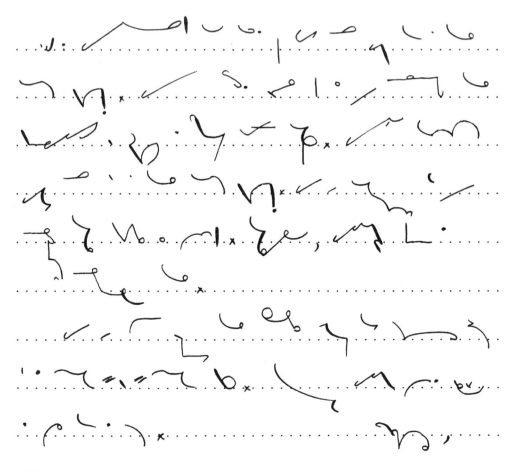

# TRANSCRIPTION LETTERS

**Preview**

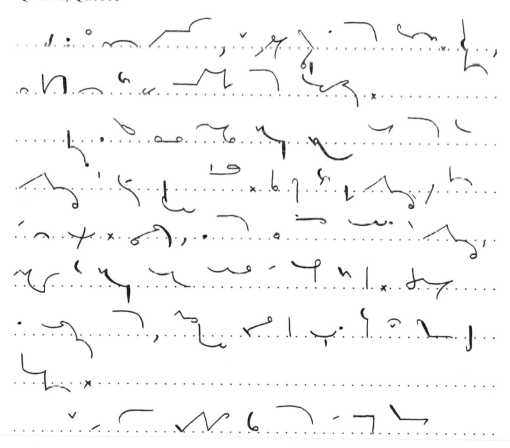

guarantee        occasions        anxiety

Morrison Automobile Agency
1242 Cartier Street
Quebec, Quebec

_(shorthand outlines)_

## Preview

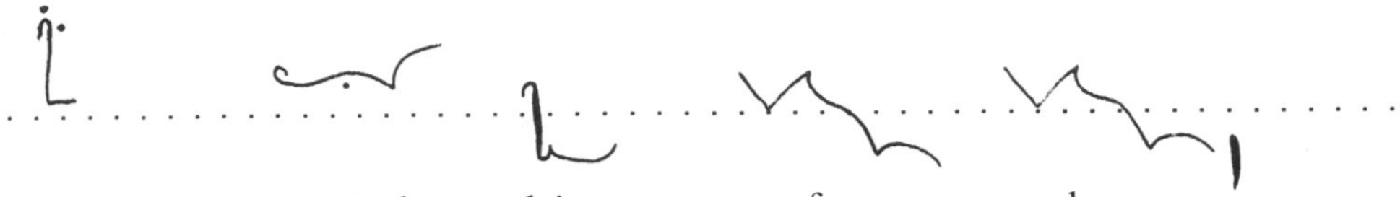

_(shorthand outline)_ contract    _(shorthand outline)_ normal    _(shorthand outline)_ driven    _(shorthand outline)_ perform    _(shorthand outline)_ -ed

_(shorthand outline)_ properly    _(shorthand outline)_ ordinary

Mr. George Jennings
322 Chandler Place
Quebec, Quebec

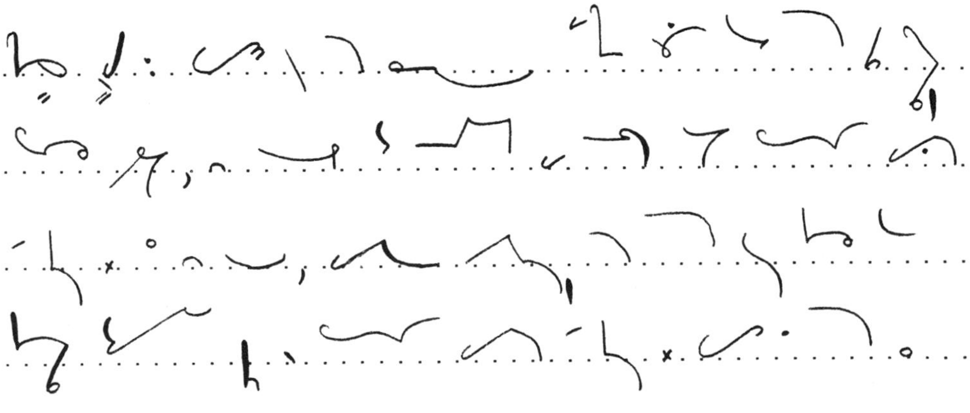

_(shorthand outlines)_

204

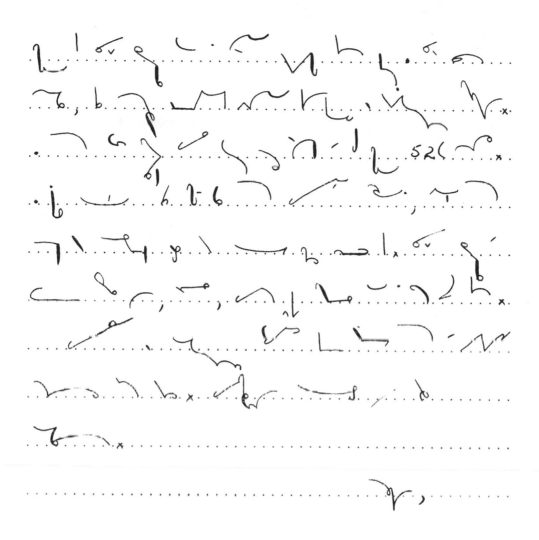

## BUSINESS UNDERSTANDING

Does a guarantee on a car mean that the car is perfect or that any repairs will be made without cost?

**Preview**

intended          exactly          definitely

Morrison Automobile Agency
1242 Cartier Street
Quebec, Quebec

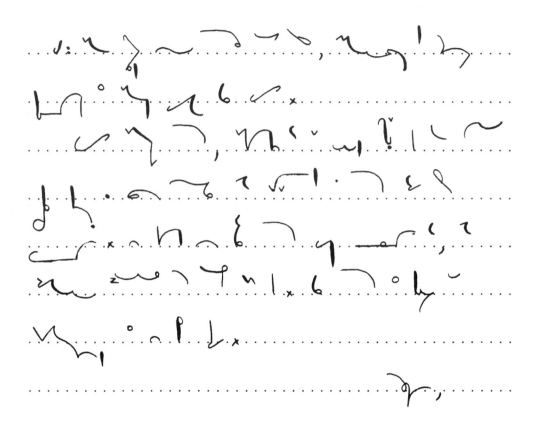

TRANSCRIPTION SKILL DEVELOPMENT

**Spelling**

1.

2.

3.

## Punctuation

Punctuate the following:

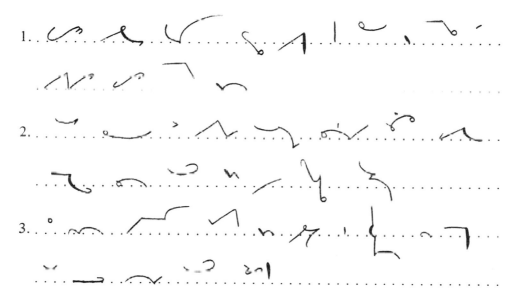

## Transcription Tips

If you are employed in an office where the correspondence is quite technical, read through letters in the files to become familiar with the vocabulary that is customarily used.

# 27

## VOCABULARY BUILDING

marvelous
reputation
    1.

simplicity
    2.

justify
    3.

fortunate
    4.

tendency
    5.

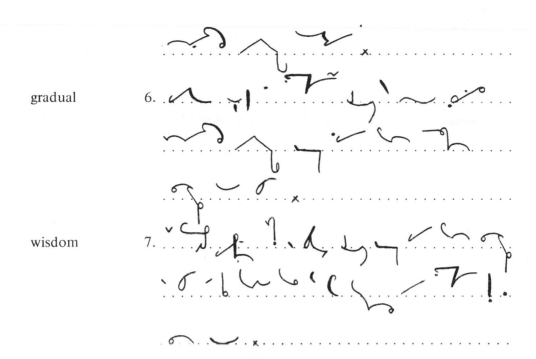

gradual  6.

wisdom  7.

## THEORY PRACTICE

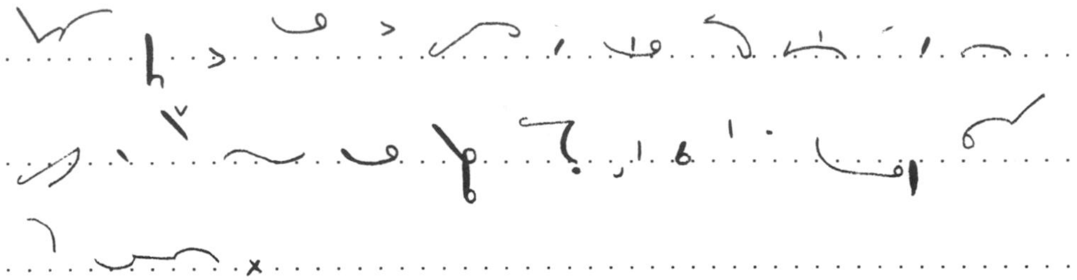

_(shorthand outlines)_

## SPEED BUILDING PRACTICE

**Preview**

_(shorthand outline)_      _(shorthand outline)_

United States          independent companies

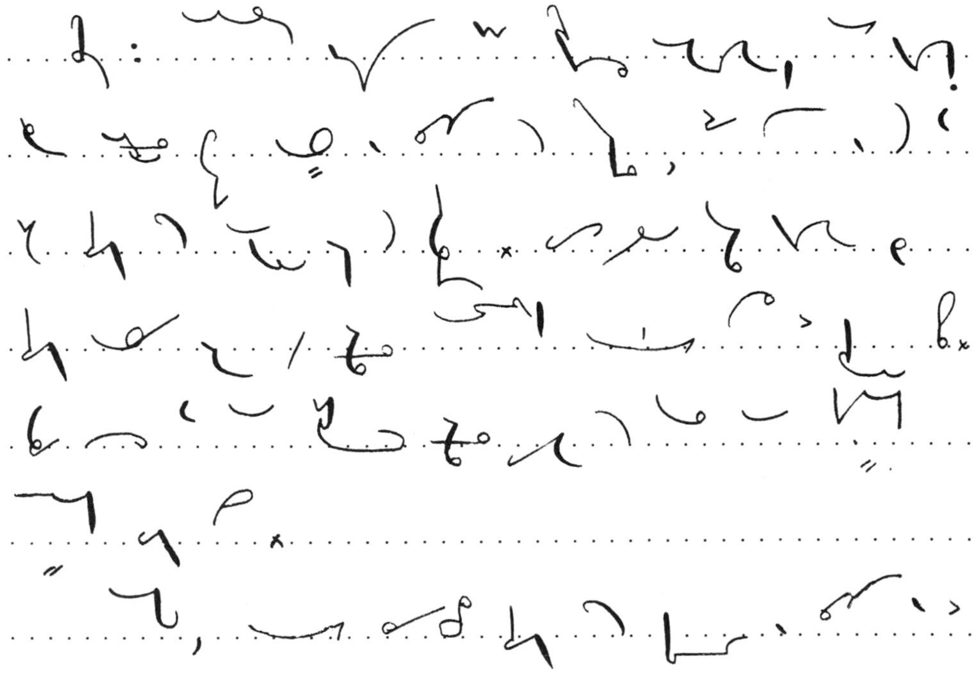

_(shorthand outlines)_

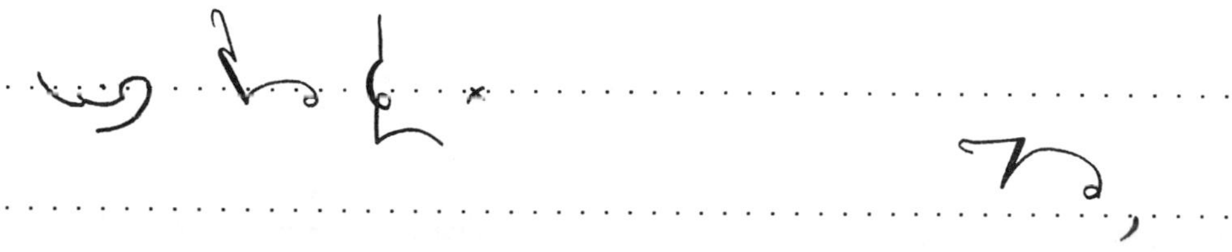

TRANSCRIPTION LETTERS

**Preview**

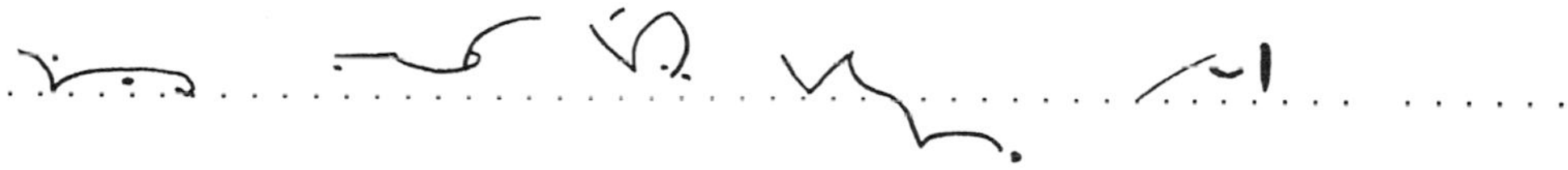

remainder cancel policy performing recommended

Phillips Car Company
110 Bank Street
Ottawa 5, Ontario

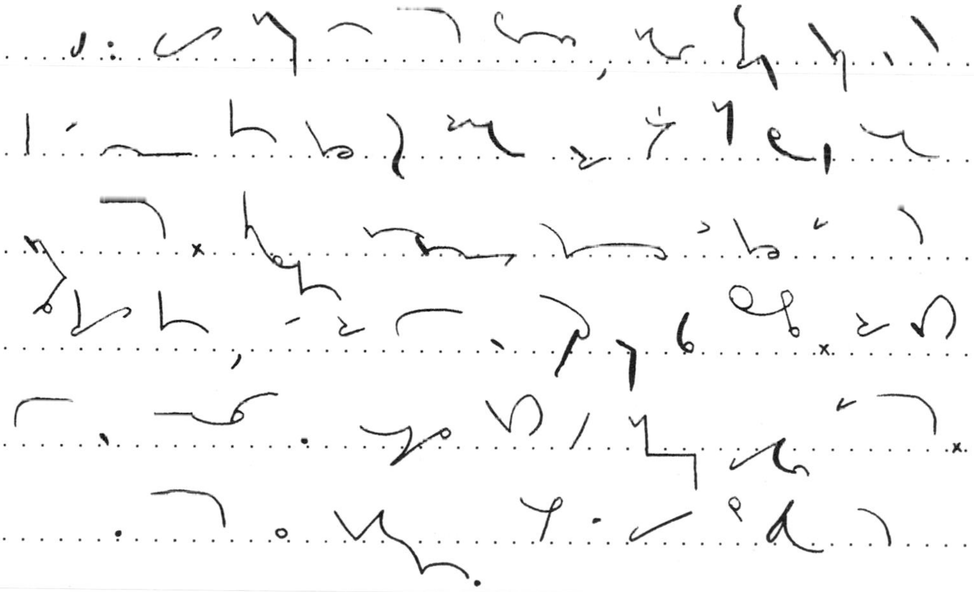

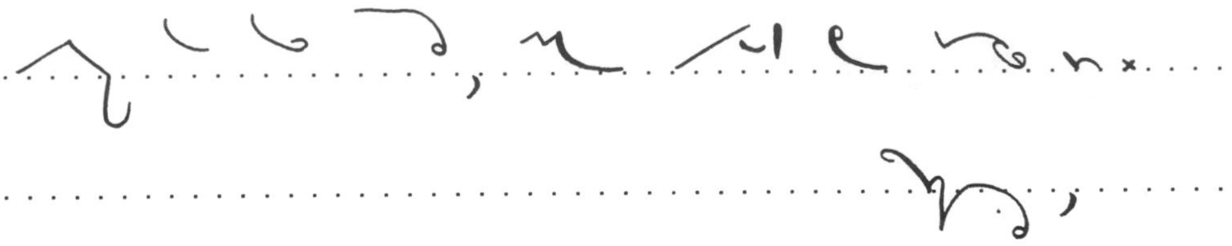

*(shorthand symbols)*

**Preview**

*(shorthand symbols)*

financing    obligation    penalty    furthermore

*(shorthand symbols)*

protection    assist

Mr. Harold Porter
404 Fourth Avenue
Ottawa 3, Ontario

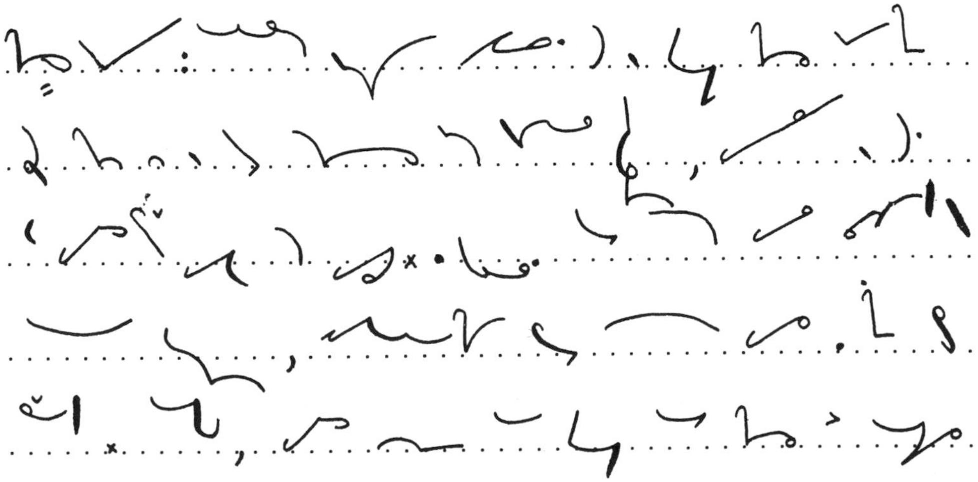

*(shorthand symbols)*

[Shorthand outlines - 7 lines]

## BUSINESS UNDERSTANDING

What is meant by making "time payments"? Why do some people prefer to pay off a loan before it is due?

**Preview**

[Shorthand outlines]

thoroughly      despite      intended

Phillips Car Company
110 Bank Street
Ottawa 5, Ontario

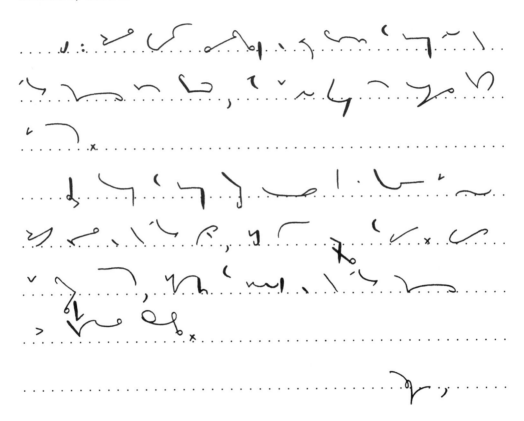

## TRANSCRIPTION SKILL DEVELOPMENT

**Spelling**

1.

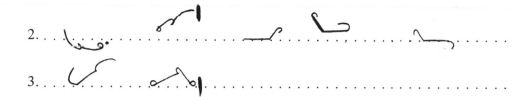

2. . . . . . . . . . . . . . . . . . . . . . . . . . . . . . . . . . . . . . . . . . . . . . . . . . . . . . . . . . . . . .

3. . . . . . . . . . . . . . . . . . . . . . . . . . . . . . . . . . . . . . . . . . . . . . . . . . . . . . . . . . . . . .

## Punctuation

Punctuate the following:

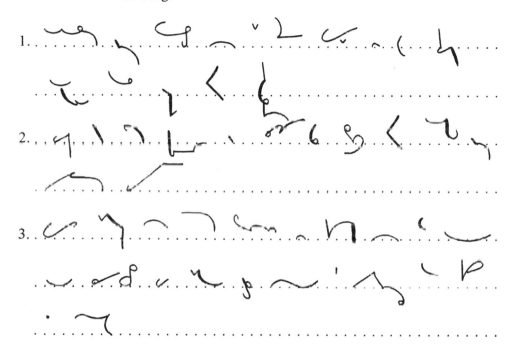

1. . . . . . . . . . . . . . . . . . . . . . . . . . . . . . . . . . . . . . . . . . . . . . . . . . . . . . . . . . . . . .

. . . . . . . . . . . . . . . . . . . . . . . . . . . . . . . . . . . . . . . . . . . . . . . . . . . . . . . . . . . . . .

2. . . . . . . . . . . . . . . . . . . . . . . . . . . . . . . . . . . . . . . . . . . . . . . . . . . . . . . . . . . . . .

. . . . . . . . . . . . . . . . . . . . . . . . . . . . . . . . . . . . . . . . . . . . . . . . . . . . . . . . . . . . . .

3. . . . . . . . . . . . . . . . . . . . . . . . . . . . . . . . . . . . . . . . . . . . . . . . . . . . . . . . . . . . . .

. . . . . . . . . . . . . . . . . . . . . . . . . . . . . . . . . . . . . . . . . . . . . . . . . . . . . . . . . . . . . .

. . . . . . . . . . . . . . . . . . . . . . . . . . . . . . . . . . . . . . . . . . . . . . . . . . . . . . . . . . . . . .

## Transcription Tips

If you are transcribing terms that are unfamiliar to you either in spelling or meaning, consult the dictionary; if necessary, ask other employees for assistance.

# 28

## VOCABULARY BUILDING

activity
comparatively

1. 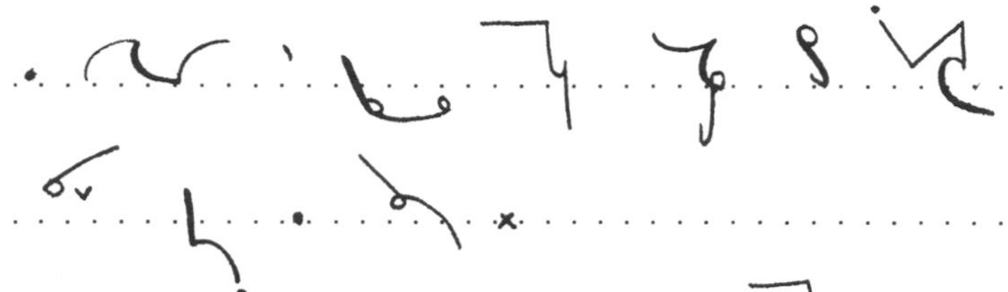 *[shorthand outlines]*

burden

2. 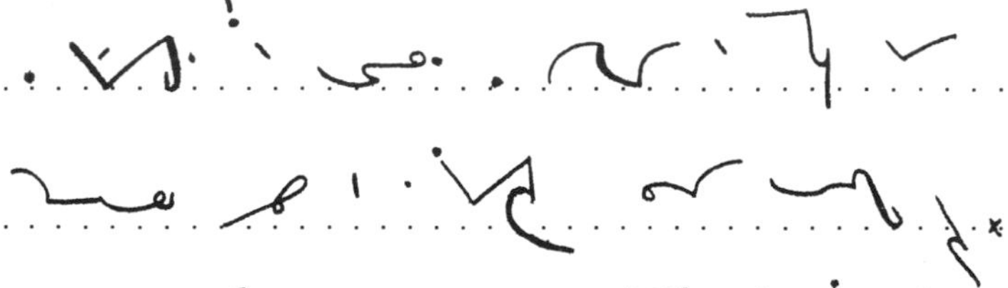 *[shorthand outlines]*

fundamental

3. 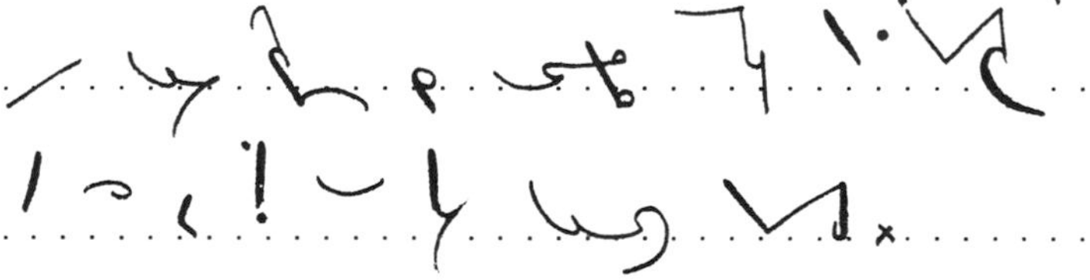 *[shorthand outlines]*

characteristic

4. 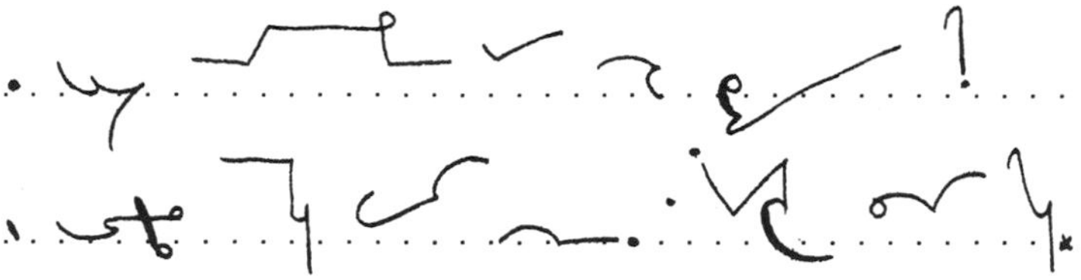 *[shorthand outlines]*

acquainted

5. 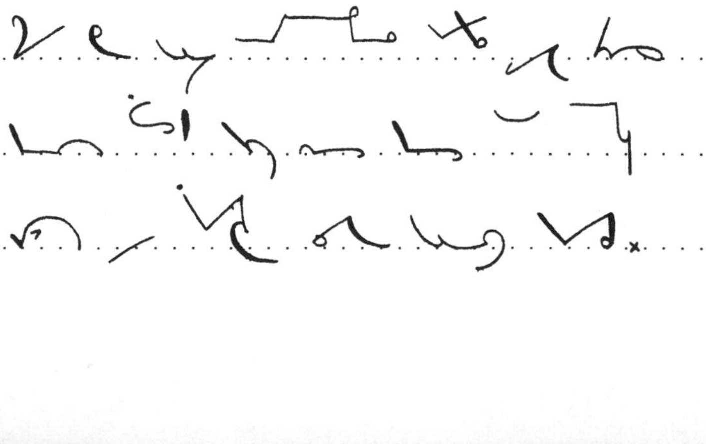 *[shorthand outlines]*

classification   6.

ignorant   7.

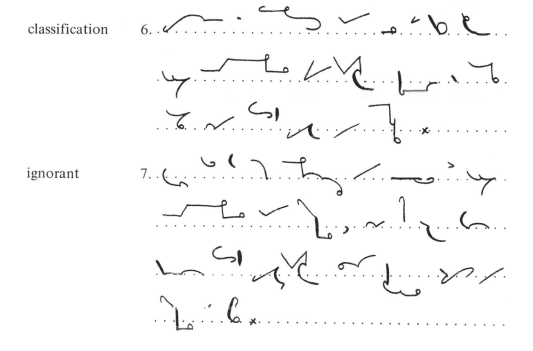

**THEORY PRACTICE**

217

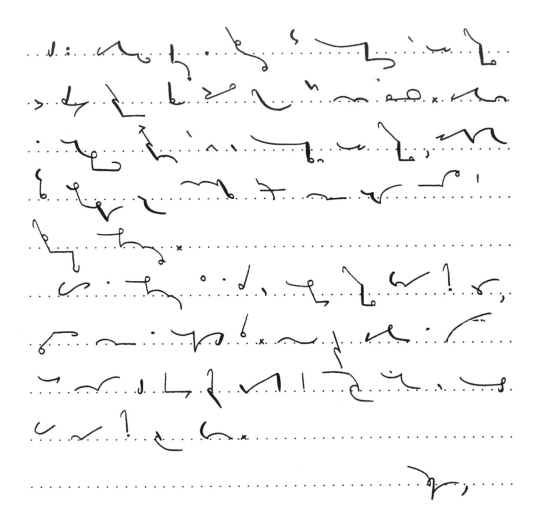

## SPEED BUILDING PRACTICE

218

# TRANSCRIPTION LETTERS

**Preview**

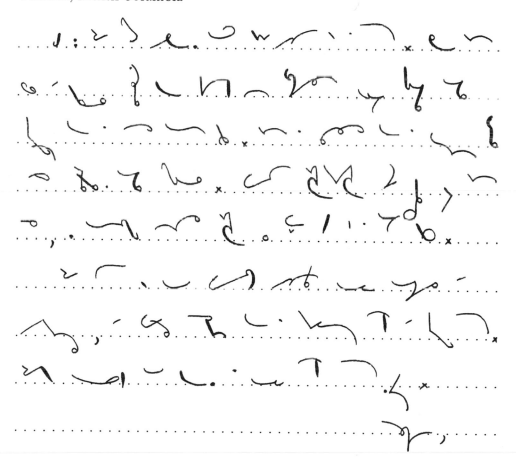

rental      position      distances      basis

Simmons Auto Rental Agency Incorporated
330 Hudson Street
Victoria, British Columbia

**Preview**

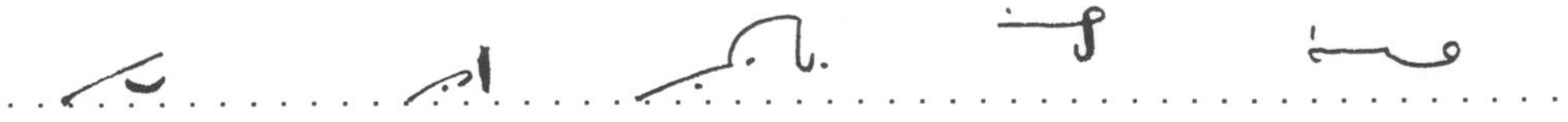

recommend rented relative accident occurrence

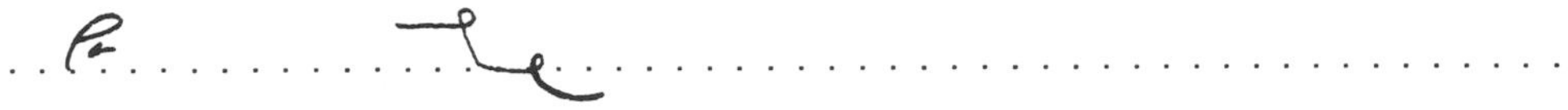

lowest expensive

Mr. Harold Prescott
412 Auburn Place
Victoria, British Columbia

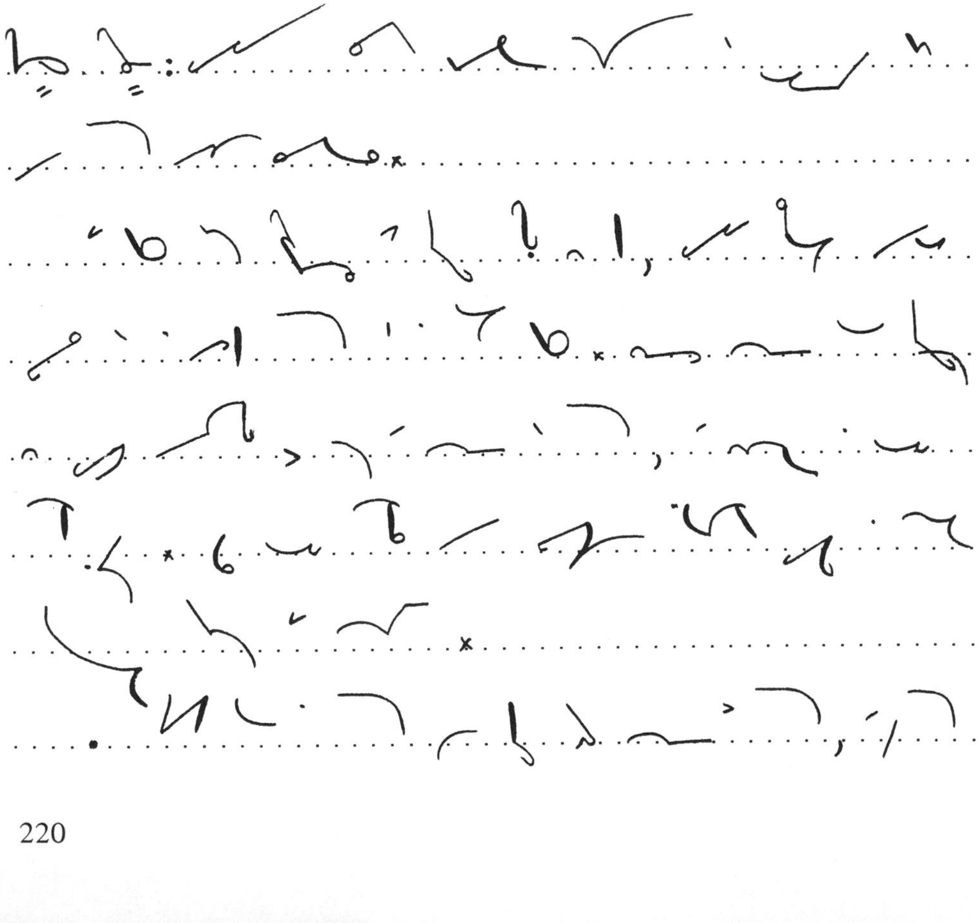

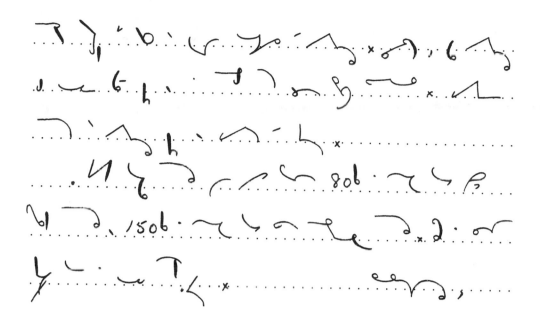

## BUSINESS UNDERSTANDING

Why might it be more desirable for a salesman to rent a car than to buy one? Would the average wage earner be better off renting a car instead of buying one?

## Preview

answered          essential

Simmons Auto Rental Agency Incorporated
330 Hudson Street
Victoria, British Columbia

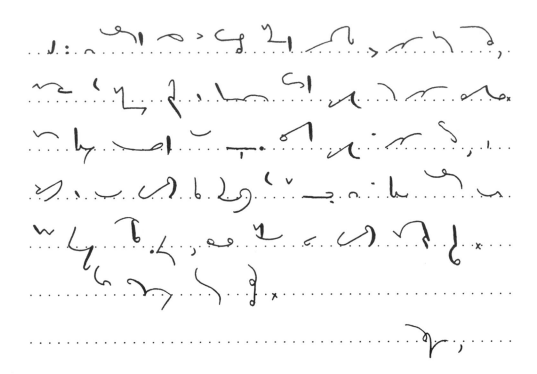

## TRANSCRIPTION SKILL DEVELOPMENT

### Spelling

1.

2.

3.

## Punctuation

Punctuate the following:

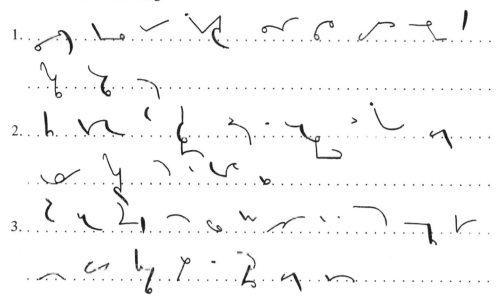

## Transcription Tips

If you have free time on your job, use the time to revise or bring up to date the files you maintain.

# 29

VOCABULARY BUILDING

illustrate

1.

permanent

2.

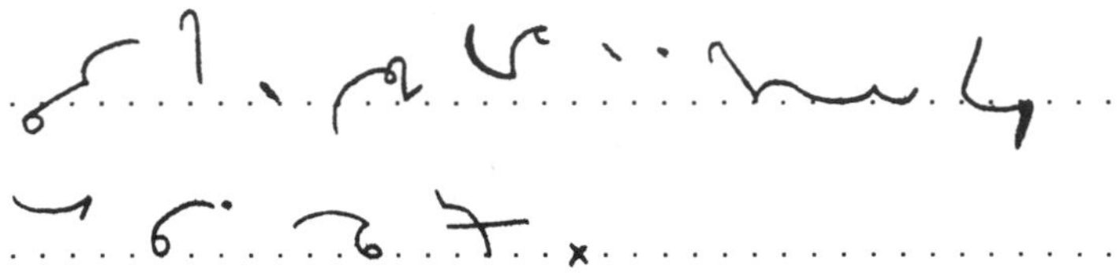

economy

3.

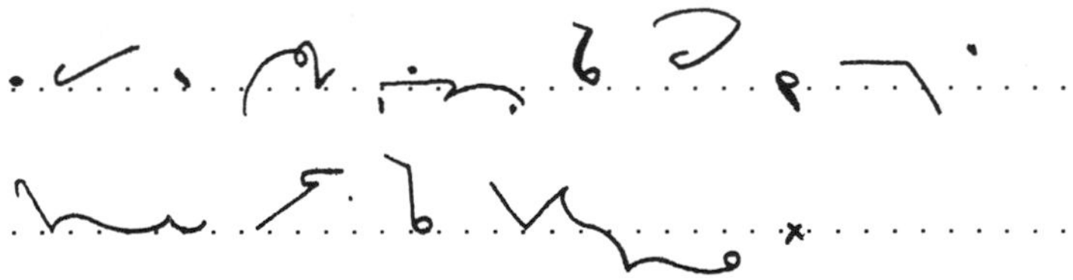

machinery

4.

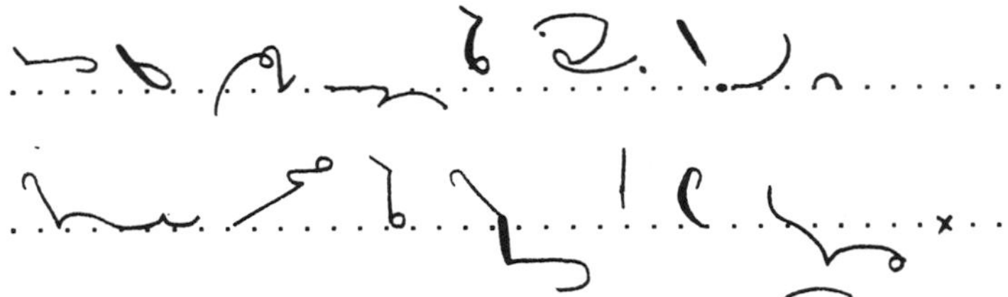

patent

5.

solution

6.

overcome        7.

specific        8.

## THEORY PRACTICE

SPEED BUILDING PRACTICE

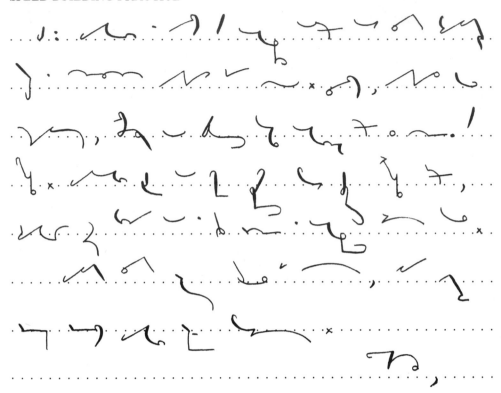

TRANSCRIPTION LETTERS

**Preview**

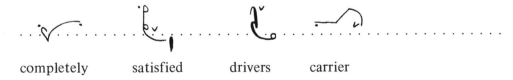

completely     satisfied     drivers     carrier

Douglas Auto Service Incorporated
306 South Drive
Lachine, Quebec

226

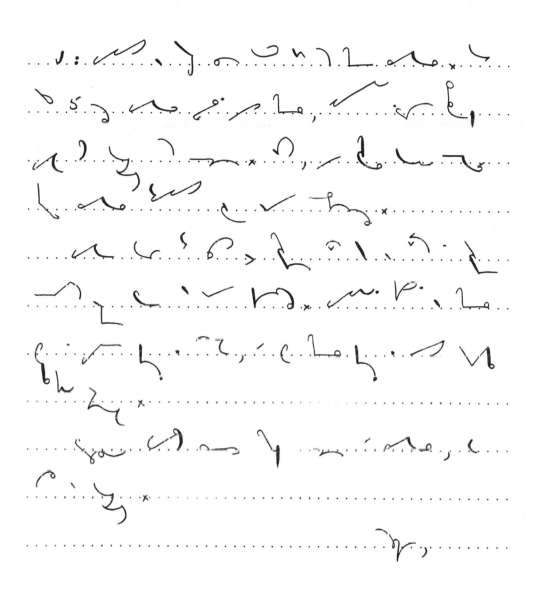

**Preview**

upkeep    greater    schedule    reference    specifically    trained

Fisher Manufacturing Company
186 Butler Street
Montreal, Quebec

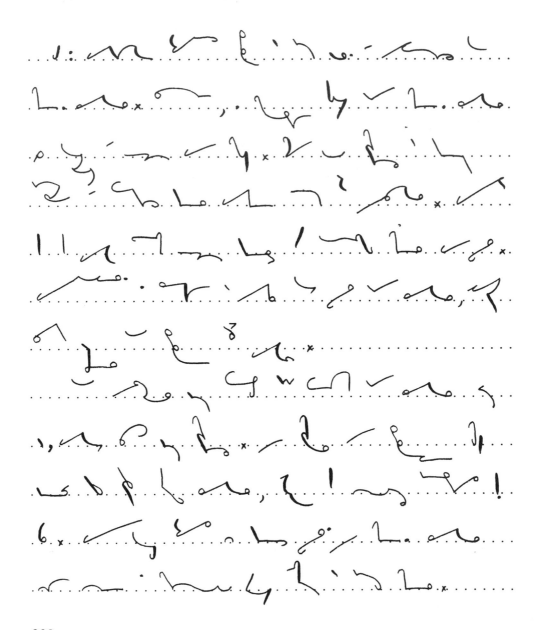

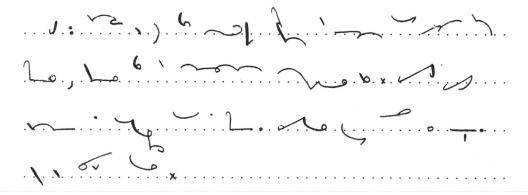

## BUSINESS UNDERSTANDING

What is the difference between a "private carrier" and a "public carrier"?
Give examples of each type of carrier.

## Preview

comments        overcome        somewhat

Douglas Auto Service Incorporated
306 South Drive
Lachine, Quebec

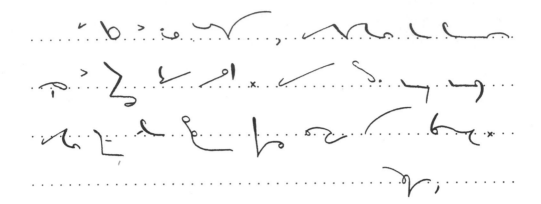

## TRANSCRIPTION SKILL DEVELOPMENT

**Spelling**

1.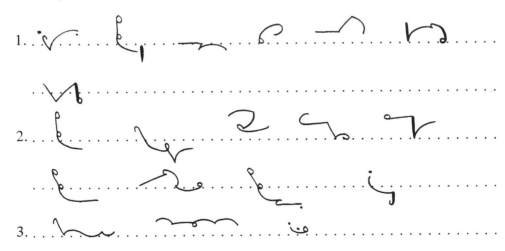

2.

3.

**Punctuation**

Punctuate the following:

1.

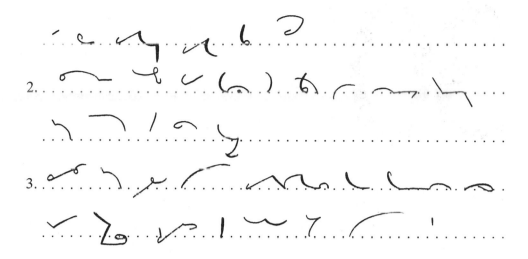

## Transcription Tips

When your employer dictates a reply to a letter, he will frequently give you the original letter. Make it a practice to clip together all papers pertaining to one letter as soon as possible.

# 30

VOCABULARY BUILDING

enormous
foreign

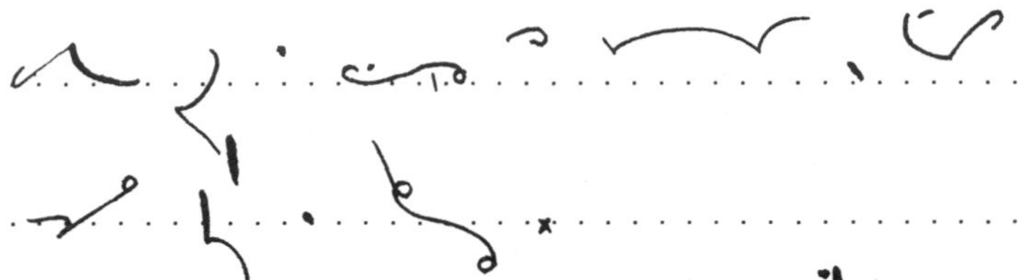

adequate

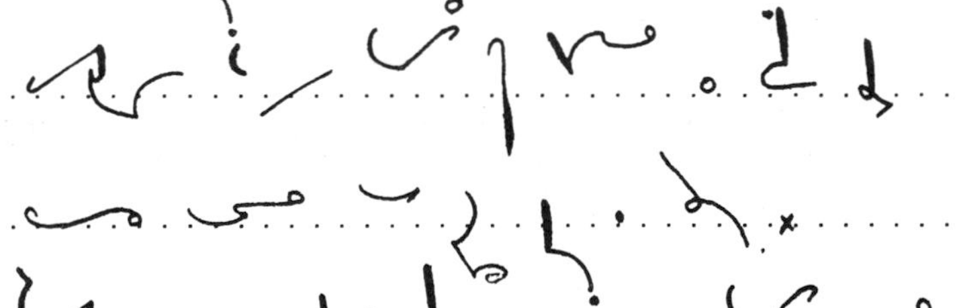

hitherto

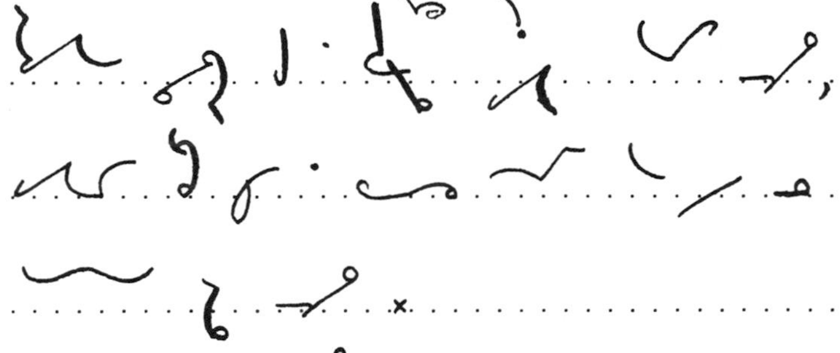

eventually

1.

2.

3.

4.

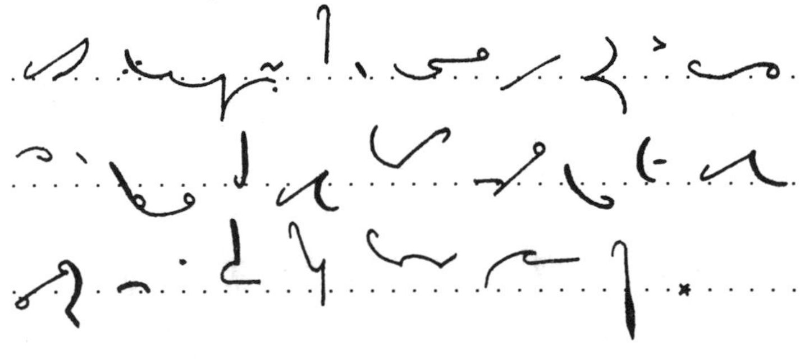

assortment    5

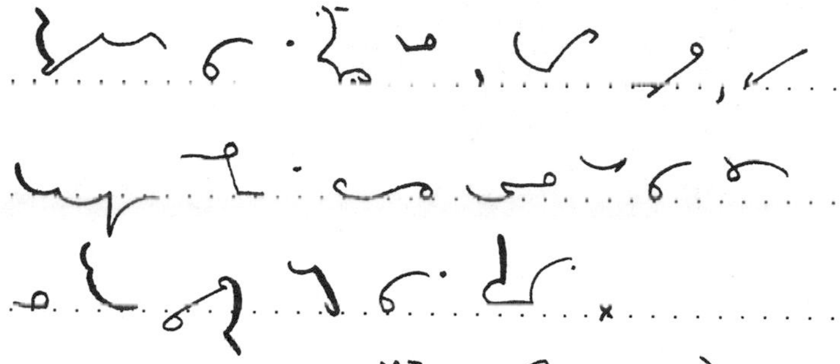

adopt    6.

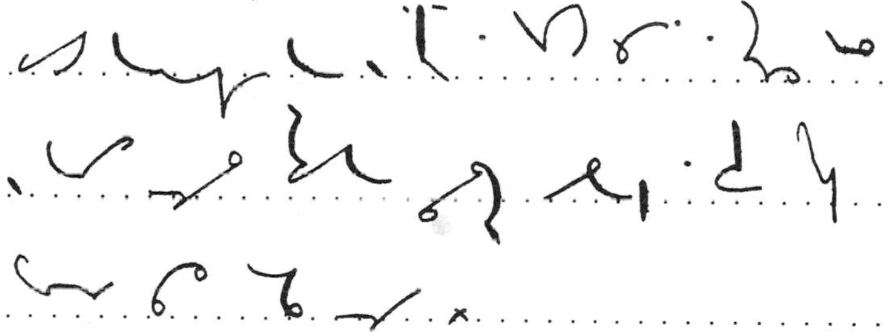

ascertain    7.

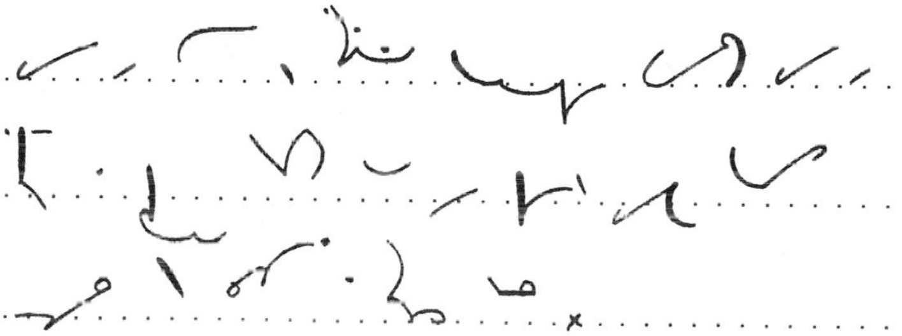

THEORY PRACTICE

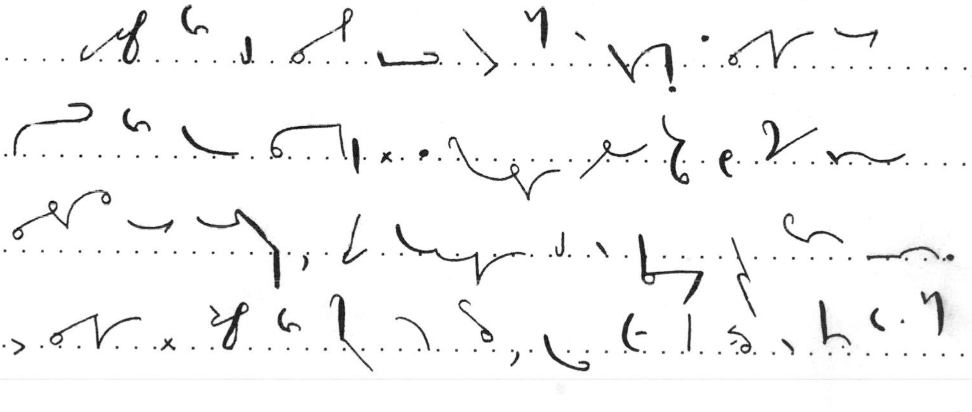

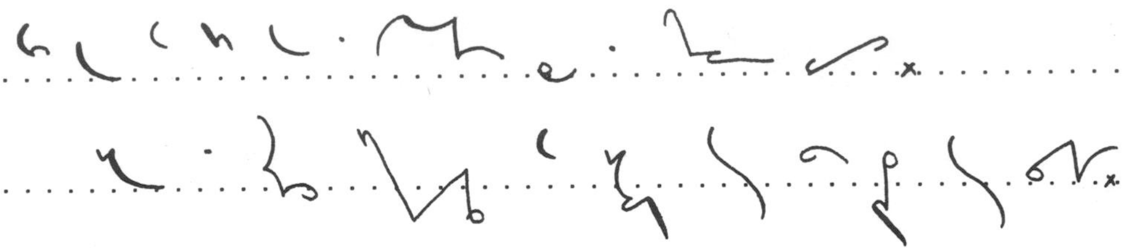

## SPEED BUILDING PRACTICE

**Preview**

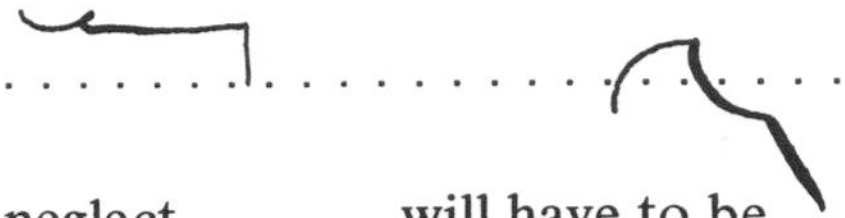

neglect       will have to be

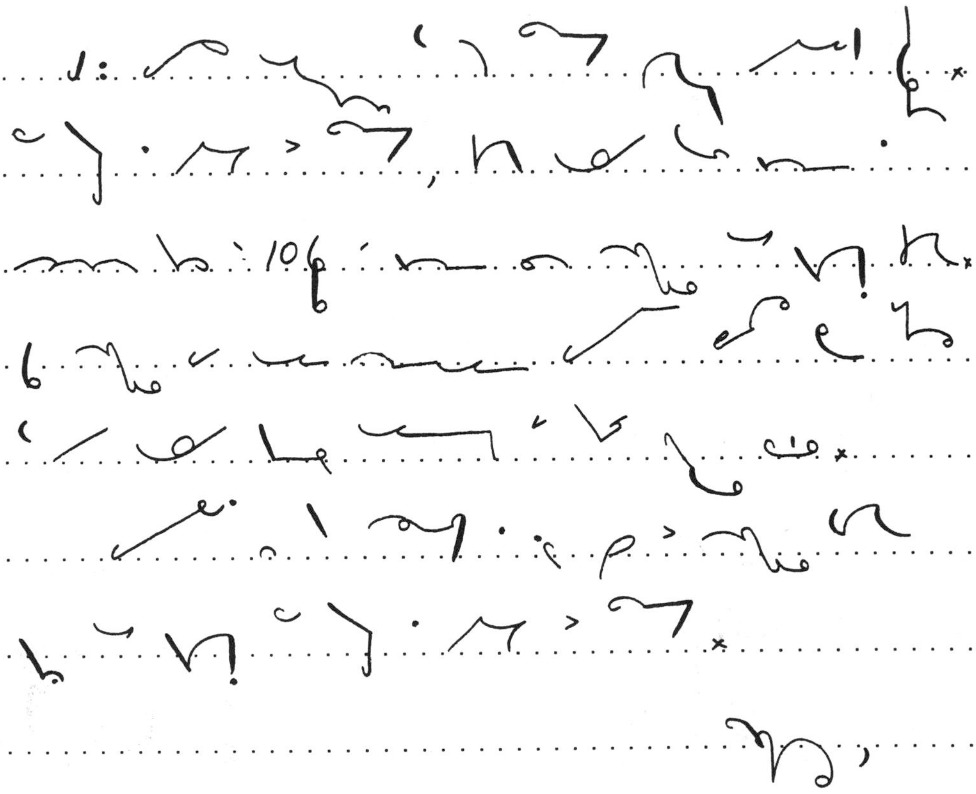

# TRANSCRIPTION LETTERS

**Preview**

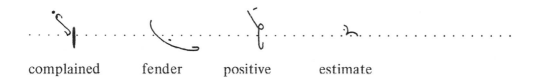

complained     fender     positive     estimate

Bryant Garage Company
196 Main Street
Thunder Bay, Ontario

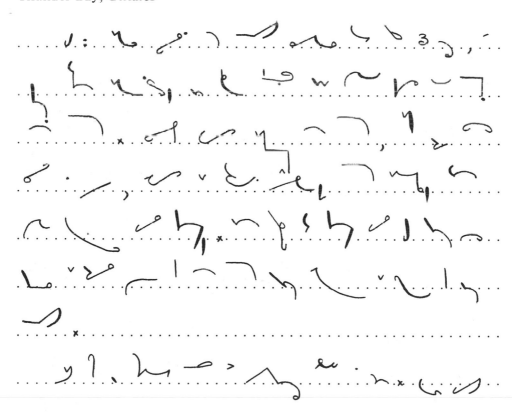

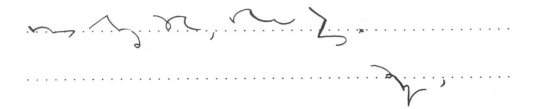

## Preview

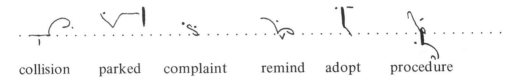

collision    parked    complaint    remind    adopt    procedure

Mr. Peter Hopkins
156 Westree Avenue
Thunder Bay, Ontario

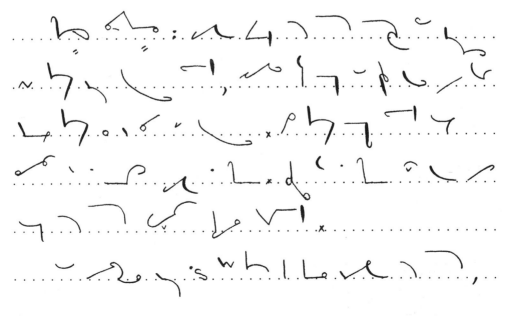

236

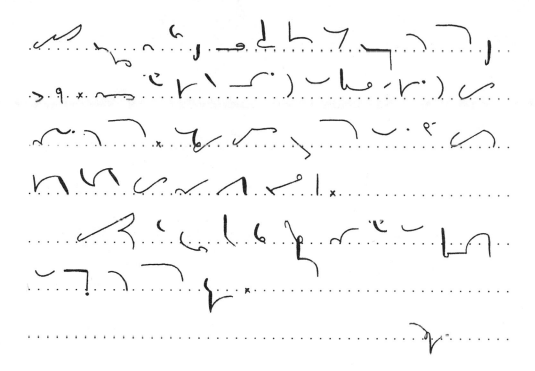

## BUSINESS UNDERSTANDING

Can a car owner obtain insurance against damage done to his car while he is not in it?

advisability        advance        cooperate

Bryant Garage Company
196 Main Street
Thunder Bay, Ontario

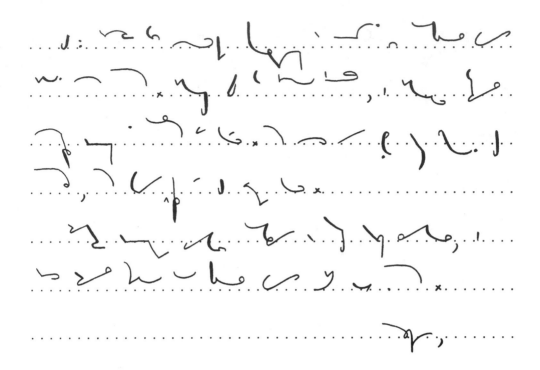

## TRANSCRIPTION SKILL DEVELOPMENT

### Spelling

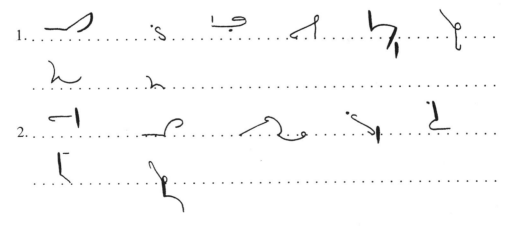

3.

## Punctuation

Punctuate the following:

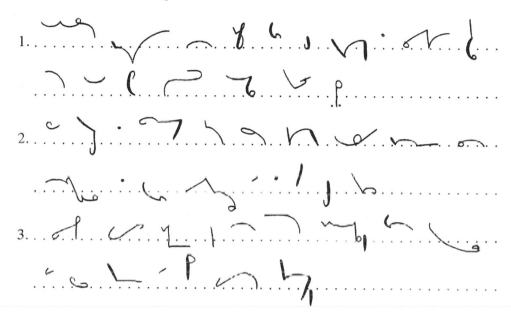

## Transcription Tips

When your employer gives you the letter that he is answering, put a number on it and the same number on your shorthand notes for the letter so that they can be identified.

# 31

VOCABULARY BUILDING

argument  1. ...

facilities  2. ...

chiefly  3. ...

hardest  4. ...

collateral  5. ...

insisted  6. ...

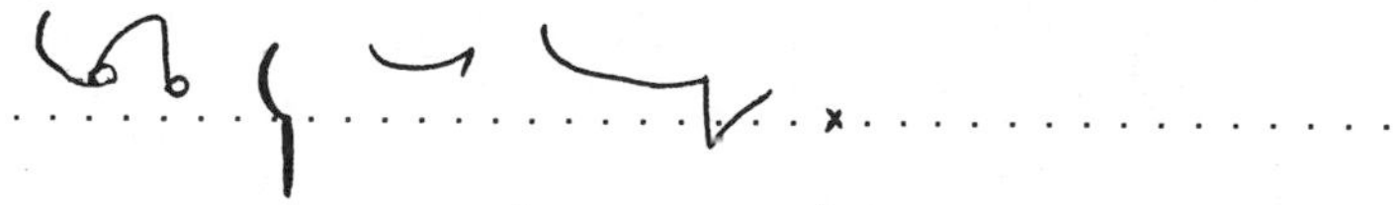

debit       7

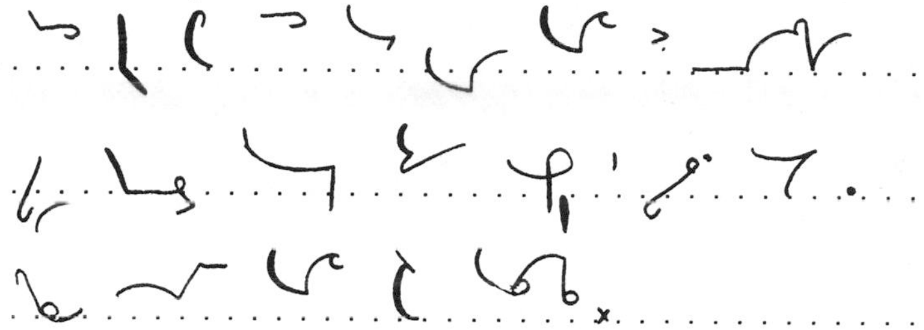

impression    8

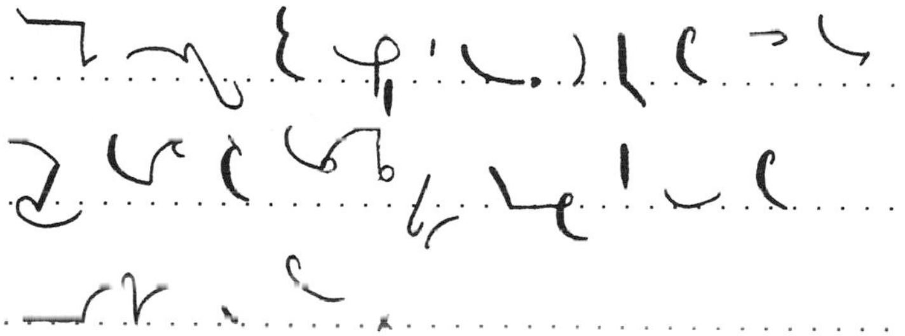

## THEORY PRACTICE

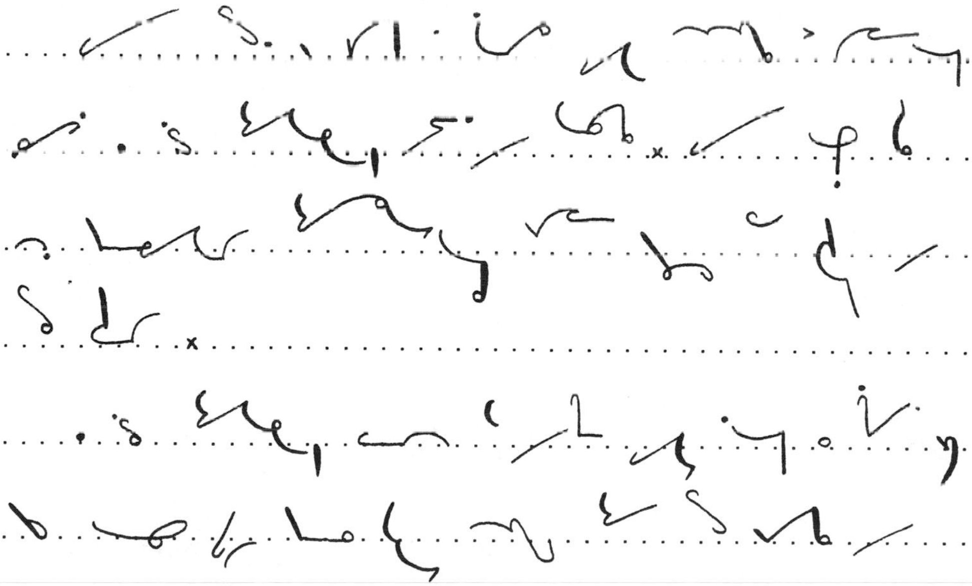

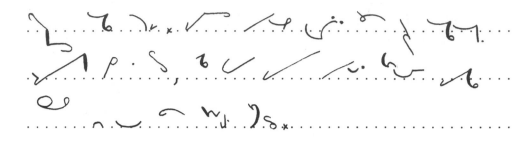

## SPEED BUILDING PRACTICE

# TRANSCRIPTION LETTERS

**Preview**

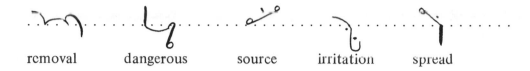

removal     dangerous     source     irritation     spread

Mrs. Doris Ross
124 Main Street
Halifax, Nova Scotia

**Preview**

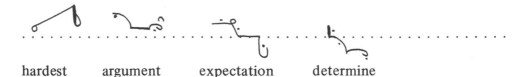

hardest    argument    expectation    determine

Dr. Harold Owen
226 Governor Road
Victoria, British Columbia

[shorthand symbols]

## BUSINESS UNDERSTANDING

What can a doctor do to get a patient to go through an operation that he
feels is necessary and which the patient does not want to have?

## Preview

[shorthand symbols]

decision    preventing    similar    medicines    prescribed

[shorthand symbols]

infection

Mrs. Doris Ross
124 Main Street
Halifax, Nova Scotia

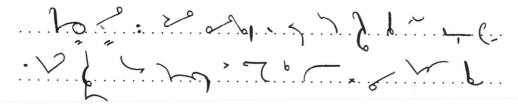

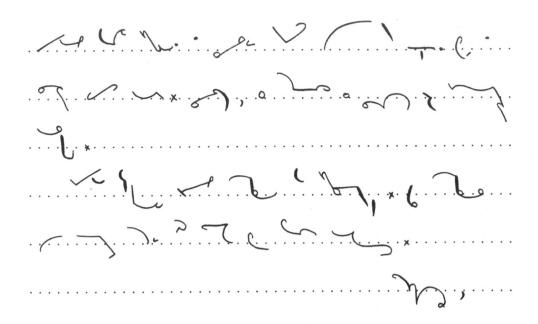

## TRANSCRIPTION SKILL DEVELOPMENT

**Spelling**

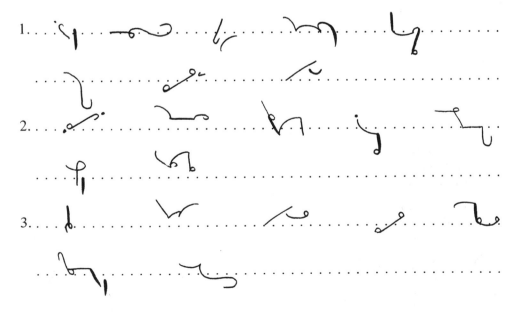

## Punctuation

Punctuate the following:

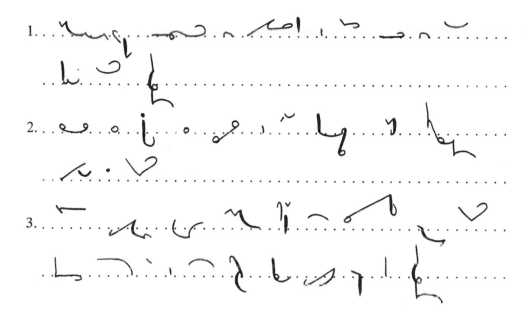

## Transcription Tips

During pauses in dictation, read your notes, inserting punctuation marks and strengthening "weak" outlines.

# 32

VOCABULARY BUILDING

assurance      1.

complaint      2.

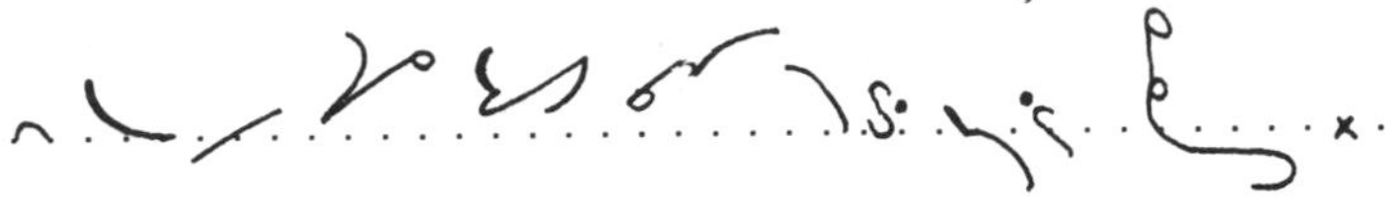

worthless      3.

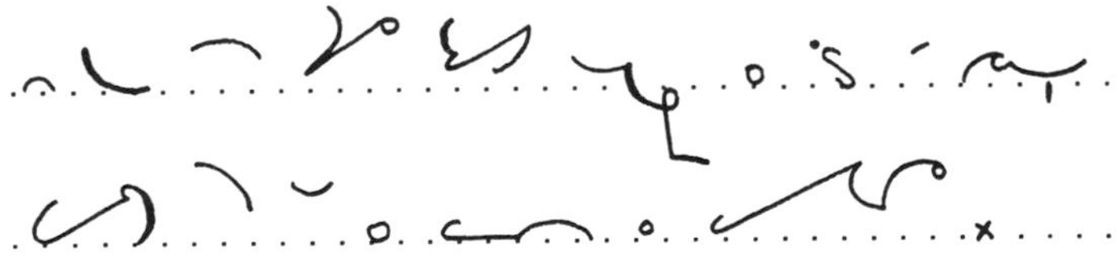

authorize      4.

compromise      5.

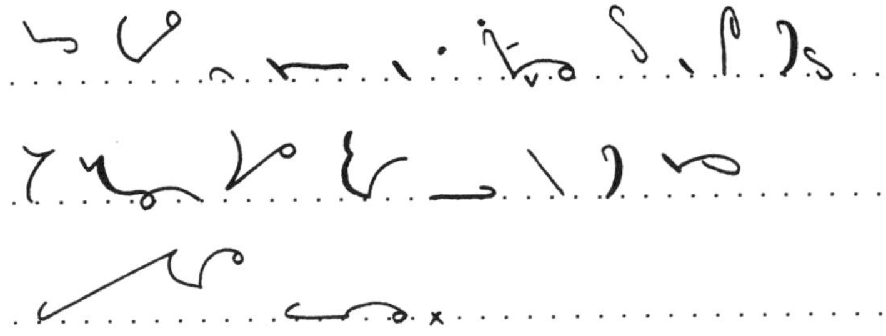

confer      6.

248

voluntary   7.

sympathize   8.

THEORY PRACTICE

## SPEED BUILDING PRACTICE

## TRANSCRIPTION LETTERS

**Preview**

X-ray        patients        discomfort        demonstration

Dr. Leo J. Snell
206 High Street
Montreal, Quebec

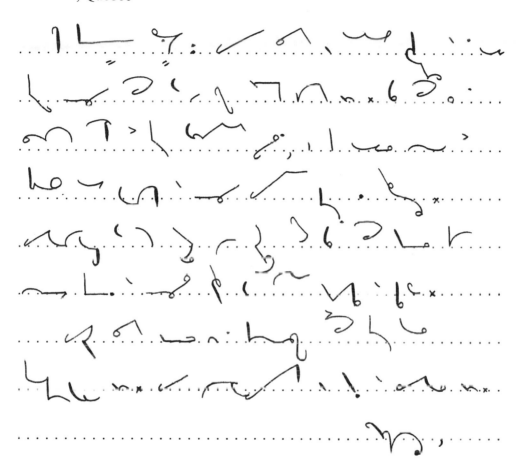

**Preview**

demonstrate    sizes    contains    adjustable    medical    journals

Mr. Henry Holmes
122 Dundas Street
London, Ontario

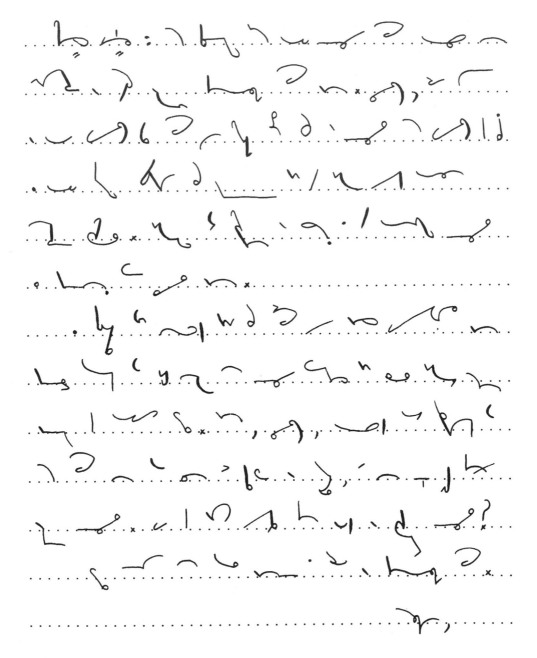

## BUSINESS UNDERSTANDING

What does an X-ray machine do? How is it used to help the patient?

**Preview**

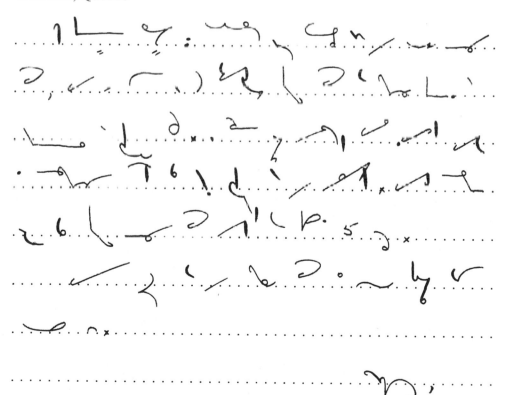

permits          referred          experimental          research

Dr. Leo J. Snell
206 High Street
Montreal, Quebec

TRANSCRIPTION SKILL DEVELOPMENT

**Spelling**

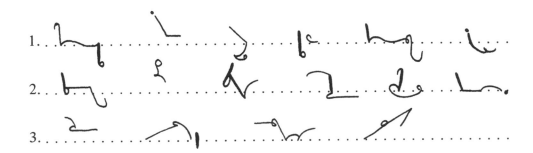

**Punctuation**

Punctuate the following:

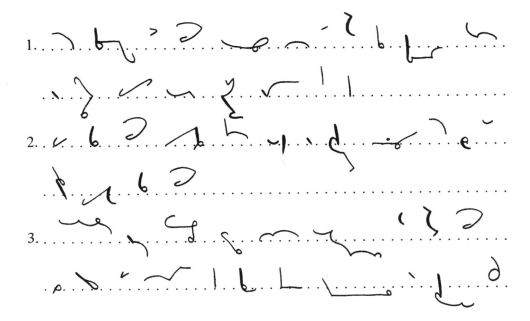

## Transcription Tips

If your employer dictates all marks of punctuation, do not resent it. His previous secretary may have been poor in this respect. Just try to show him, whenever the opportunity presents itself, that you can use correct punctuation.

# 33

VOCABULARY BUILDING

ashamed
departure

1.

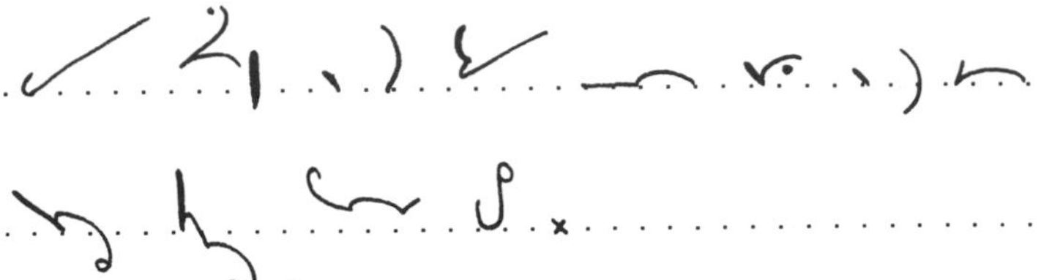

calendar

2.

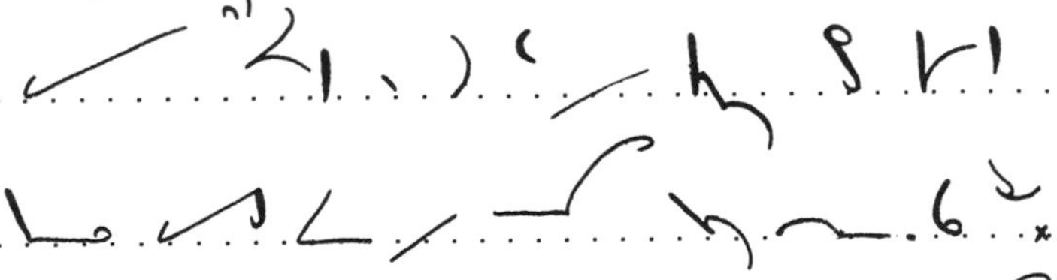

behavior

3.

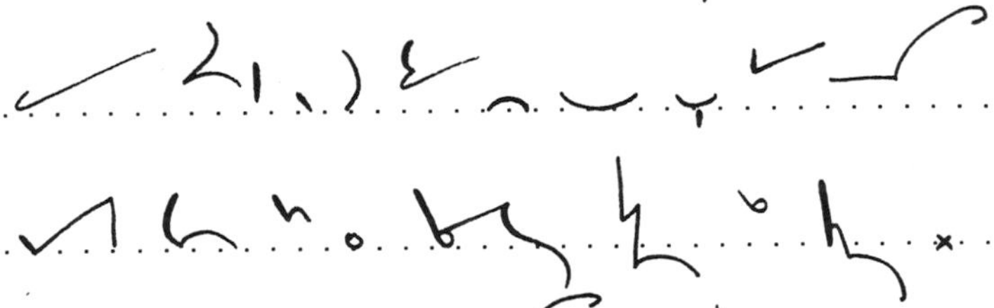

notation

4.

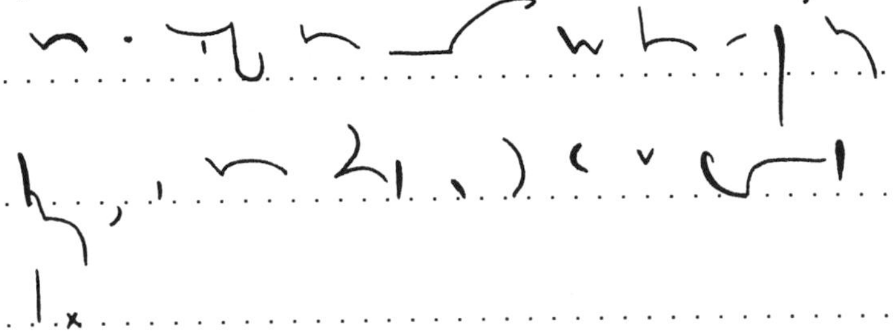

contemplate
next week

5.

journal 6.

fortnight 7.

THEORY PRACTICE

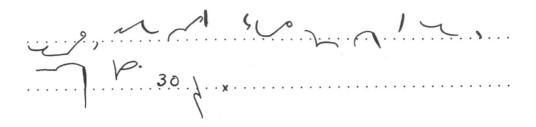

SPEED BUILDING PRACTICE

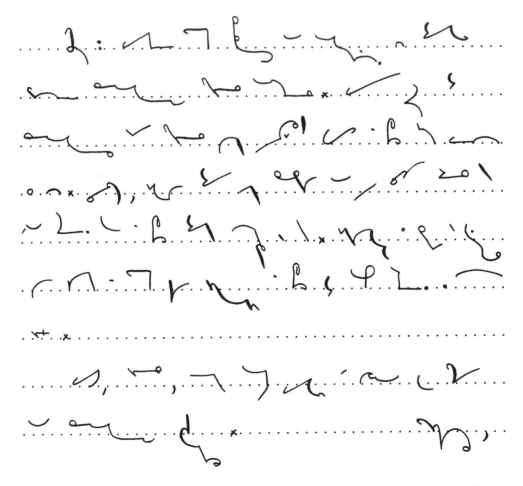

# TRANSCRIPTION LETTERS

## Preview

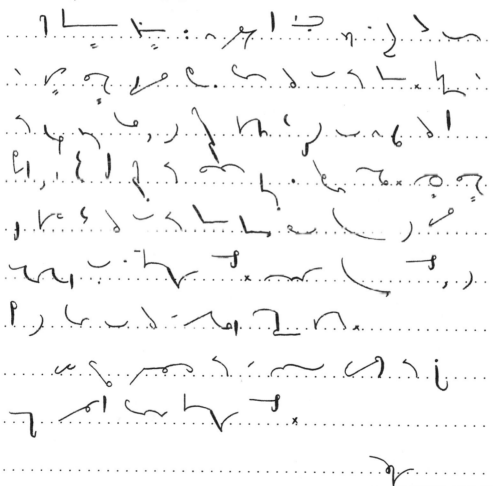

| treat | suffering | pains | troubling | medical | re-examine |

Dr. Alvin Baker
68 Haro Avenue
Vancouver, British Columbia

**Preview**

*[shorthand symbols]*

husband     secondly     nurse     inclined     conclusions

Mr. Samuel Smith
22 James Street
Montreal, Quebec

*[shorthand text]*

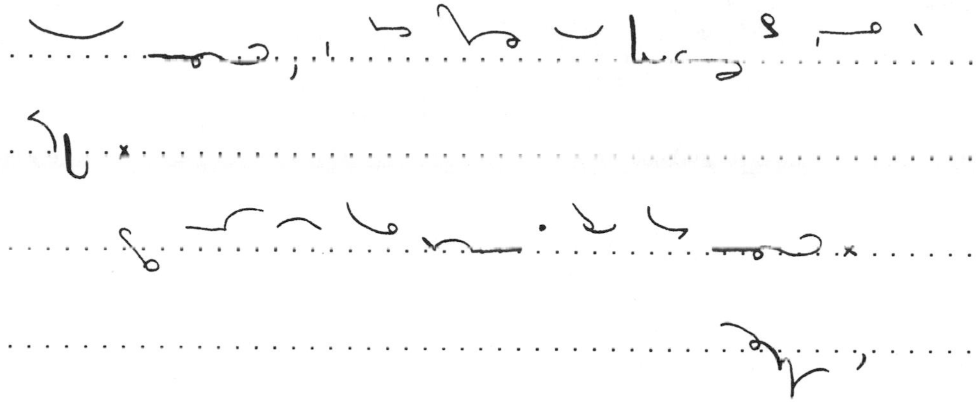

## BUSINESS UNDERSTANDING

Can a doctor be compelled to testify in a court about the condition of one of his patients? Can a doctor be compelled to reveal medical information told to him by a patient?

### Preview

concerning    encouraging    gathered    process    suffer

Dr. Alvin Baker
68 Haro Avenue
Vancouver, British Columbia

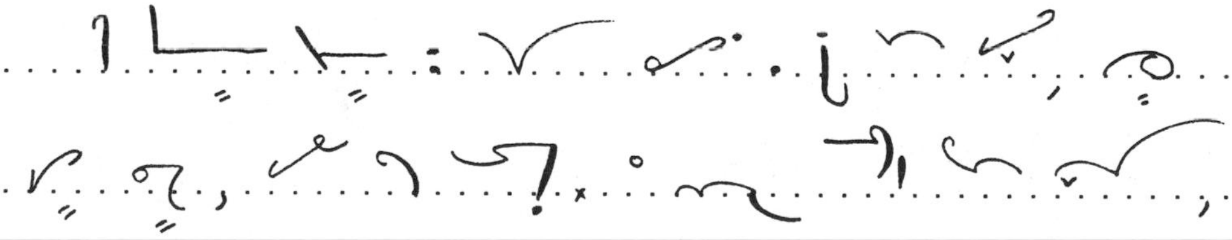

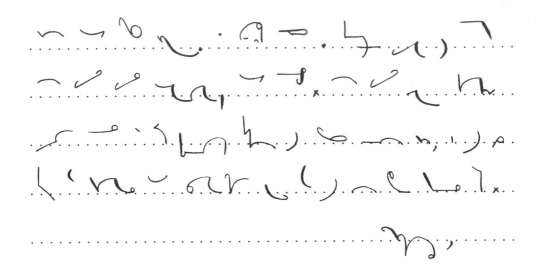

## TRANSCRIPTION SKILL DEVELOPMENT

### Spelling

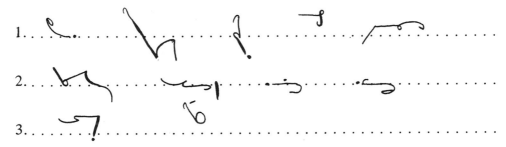

1.

2.

3.

### Punctuation

Punctuate the following:

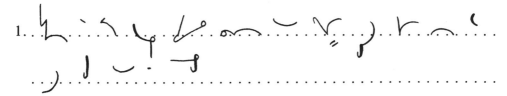

1.

262

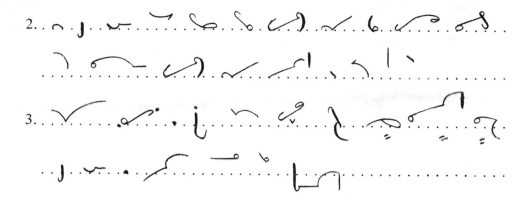

2.

3.

## Transcription Tips

Occasionally you will be asked to type a rough draft of material that has been dictated. Use double spacing and generous margins for such work.

# 34

## VOCABULARY BUILDING

ordinarily 1. 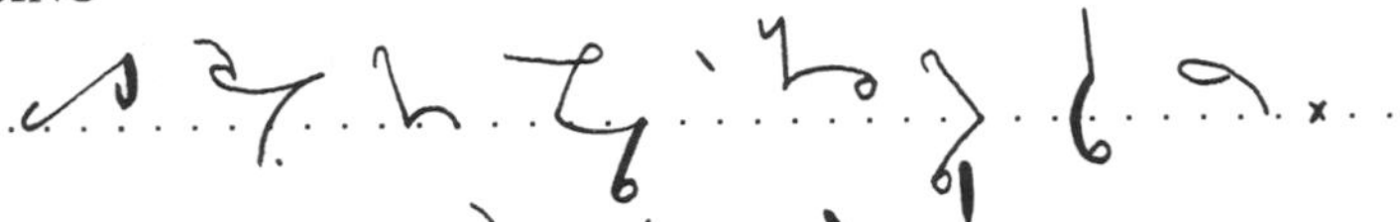

certified 2. 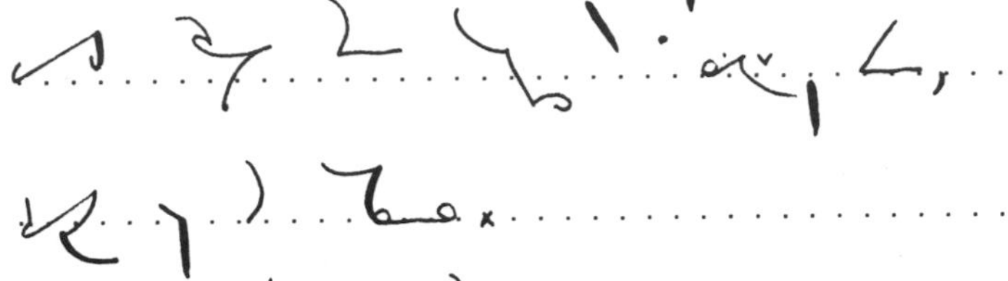

peculiar 3. 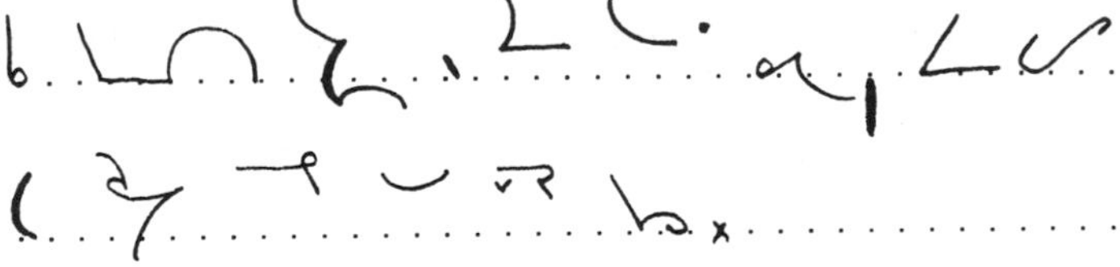

background
membership 4. 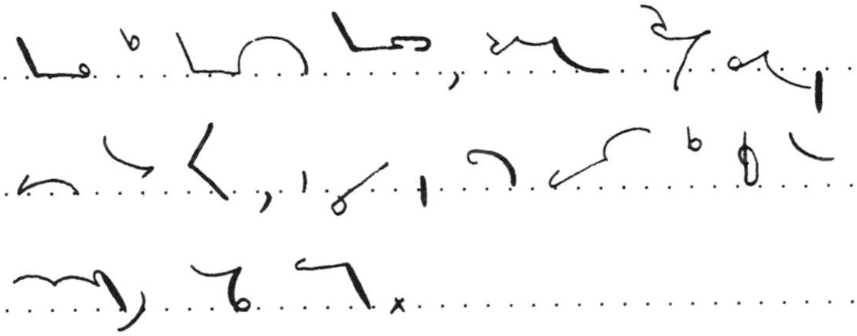

briefly 5. 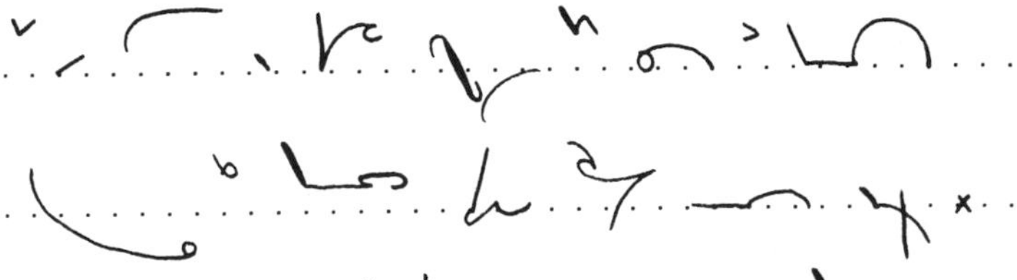

pertaining 6. 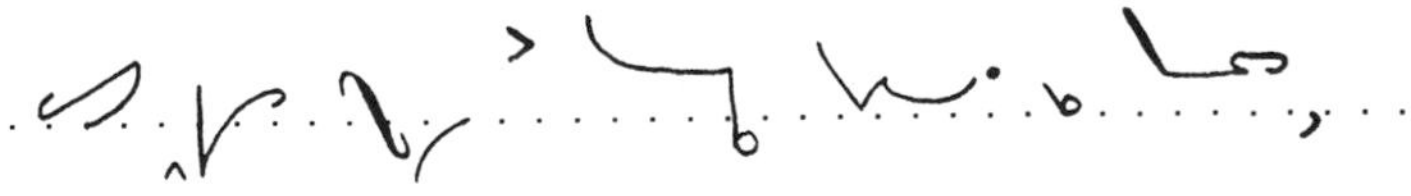

phase 7.

awkward 8.

## THEORY PRACTICE

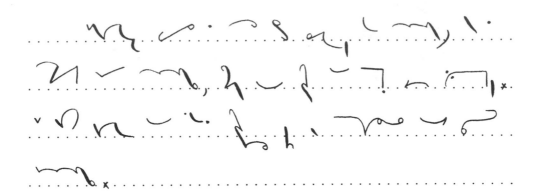

SPEED BUILDING PRACTICE

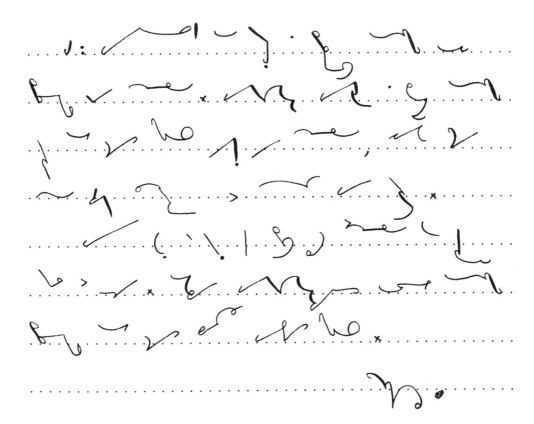

# TRANSCRIPTION LETTERS

**Preview**

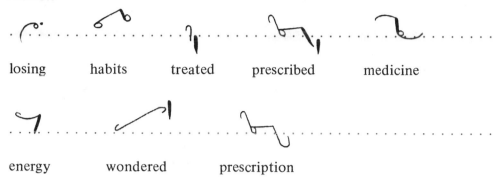

losing      habits      treated      prescribed      medicine

energy      wondered      prescription

Dr. Morris Jaffe
Box 29
Swift Current, Saskatchewan

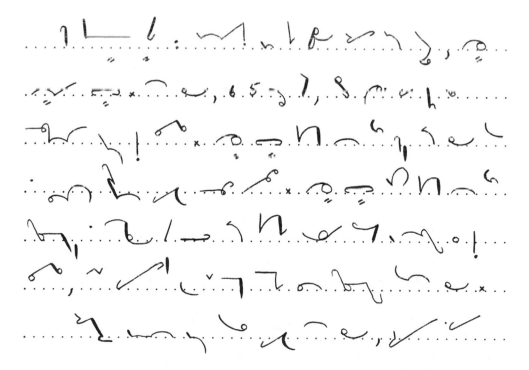

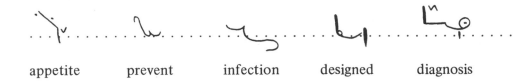

**Preview**

| appetite | prevent | infection | designed | diagnosis |

Mrs. Caroline Johnson
39 Sommerville Avenue
Oakville, Ontario

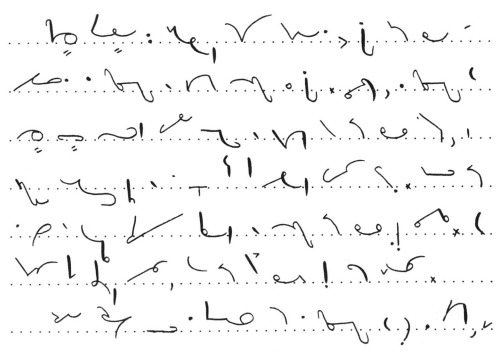

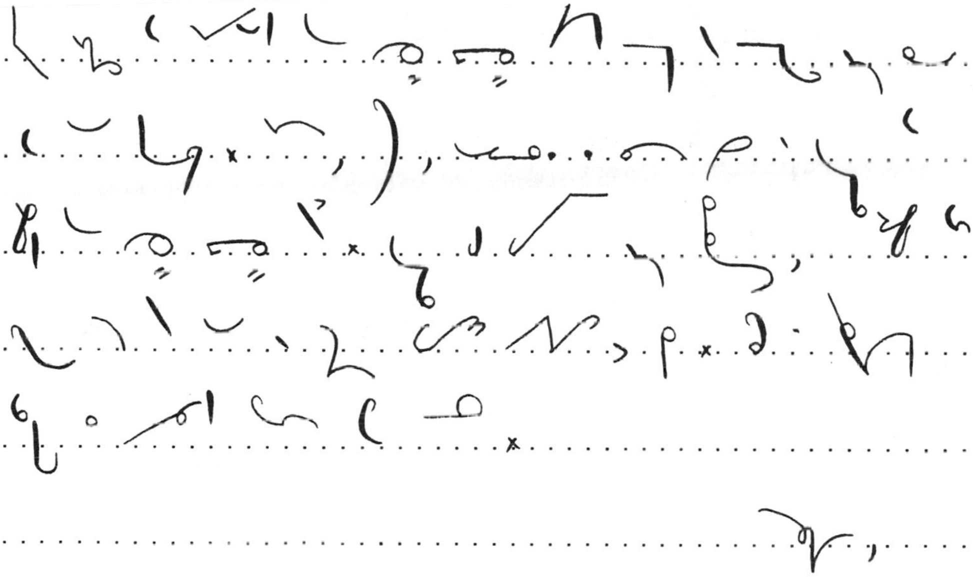

_[shorthand outlines]_

## BUSINESS UNDERSTANDING

Can a prescription be renewed without consulting the doctor who wrote it originally?

## Preview

_[shorthand outline]_          _[shorthand outline]_

included          this week

Dr. Morris Jaffe
Box 29
Swift Current, Saskatchewan

## TRANSCRIPTION SKILL DEVELOPMENT

### Spelling

1. . . . . . . . . . . . . . . . . . . . . . . . . . . . . . . . . . . . . . . . . . . . . . . . . . . . . . . . . . . . . . . . . . . . . . . . . . . . . . .

2. . . . . . . . . . . . . . . . . . . . . . . . . . . . . . . . . . . . . . . . . . . . . . . . . . . . . . . . . . . . . . . . . . . . . . . . . . . . . . .

. . . . . . . . . . . . . . . . . . . . . . . . . . . . . . . . . . . . . . . . . . . . . . . . . . . . . . . . . . . . . . . . . . . . . . . . . . . . . .

3. . . . . . . . . . . . . . . . . . . . . . . . . . . . . . . . . . . . . . . . . . . . . . . . . . . . . . . . . . . . . . . . . . . . . . . . . . . . . . .

270

## Punctuation

Punctuate the following:

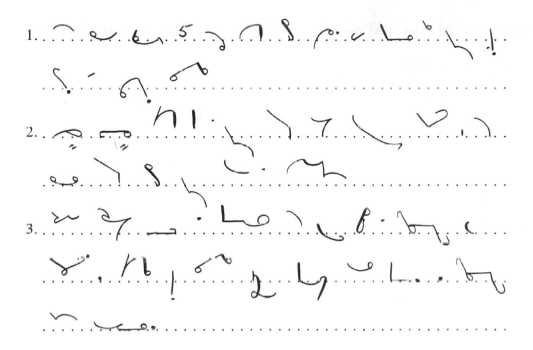

## Transcription Tips

If carbon copies of a letter are to be sent to, say, four persons, type "cc-4" at the margin below the identification initials. On the successive lines below, indented two spaces, type the names of the addressees.

# 35

## VOCABULARY BUILDING

data        1. ....................................................

concrete    2. ....................................................

            ....................................................

evidence    3. ....................................................

            ....................................................

habit       4. ....................................................

            ....................................................

bonus       5. ....................................................

            ....................................................

brilliant   6. ....................................................

            ....................................................

heartily 7.

preserve 8.

## THEORY PRACTICE

Note: a joined or disjoined  ...⌣... stroke may be used for
the suffix *ship*.

SPEED BUILDING PRACTICE

**Preview**

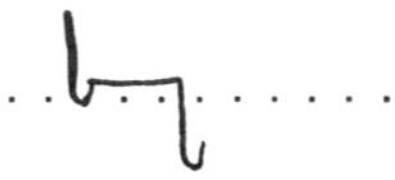

defective

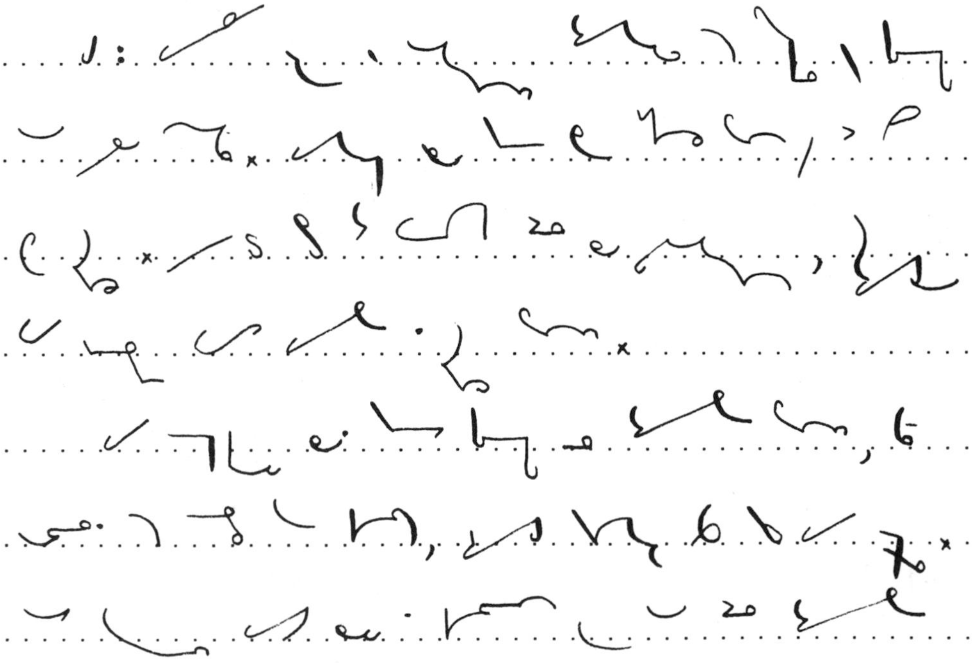

274

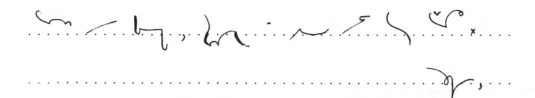

## TRANSCRIPTION LETTERS

**Preview**

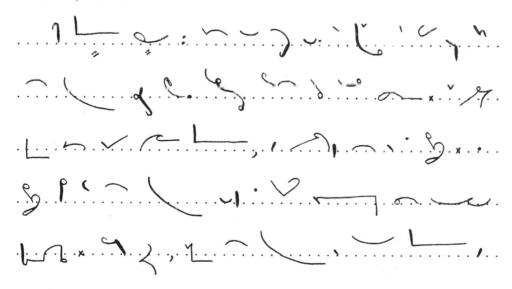

urgent   suffering   stomach   specialist   lnternal   physical

Dr. Howard Stone
1 Markland
Hamilton, Ontario

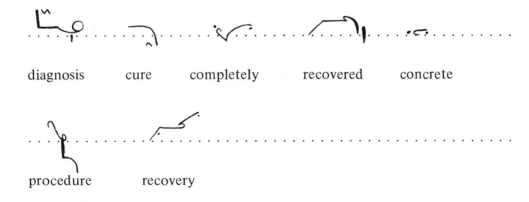

**Preview**

diagnosis    cure    completely    recovered    concrete

procedure    recovery

Mr. Gilbert Tyler
35 Thornridge Drive
Thornhill, Ontario

276

## BUSINESS UNDERSTANDING

If an operation does not result in the cure promised or predicted by a doctor, can he be held legally responsible?

**Preview**

proposal      proposed

Dr. Howard Stone
1 Markland
Hamilton, Ontario

278

TRANSCRIPTION SKILL DEVELOPMENT

**Spelling**

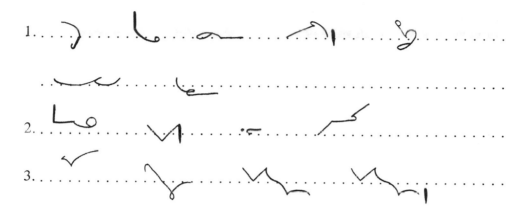

**Punctuation**

Punctuate the following:

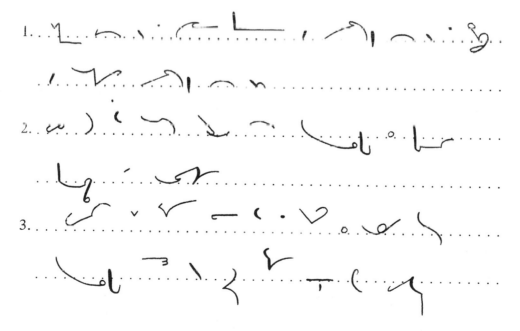

**Transcription Tips**

If your employer says nothing to you about the form or setup of the letters you are to transcribe, check the files for previous correspondence and follow the same form. If you feel that the form is not a good one, ask your employer if it will be all right to use a different form.

# 36

## VOCABULARY BUILDING

budget     1. ...................................................................

capital     2. ...................................................................

                   ...................................................................

inability     3. ...................................................................

                   ...................................................................

deduct     4. ...................................................................

                   ...................................................................

comparison     5. ...................................................................

                   ...................................................................

                   ...................................................................

liability     6. ...................................................................

expiration  7.

negotiations  8.

## THEORY PRACTICE

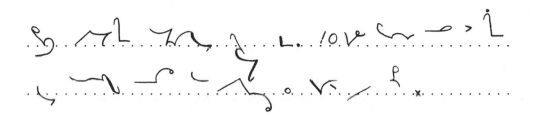

## SPEED BUILDING PRACTICE

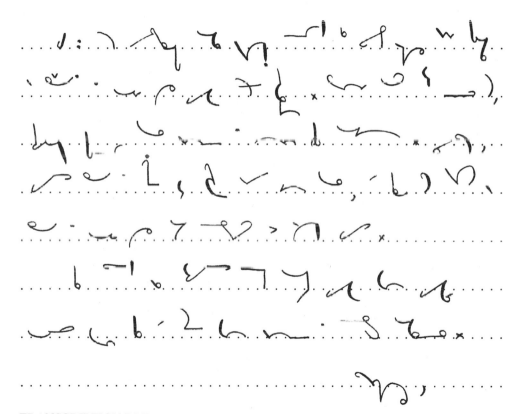

## TRANSCRIPTION LETTERS

**Preview**

conducting      survey      sponsored      association      television listening          entertainment          at the moment

Mrs. Florence Gilmore
31 Hewitt Avenue
Windsor 8, Ontario

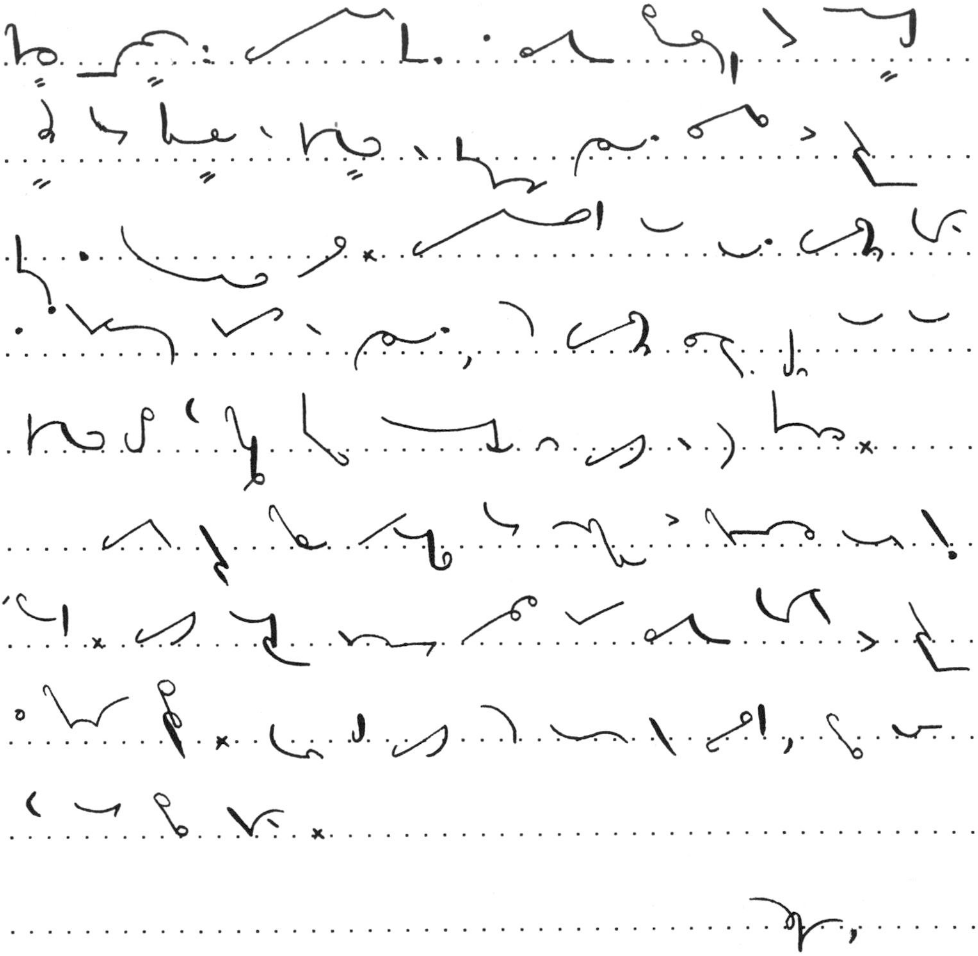

**Preview**

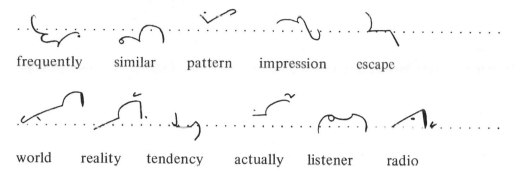

frequently    similar    pattern    impression    escape

world    reality    tendency    actually    listener    radio

Emerson and Franklin Incorporated
2489 Broadway
New York 61, New York

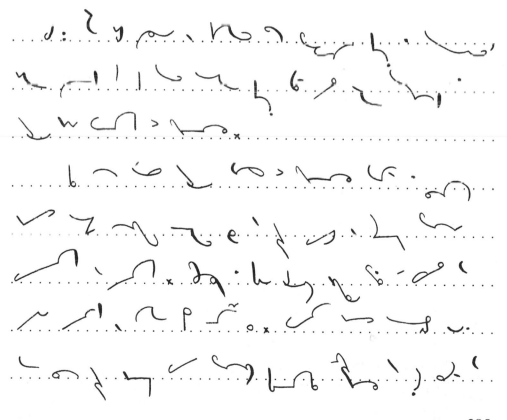

285

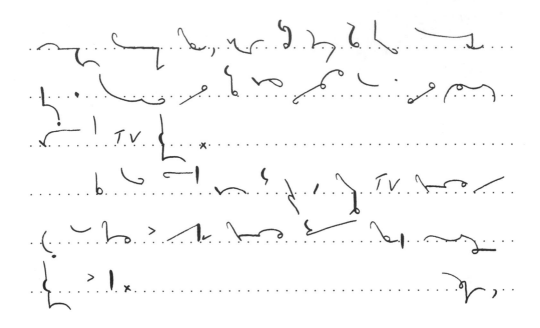

## BUSINESS UNDERSTANDING

Why would the type of TV programs tend to differ at different times during the day?

## Preview

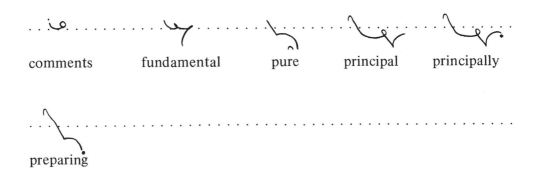

comments     fundamental     pure     principal     principally

preparing

Mrs. Florence Gilmore
31 Hewitt Avenue
Windsor 8, Ontario

286

TRANSCRIPTION SKILL DEVELOPMENT

**Spelling**

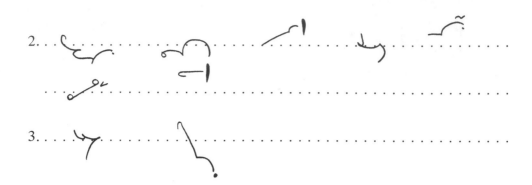

2.

3.

## Punctuation

Punctuate the following:

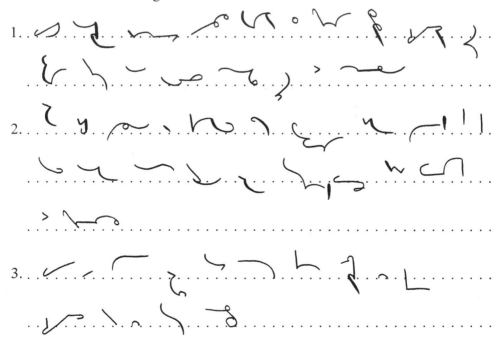

1.

2.

3.

## Transcription Tips

After you finish transcribing a letter, and while it is still in the typewriter, proofread it.

288

# 37

## VOCABULARY BUILDING

recover
outstanding

1. 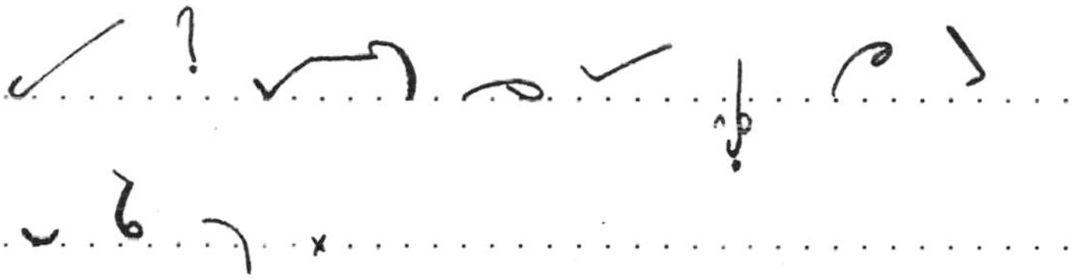 [shorthand outline]

pending
economic

2. 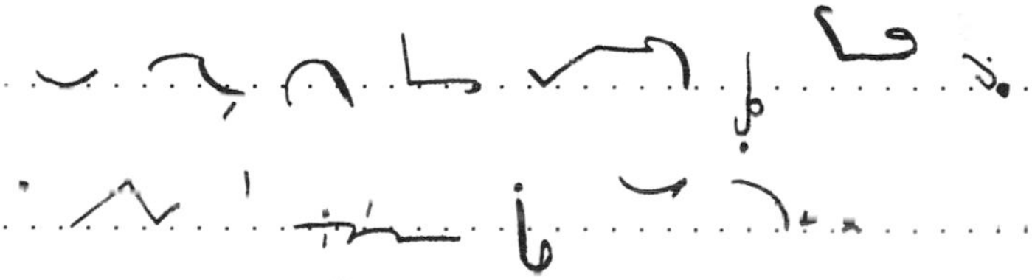 [shorthand outline]

partial

3. 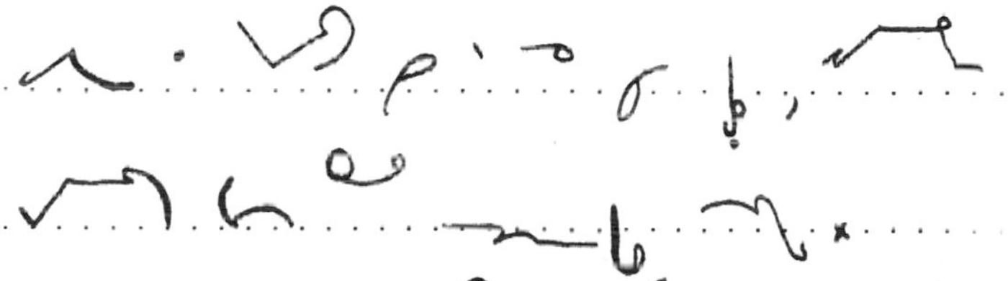 [shorthand outline]

entitled

4. 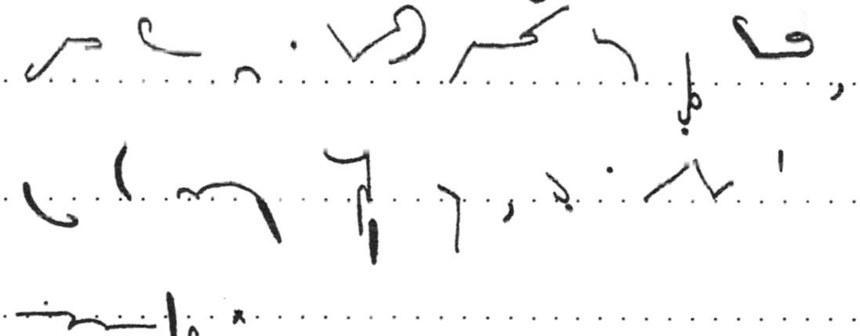 [shorthand outline]

reduction

5. 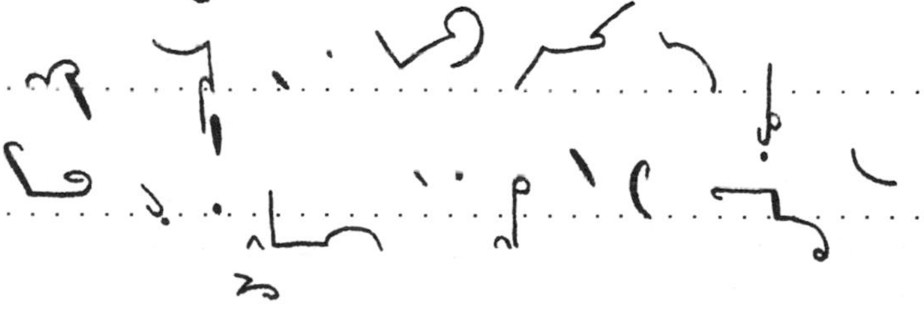 [shorthand outline]

compensation    6.

## THEORY PRACTICE

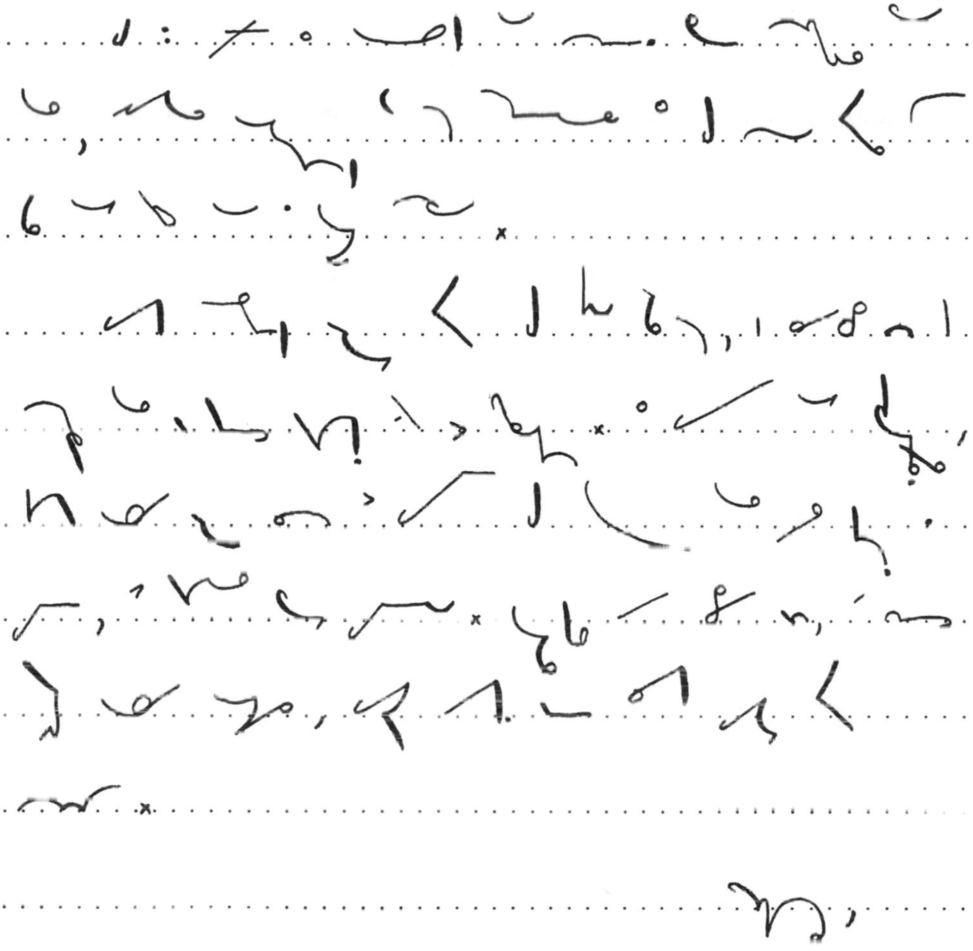

# SPEED BUILDING PRACTICE

*[Shorthand outlines]*

## TRANSCRIPTION LETTERS

### Preview

*[Shorthand outlines]*

approximately    metropolitan    facilities    announcements

audience          housewives

Central Broadcasting Company
312 Madison Avenue
New York 3, New York 10017

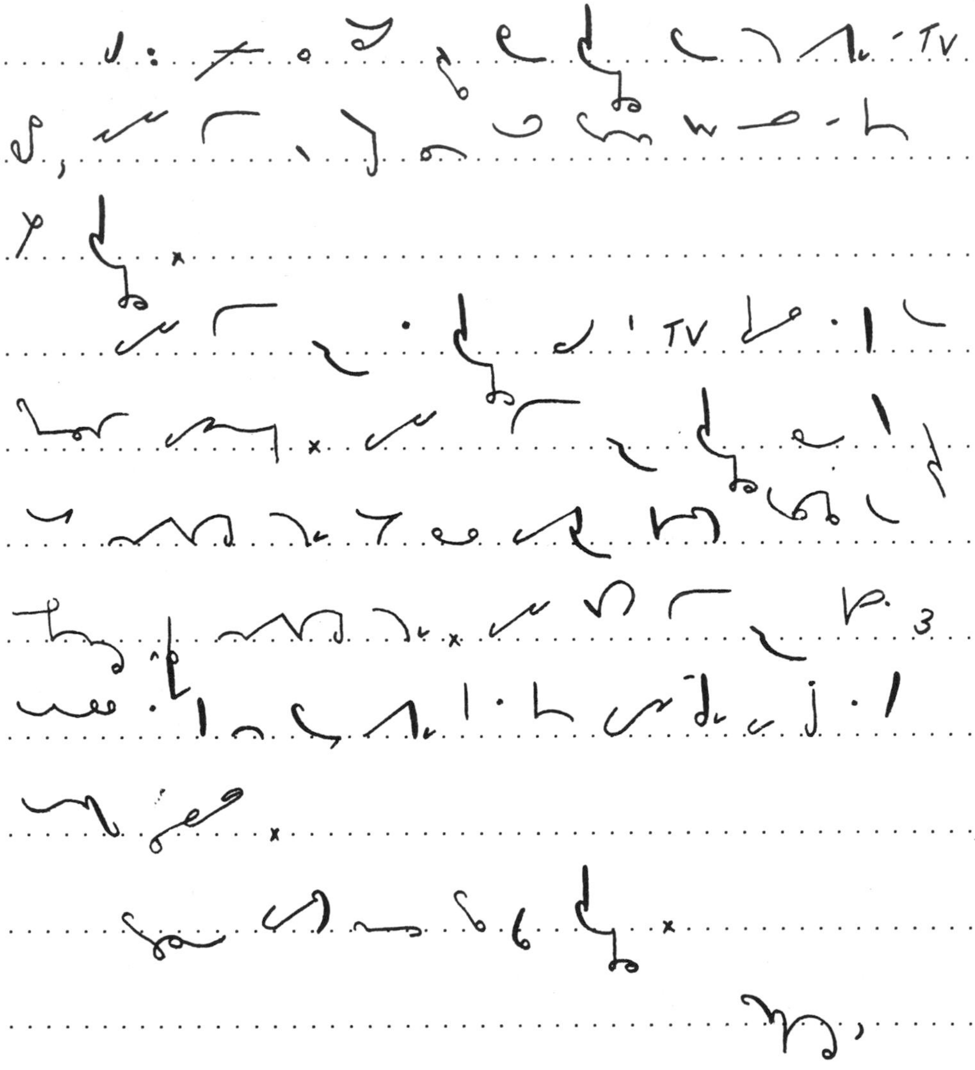

**Preview**

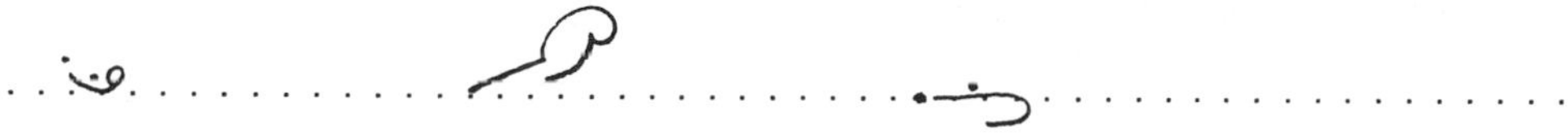

comments          relationship          connection


Carter Manufacturing Company
64 Hastings Street
Vancouver, British Columbia

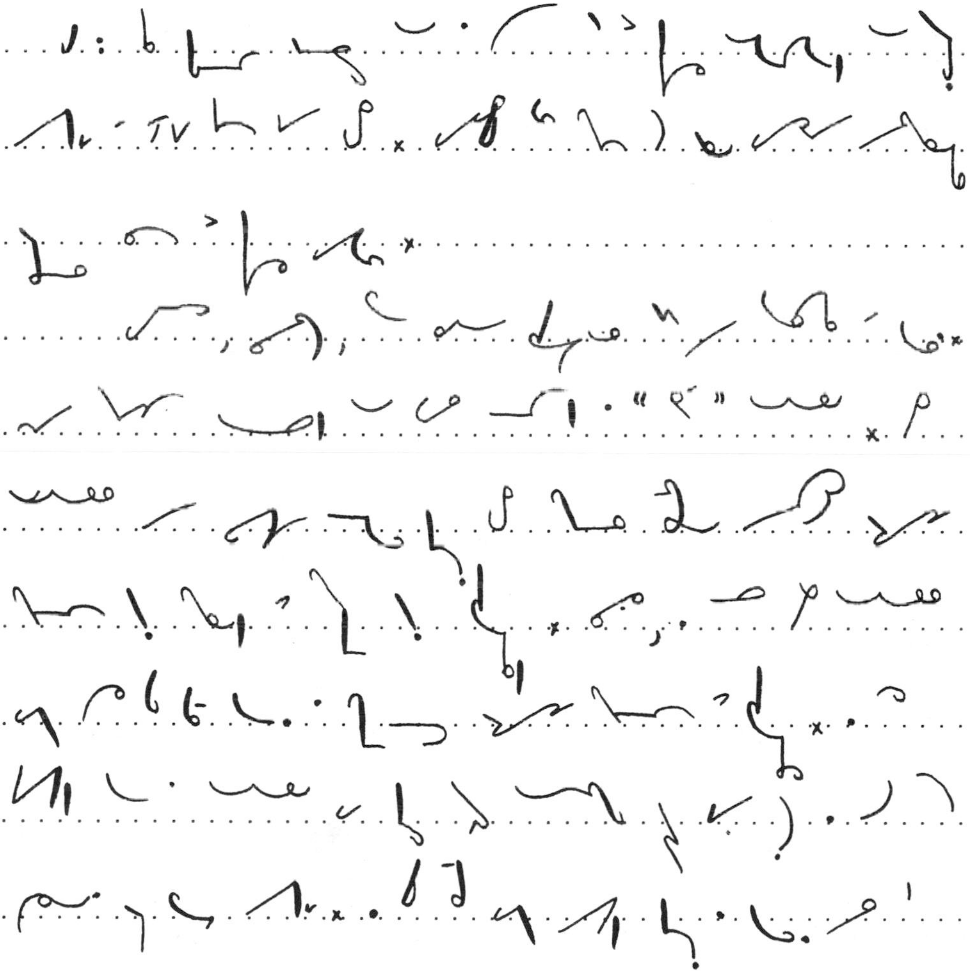

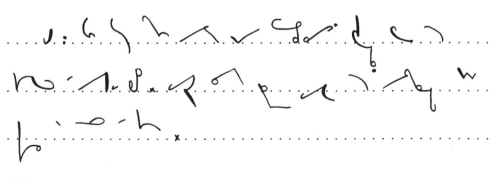

## BUSINESS UNDERSTANDING

How do TV and radio stations know what type of audience is watching or listening to their programs at any given time?

### Preview

concerning          decided

Central Broadcasting Company
312 Madison Avenue
New York 3, New York 10017

294

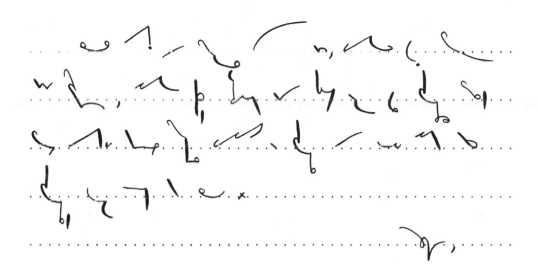

## TRANSCRIPTION SKILL DEVELOPMENT

### Spelling

1.

2.

3.

### Punctuation

Punctuate the following:

1.

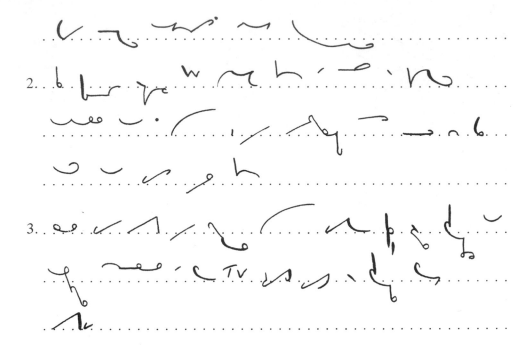

**Transcription Tips**

If while transcribing you find that the letter will be longer than you had estimated and that you will probably have part of the letter going onto a second page, end the first page a little higher than you ordinarily would.

# 38

## VOCABULARY BUILDING

confirm
existence

1.

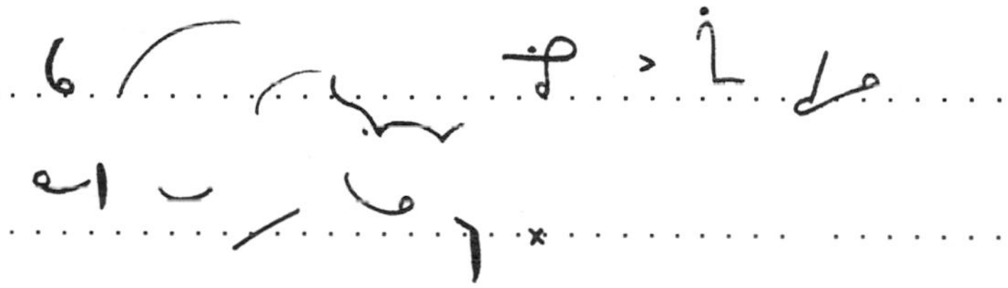

consult

2.

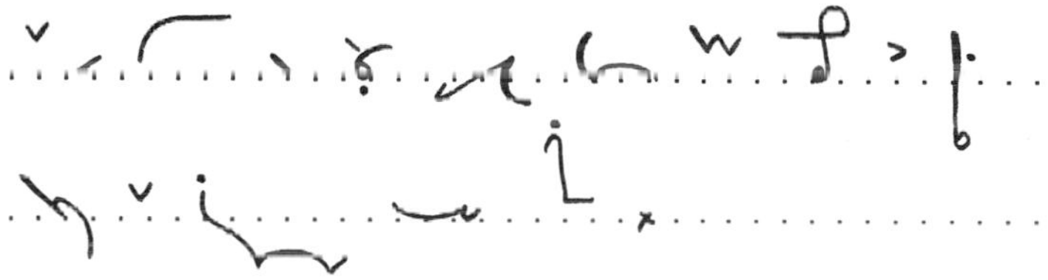

liable

3.

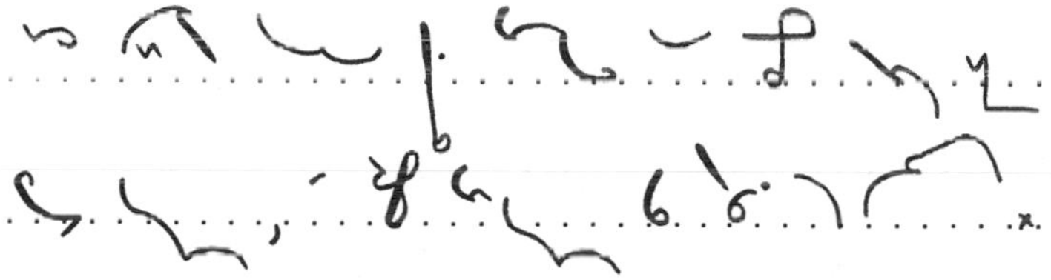

mechanical

4

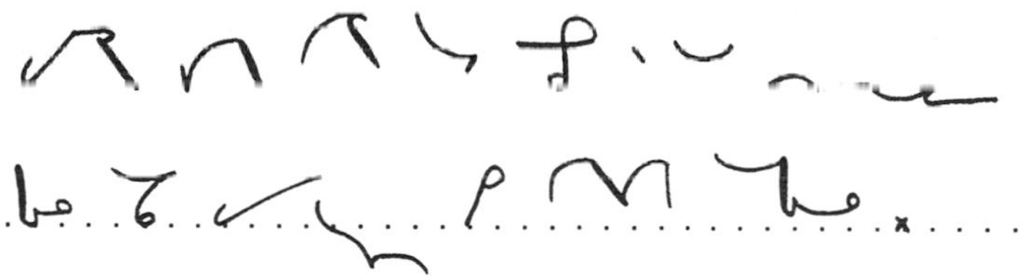

extensive

5.

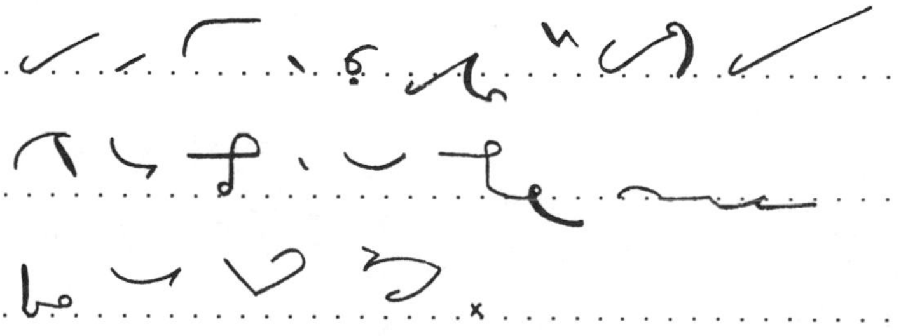

induce 6.

miserable 7.

**THEORY PRACTICE**

## SPEED BUILDING PRACTICE

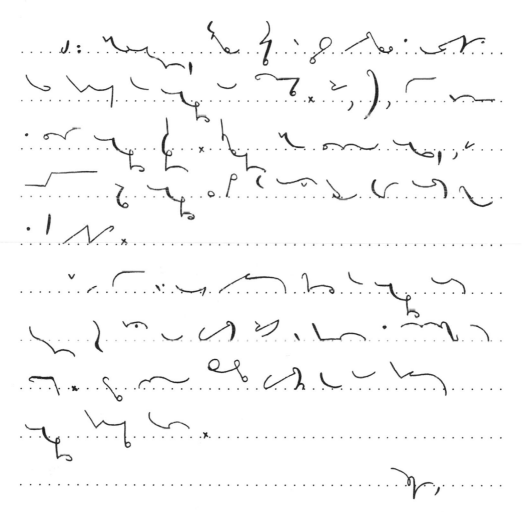

## TRANSCRIPTION LETTERS

**Preview**

considerable    sponsored    encouraging    sharp

inquiries    unlikely

Atlantic Broadcasting System
73 Ontario Street
Stratford, Ontario

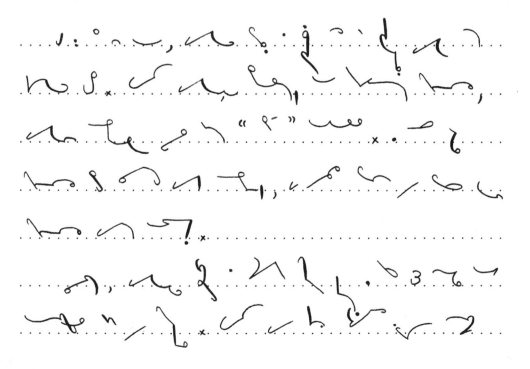

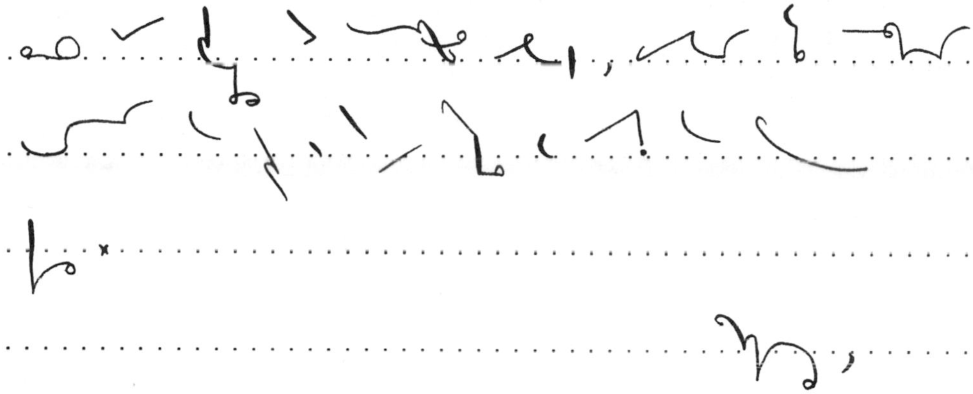

**Preview**

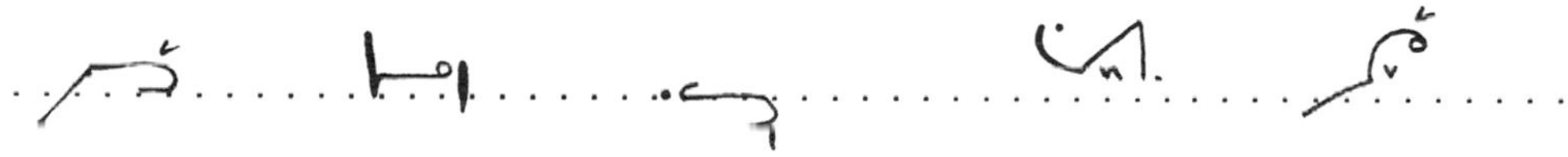

reaction decreased conclusion variety realize

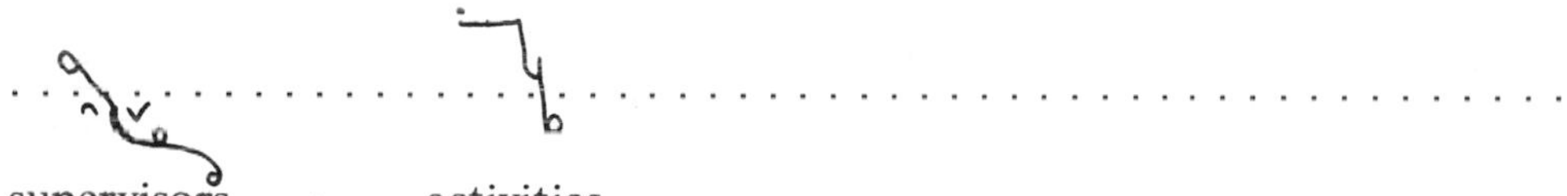

supervisors activities

Griffith Carpet Company Incorporated
25 Caledonia Road
Toronto, Ontario

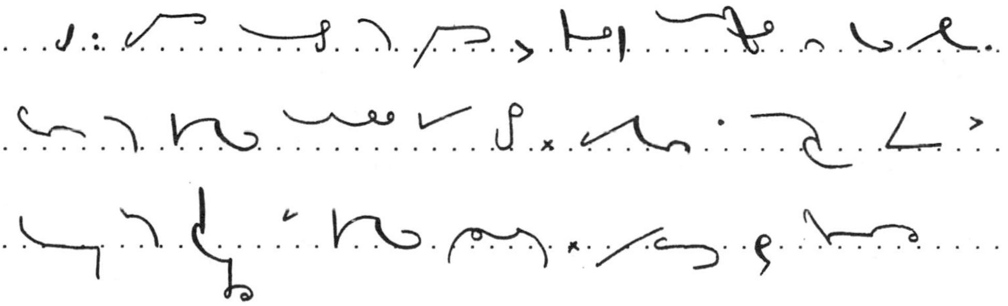

BUSINESS UNDERSTANDING

Can an advertiser suddenly stop his advertising on TV or radio if he decides
that he is not getting the type of results he expected?

**Preview**

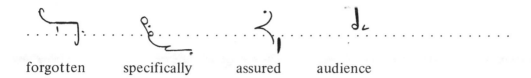

forgotten      specifically      assured      audience

Atlantic Broadcasting System
73 Ontario Street
Stratford, Ontario

## Spelling

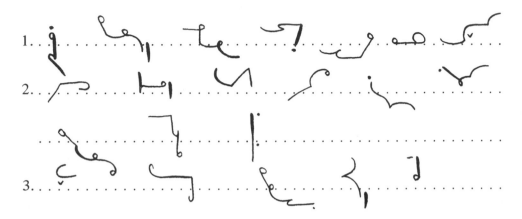

## Punctuation

Punctuate the following:

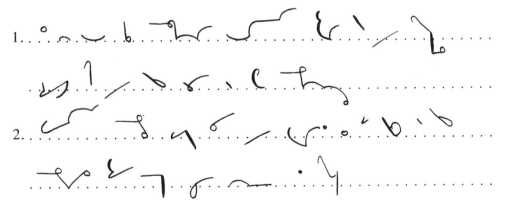

## Transcription Tips

If you are given a great many letters in dictation and you find that you will not be able to finish all of them, select those that are urgent or important and do those first. If letters are not urgent or important, but time is short, select the short letters and do them first. Leave the long letters for the first thing the next day.

304

# 39

VOCABULARY BUILDING

opposed
preliminary          1. *[shorthand outlines]*

intense
publicity            2. *[shorthand outlines]*

indulge              3. *[shorthand outlines]*

finance              4. *[shorthand outlines]*

questionnaire        5. *[shorthand outlines]*

interval   6.

THEORY PRACTICE

# SPEED BUILDING PRACTICE

# TRANSCRIPTION LETTERS

## Preview

communicate      introducing      educational      entertainment

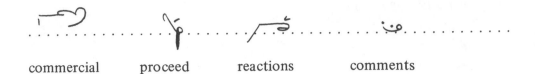

commercial      proceed      reactions      comments

Empire Broadcasting System
109 Walker Street
Boston 16, Massachusetts 10019

**Preview**

possibilities    influencing    slightest    realizing

actually    films       frankly

Dr. Harry Perkins
24 Herser Street
Los Angeles, California 21956

*[Shorthand notation]*

**BUSINESS UNDERSTANDING**

How can educational TV assist in improving student learning?

**Preview**

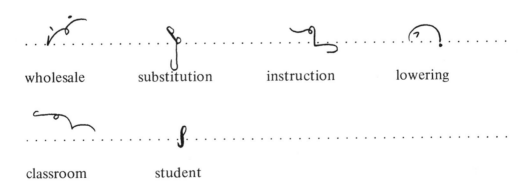

wholesale    substitution    instruction    lowering

classroom    student

Empire Broadcasting System
109 Walker Street
Boston 16, Massachusetts 10019

310

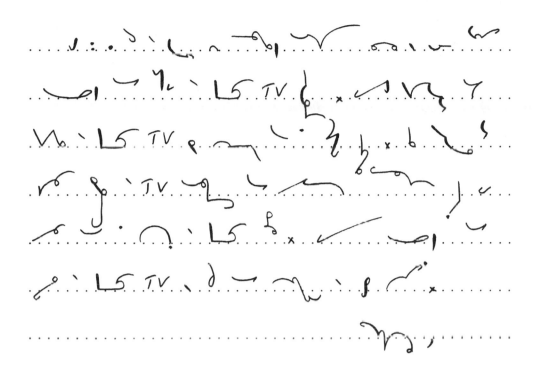

## TRANSCRIPTION SKILL DEVELOPMENT

**Spelling**

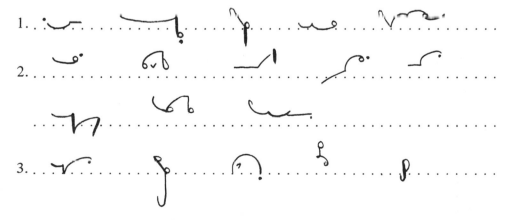

## Punctuation

Punctuate the following:

## Transcription Tips

If your employer asks you to send the same letter to two different people, it is better to make two originals unless you are specifically told to send a carbon copy to one of them. If a carbon copy is requested, find out which person is to get the carbon copy.

# 40

VOCABULARY BUILDING

compel
artificial

1.

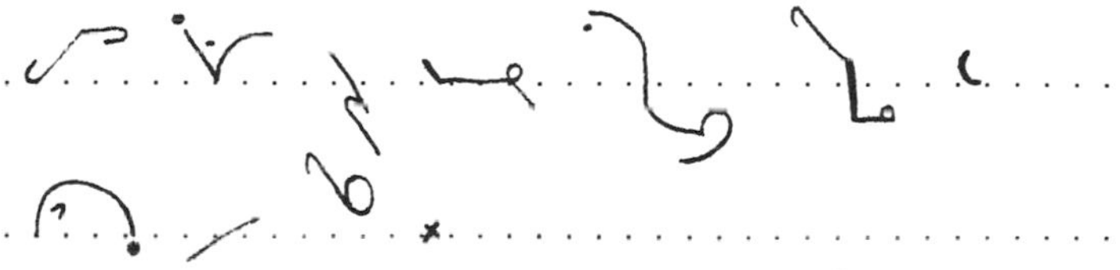

distinct
genuine

2.

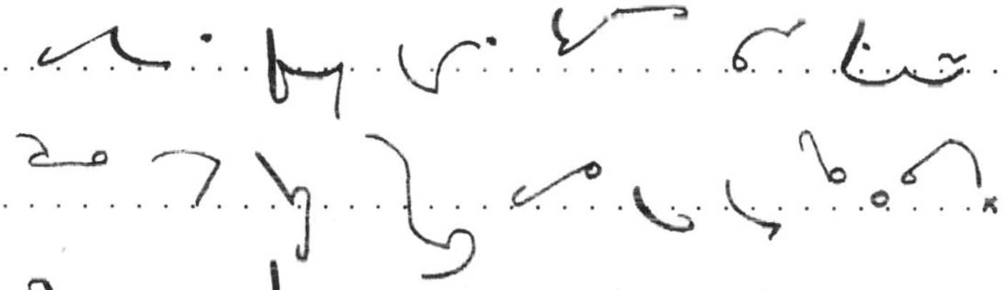

outcome

3.

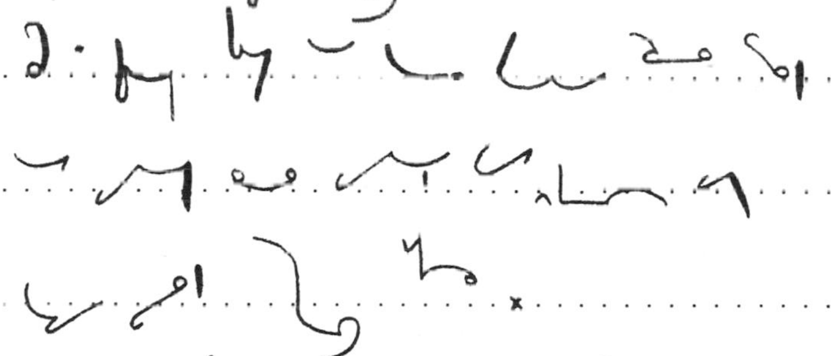

beneficial

4.

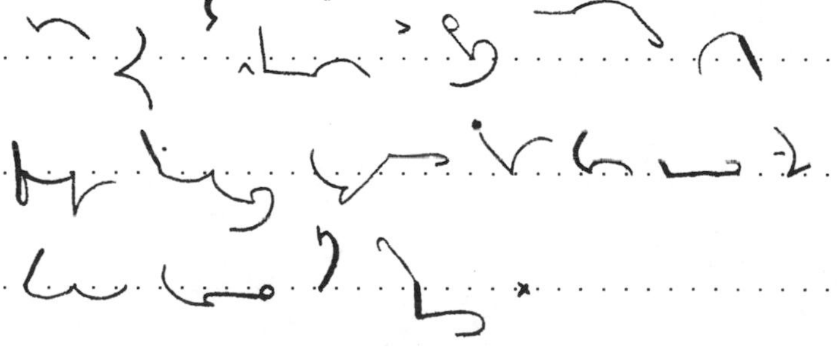

313

controversy 5.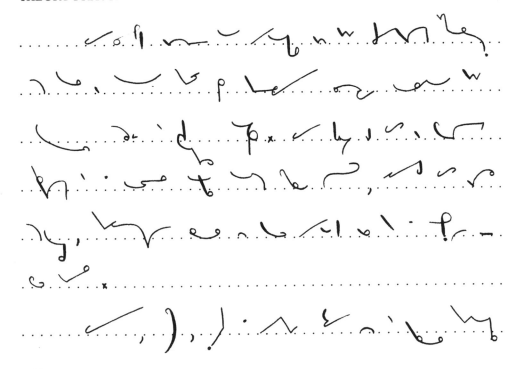

reality 6.

THEORY PRACTICE

314

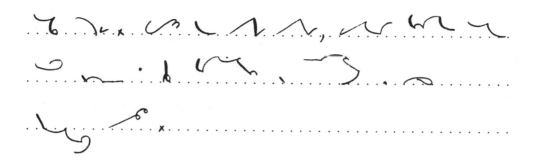

## SPEED BUILDING PRACTICE

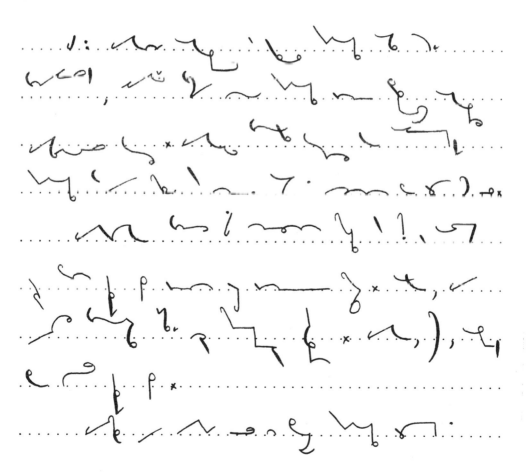

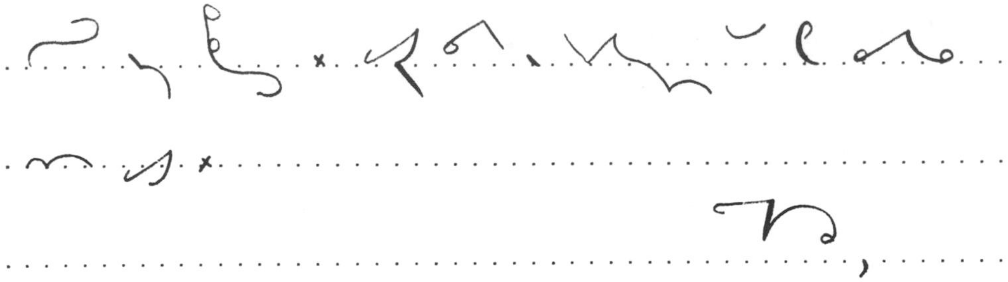

TRANSCRIPTION LETTERS

**Preview**

summary background contestants

Southern Broadcasting System
15 Rosemount Avenue
Rochester, New York 20136

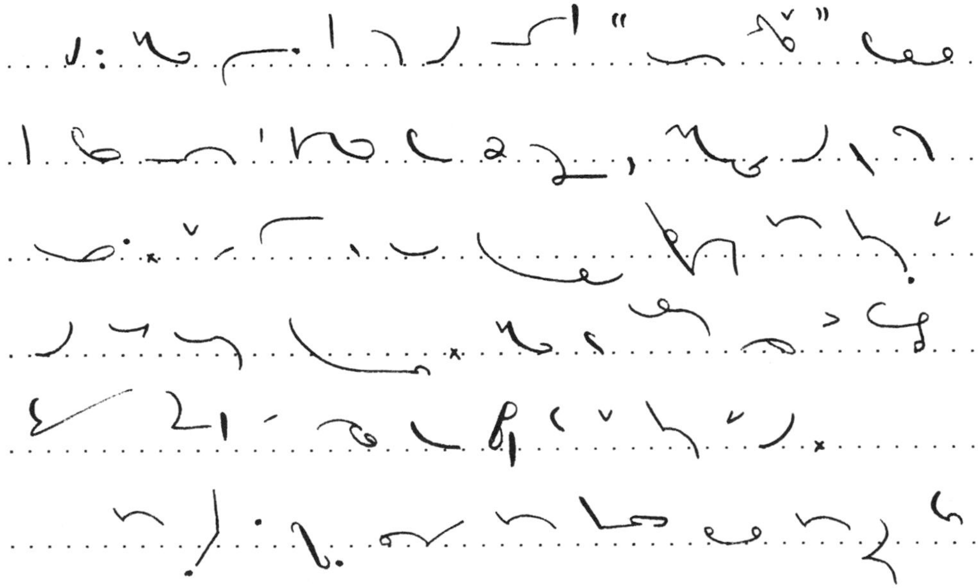

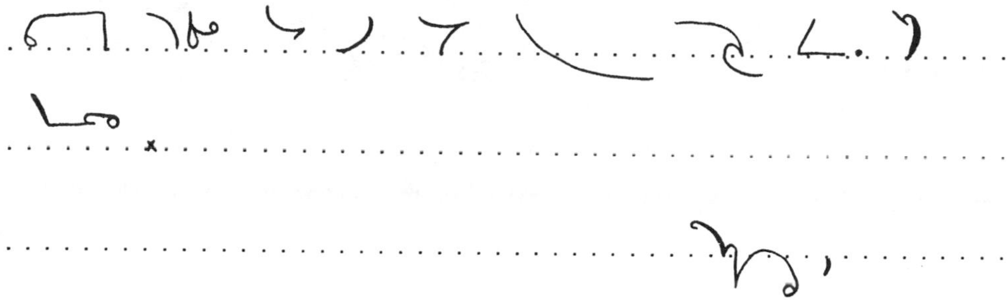

**Preview**

performance decision investigation investigate

suit provision accepted

Mr. Alvin Moore
109 King Street
London, Ontario

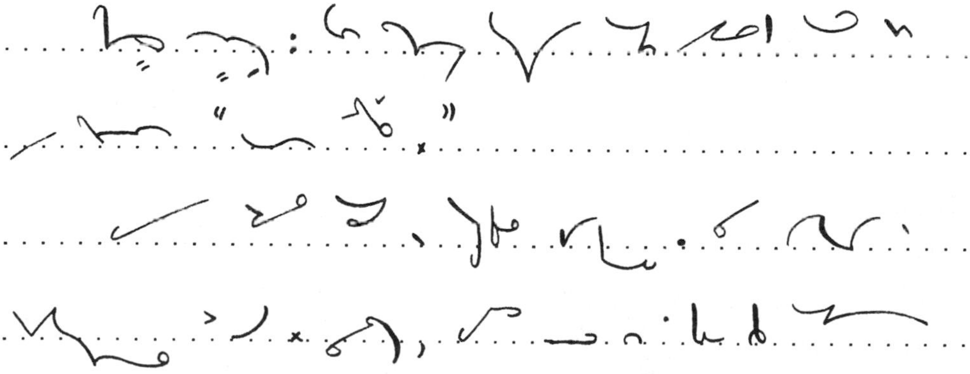

## BUSINESS UNDERSTANDING

Why would it be desirable for a TV station to check the background of a person appearing on one of its shows?

**Preview**

originally      withdraw      application

318

Southern Broadcasting System
15 Rosemount Avenue
Rochester, New York 20136

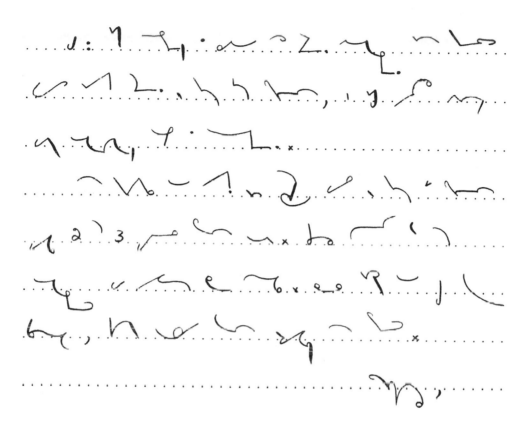

TRANSCRIPTION SKILL DEVELOPMENT

**Spelling**

1.

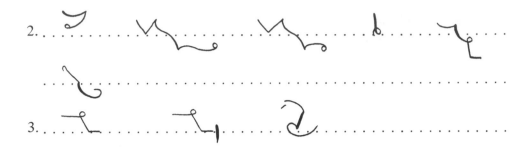

## Punctuation

Punctuate the following:

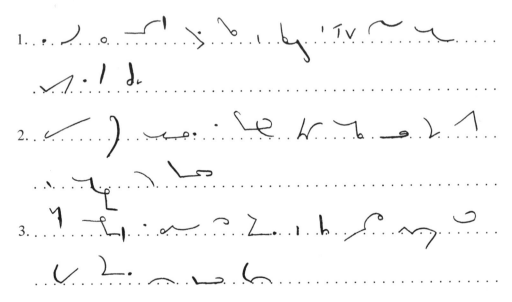

## Transcription Tips

If your employer is sending a business letter to a close personal friend, he may want to sign it with just his first name. Find out from your employer whether he wants you to type his full name or just leave the typed name out completely.

320

# SHORTERHAND SKILLS FOR THE FUTURE

# KEY

# 1

## VOCABULARY BUILDING

*delightful* 1. It was delightful to have you visit us during the week.

*exciting* 2. We have just finished reading a delightful and exciting book.

*concerned* 3. He did not seem to be concerned about the talk even though everyone agreed it was delightful and exciting.

*volume* 4. We are very much concerned about the exciting news that the volume of your business has gone up.

*supervision* 5. It was delightful to receive your letter and to know that you were concerned about the effect of their supervision practices on the volume of their business.

*former* 6. It was our former policy not to be concerned about the supervision of our sales staff so long as the volume of sales went up.

*exceed* 7. Our home office is very much concerned with our failure to exceed our former volume of business.

*substantial* 8. We have been able to make a substantial improvement in the volume of our business through a change in our supervision practices.

## THEORY PRACTICE

The question of the volume of our business in your[10] area has concerned us very much recently because of the[20] substantial quantity of equipment that we have sent to you.[30] We had hoped that you would be able to exceed[40] your former volume of business by the use of this[50] new equipment.

It is our feeling at this time that[60] if some improvement is not made quickly in your volume[70] of sales, we shall have to make substantial changes in[80] our methods of distribution. Meanwhile, please keep us informed of[90] any new developments.     (93)

## SPEED BUILDING PRACTICE

Dear Sir:

We were informed by your representative that you[10] are putting up a new building which will have stores[20] as well as offices. We would be interested in taking[30] a substantial amount of space so that we can move[40] our main office to your new building.

Would you please[50] send us more information about the cost of the offices,[60] together with the dates on which these offices are expected[70] to be ready.

Very truly yours, (76)


## TRANSCRIPTION LETTERS

Western Savings and Loan Association
58 Portage Avenue
Winnipeg, Manitoba

Gentlemen:

We have been requested by a group of investors[10] to provide information on the costs of remodeling an office[20] building in this city. At the present time we are[30] especially concerned with the questions of financing because we shall[40] have to obtain a substantial mortgage on the building. However,[50] we are convinced that the income which the building will[60] bring when remodeled will exceed all former returns from the[70] property as it is now.

We should appreciate the opportunity[80] of getting together with a representative of the bank as[90] quickly as possible to discuss arrangements for a mortgage.

We[100] look forward to hearing from you very soon.

Sincerely yours, (110)


Mr. J.A. Holmes
1090 Don Mills Road
Don Mills, Ontario

Dear Mr. Holmes:

We shall be happy to have a[10] representative of the bank get together with you to discuss[20] the remodeling of the office building about which you wrote[30] to us recently. Mr. Arthur Brown, who has supervision of[40] our mortgage investments, will contact you soon to arrange this[50] meeting.

In the meanwhile, we feel that you might assist⁶⁰ us by giving us some of the details of your⁷⁰ plans. The questions about which we are most concerned involve⁸⁰ the size of the building and the number of offices⁹⁰ to be available after the remodeling has been completed. We¹⁰⁰ would also like to know your plans for obtaining tenants,¹¹⁰ and the quantity and quality of equipment that you plan¹²⁰ to use.

Often a substantial increase in rentals can be¹³⁰ obtained after a building has been remodeled. We are looking¹⁴⁰ forward to hearing from you. We trust that we can¹⁵⁰ come to a mutually satisfactory arrangement.

Very truly yours,      (159)

Western Savings and Loan Association
58 Portage Avenue
Winnipeg, Manitoba

Gentlemen:

We can perhaps answer your questions about our proposed¹⁰ remodeling of an office building by informing you that we²⁰ estimate that the project will require a maximum of³⁰ $500,000 for the complete job, and we⁴⁰ do not expect to have to exceed this figure. We⁵⁰ expect to attract many desirable tenants from this city and⁶⁰ from nearby cities. It is our intention to make our⁷⁰ offices up to date in every respect, and to provide⁸⁰ modern equipment throughout the building.

Yours truly,      (87)

## SPELLING

(1) remodeling, concerned, mortgage-d, convinced, volume, exceed
(2) recently, supervision, tenants, equipment, mutually
(3) estimate, maximum, exceed

## PUNCTUATION

(1) Mr. Arthur Smith, our sales manager, will contact you about our plans for our regular salesmen's meeting next month.
(2) We would like to know your plans for advertising, together with any plans you may have for changes in our delivery service.
(3) Can we make an appointment to see your sales representative within two weeks?

# 2

## VOCABULARY BUILDING

*permission* 1. We should like permission to visit your factory next week.

*publicity* 2. We will need their permission to use this information for publicity purposes.

*examine* 3. We should like to have your permission to examine these reports without unnecessary publicity.

*render* 4. If you will examine our last letter, you will note that we agreed to render this service to you provided we had your permission to work without publicity.

*assistance* 5. I shall be glad to render whatever assistance you may desire in your new publicity campaign provided I have permission from my firm.

*supporting* 6. With your permission and assistance, we can obtain publicity supporting your point of view in this matter.

*recognize* 7. I recognize how much assistance they can render by supporting us, but I would like your permission to examine their information without too much publicity.

## THEORY PRACTICE

We are now planning a publicity campaign to sell several[10] new investments, and we shall need your assistance.

Our investment[20] manager is agreeable to the idea of your rendering this[30] assistance, provided you recognize that he remains responsible for the[40] sale of the stocks. I am sure, however, that any[50] reasonable suggestion for handling the problem will be welcome to[60] our manager. **(62)**

# SPEED BUILDING PRACTICE

Gentlemen:

We are interested in your proposal, and we shall[10] begin immediately to make the necessary inquiries. We expect to[20] have a sufficient number of replies very shortly so that[30] we can examine the answers and be able to present[40] a plan for handling your problems.

We shall send you[50] what we feel is a reasonable request for financial assistance.[60] We are sure that you recognize that such a report[70] will cost a great deal of money. We would suggest[80] that you let us know promptly how much you expect[90] to be able to spend for the study.

Cordially yours,     (100)

# TRANSCRIPTION LETTERS

Standard Investment Corporation
56 Church Street
Toronto 1, Ontario

Gentlemen:

We are interested in making an investment in real[10] estate and we need the assistance of someone who is[20] familiar with real estate and who would be agreeable to[30] rendering a service of this type at a reasonable price.[40] We have had no previous experience in the real estate[50] field, but many of our business friends have made some[60] profitable investments in real estate.

If you can render any[70] assistance in this connection, please send the details of[80] your proposals so that we can examine them promptly. If[90] we like your proposals, I am sure that we can[100] come to a reasonable agreement without delay.

Cordially yours,     (109)

Mr. Fred Williams
67 Willingdon Blvd.
Toronto 18, Ontario

Dear Mr. Williams:

It was a pleasure to receive your[10] letter of inquiry about our investment opportunities. We have available[20] a large number of choice investments which may be suitable[30] for you. Some of these investments are in office buildings[40] and many are in apartment houses. We also have some[50] land for sale if you are interested in obtaining property[60] for a long-term investment.

What we propose to do[70] is to send you immediately a list of properties which[80] are now available for investment so that you can examine[90] them to see if they meet your needs. In addition,[100] if it is agreeable to you, we should like to[110] have our ~~New York~~ *Toronto* representative give you further details about[120] properties that are not on the enclosed list. We assure[130] you that you will get a reasonable return on any[140] of these investments.

If we can render any further assistance,[150] please be sure to call on us.

Very truly yours,          (160)

Standard Investment Corporation
56 Church Street
Toronto 1, Ontario

Gentlemen:

Your list of available properties was very interesting to[10] me and to the members of my investment group. We[20] recognize the difficulty of giving us full details through the[30] mail and we would, therefore, be agreeable to having your[40] ~~New York~~ *Toronto* representative come to speak to us. However, we[50] would like him to bring along any other information he[60] may have about the properties you list for long-term[70] investment.

Please have him call at his convenience and ask[80] for Mr. Fred Smith, our investment manager.

Very truly yours,          (90)

## SPELLING
(1) assistance, reasonable, previous, experience, profitable, proposals, promptly
(2) suitable, properties, immediately
(3) recognize, convenience, manager

## PUNCTUATION
(1) If you are interested, we also have some land for long term investments.
(2) Furthermore, if you wish us to do so, we can send you information about properties not on the enclosed list.
(3) If we can be of any further help, please do not hesitate to call on us.

# 3

## VOCABULARY BUILDING

*outstanding*  1. We are glad to inform you that all of their outstanding bills have been paid.

*consult*  2. We should like to consult you about the matter of their outstanding bills.

*financial*  3. It will not be necessary for us to consult anyone about your financial condition because we have already heard that it is outstanding.

*obligations*  4. The manner in which you have made settlement of your financial obligations has given you an outstanding record.

*adopted*  5. We have adopted certain changes in our method of handling outstanding financial obligations, and we should like to consult you about them.

*deferred*  6. We had deferred making any changes in our methods of collecting outstanding financial obligations, but we have now adopted several new procedures.

*personnel*  7. We deferred adopting any changes in our methods of handling financial obligations until we could consult you about getting outstanding personnel for the job.

*qualifications*  8. We wish to consult you about some changes we have adopted in our personnel office regarding qualifications for positions.

## THEORY PRACTICE

We should like to have the opportunity of becoming the[10] agent to handle your financial obligations. Our charge for such[20] services is small, and we have had favorable approval of[30] our methods from other companies who have also had outstanding[40] financial obligations.

If you will favor us with your business,[50] we shall endeavor to handle your obligations in a manner[60] that will be both helpful and

efficient. We would, of$^{70}$ course, consult you about any special financial matters, but it$^{80}$ would be our policy to pay all deferred accounts
as$^{90}$ soon as possible so as to be able to take$^{100}$ advantage of further
credit privileges.                                                        (105)


## SPEED BUILDING PRACTICE

Dear Sir:

I would like to have the opportunity of$^{10}$ speaking to a representative of your personnel department about a$^{20}$ position. I am
enclosing a list of my qualifications which$^{30}$ shows favorable experience in my other jobs. I am interested$^{40}$ in a position in the
financial section of your investment$^{50}$ department. I feel sure that I
can win approval for$^{60}$ a job if I am given the opportunity of an$^{70}$
interview with you.

I feel confident that my qualifications can$^{80}$ be used to advantage in your company.

Respectfully yours,          (89)


## TRANSCRIPTION LETTERS


Queens Realty Company
104 Main Street
Hamilton, Ontario

Gentlemen:

I am interested in purchasing either a small house$^{10}$ or a cooperative apartment in the Jamaica section of Queens.$^{20}$ Our present
apartment is beautiful, but it is now too$^{30}$ small for our family. I
can make a moderate down$^{40}$ payment either on the house or the
cooperative apartment. I$^{50}$ would personally prefer the cooperative
apartment because the financial obligations$^{60}$ would be less.

We have deferred making this change until$^{70}$ now because of
our pleasant situation. If you have any$^{80}$ outstanding offers, please
get in touch with me.

Yours truly,          (90)

Mr. Leslie Green
P.O. Box 36
Hamilton, Ontario

Dear Mr. Green:

We understand perfectly your desire to obtain[10] a cooperative apartment or a small house for your family[20] without taking on too much additional financial obligation. However, there[30] is a shortage of good cooperative apartments at the present[40] time. We can offer some outstanding buys in small houses[50] just outside the Jamaica area. We have one house in[60] mind that we feel sure will win your approval once[70] you have looked at it. However, our previous experience in[80] these matters has shown that it is best to look[90] at a number of houses before coming to a decision.[100] We would, therefore, suggest that you and your wife make[110] an appointment to come to our offices so that we[120] may have the privilege of showing you our houses.

It[130] is our policy to be as helpful as possible in[140] the selection of a home and that is why we[150] are sure we can be of assistance to you.

Cordially[160] yours,            (161)


Queens Realty Company
104 Main Street
Hamilton, Ontario

Gentlemen:

I am rather disappointed that you are not in[10] a position to offer the type of cooperative apartment in[20] which we are interested. However, after consulting my wife, I[30] have decided that it would be better for us to[40] look at a small house even though the financial obligations[50] might be higher than I had expected them to be.[60]

If you wish, we can meet with one of your[70] representatives on Saturday of this week and look at some[80] of the houses that you have to offer.

Very truly[90] yours,            (91)

## SPELLING

(1) cooperative, apartment, beautiful, moderate, personally, deferred, pleasant

(2) favorable, approval, previous, decision, privilege, assistance

(3) disappointed, position, decided

## PUNCTUATION

(1) As you know, our present apartment is too small for our family's needs.

(2) We are sorry to have to tell you that there is a shortage of good apartments at the present time.

(3) If you wish, we can have our representative get together with you within a day or two.

# 4

## VOCABULARY BUILDING

*expansion*   1. We are happy to announce the expansion of our sales department.

*interview*   2. In a recent interview he spoke about the expansion of the firm in this city.

*demonstration*   3. During the interview he gave a demonstration of what the expansion of his store would mean to the people of the town.

*specify*   4. He spoke of the expansion plans of his firm during the interview and then he was asked to specify how it would affect other firms in the city.

*conference*
*facilities*   5. As a result of my interview and conference with the officers of the firm, I can now specify how they will proceed with the expansion of their facilities.

*patronage*   6. The patronage of our store by the people of this town is a demonstration of their faith in our products and has resulted in our making specific plans for the expansion of our facilities.

*signature*   7. He added his signature to the report of the conference, but he told me later that the loss of patronage by his firm will prevent further expansion.

*privilege*

8. May I have the privilege of your signature on this report so that I can specify to the members of the conference which people are in favor of the expansion of our facilities.

## THEORY PRACTICE

Since our recent interview with you, it has occurred to[10] us that an expansion of your delivery facilities might result[20] in an increase in patronage by many customers who wish[30] to make purchases by telephone. Furthermore, according to our experience[40] in this town, the people would welcome a circular from[50] you each month in which you specify the particular items[60] that you have to offer, together with pictures of each[70] of the items.          (73)

## SPEED BUILDING PRACTICE

Gentlemen:

It has been difficult for us to take advantage[10] of your recent offer to come in and look at[20] your special showing of dresses for the fall. It occurred[30] to us that you may have been under the impression[40] that we were not interested in your offerings because we[50] have not come to see you recently. However, we have[60] been busy during the past few days getting ready our[70] new fall circular.

We shall be glad to come to[80] a demonstration of your new fashions at any time that[90] you specify.

Very truly yours,          (95)

## TRANSCRIPTION LETTERS

Union Realty Company
P.O. Box 2006
Hamilton, Ontario
Gentlemen:

As you know, we are a tenant in one[10] of your stores, and we are interested in the possibility[20] of an expansion of our store. It has occurred to[30] us that it might be possible to take over one[40] of the neighboring stores if the terms of the lease[50] permit. We are prepared to pay a reasonable sum for[60] this privilege. We would be interested in a thirty-year[70] lease, and we would require the privilege of a renewal[80] of the lease at the end of that period of[90] time.

333

May we suggest that you arrange a conference with[100] us as soon as possible to discuss the matter further.[110]

Sincerely yours,   (112)

Madison Dry Cleaning Company
98 Sparks Street
Ottawa, Ontario
Gentlemen:

According to your letter of March 12, you are[10] interested in an expansion of your store by taking a[20] lease on a neighboring store.

It has occurred to us[30] that you have been in contact with the present owners[40] of these stores so that you are aware of the[50] fact that their leases expire within three years. We are[60] willing to have you take over either or both of[70] your neighboring stores. However, we cannot grant a thirty-year[80] lease because our mortgage agreement with the bank forbids leases[90] of more than twenty years. This would not prevent a[100] twenty-year lease with the privilege of renewal at the[110] end of that time.

The other terms of your offer[120] seem to be acceptable to us. We are agreeable to[130] a conference with you at any time that you find[140] convenient.

We look forward to hearing from you.

Yours truly,   (150)

Union Realty Company
P.O. Box 2006
Hamilton, Ontario
Gentlemen:

We were surprised to learn that you cannot grant[10] a lease of more than twenty years because of the[20] terms of your mortgage agreement with the bank. However, we[30] may be interested in the twenty-year lease with the[40] privilege of renewal.

In view of this special condition, it[50] has occurred to us that a representative of the bank[60] should attend our conference. In this way we can be[70] made aware of any other conditions which might affect the[80] granting of the lease.

Sincerely yours,   (86)

334

## SPELLING

(1) tenant, possibility, expansion, occurred, neighboring, prepared, reasonable, privilege, renewal, period, conference, convenience

(2) specify, forbids, acceptable

(3) surprised

## PUNCTUATION

(1) We are willing to have you take over this store, but we cannot give you more than a five-year lease.

(2) However, we would like to know whether a renewal of the lease would be possible after ten years.

(3) Because of the terms of our agreement with you, we cannot meet the bank's terms.

# 5

## VOCABULARY BUILDING

*convinced*   1. We are convinced that he did the right thing.

*budget*
*experiment*   2. It was difficult to convince them that we would need a larger budget to carry out the experiment.

*employees*   3. Our employees are convinced that we should experiment with the new sales plan for people who buy on a budget.

*steadily*   4. We have steadily convinced more and more of our employees that they should try to sell more goods to people who buy on a budget plan.

*impressed*   5. I was very much impressed with the steadily increasing number of people who are buying on a budget, and I am convinced that our employees should know about this.

*private*   6. In private talks with our employees I was impressed by their desire to experiment with special sales for customers who buy on a budget.

*unfortunately*   7. I shall unfortunately not be able to attend your private conferences with your employees, but I have been steadily convinced of their desire to keep expenses within your budget.

335

## THEORY PRACTICE

The relations that we have maintained with our employees have[10] unfortunately taken a turn for the worse because of their[20] unwillingness to work extra hours. I am convinced that we[30] must experiment with the plan to have the store open[40] in the evening at least two or three days a[50] week until nine.

We have known for a long time[60] that we have been losing patronage steadily because many of[70] our customers like to do their shopping in the evening.[80] If we cannot obtain the cooperation of our employees, it[90] may mean that the entire experiment will have to be[100] dropped, and this will mean a further loss of business[110] for us. (112)

## SPEED BUILDING PRACTICE

Dear Madam:

The goods you ordered recently will be delivered[10] by next Monday without fail.

According to the information we[20] have received, there have been several delays in freight service[30] between our factory and this city. Because of these delays,[40] it may be necessary for us to change our methods[50] of delivery. This would, unfortunately, cause us to lose the[60] patronage of several of our best customers.

We shall make[70] sure that the railroad is impressed with the importance of[80] prompt delivery and the effect of slow deliveries on our[90] business with them in the future.

Very truly yours, (99)

## TRANSCRIPTION LETTERS

Metropolitan Realty Corporation
504 Princess Avenue
Brandon, Manitoba

Gentlemen:

According to the terms of our lease, we are[10] obligated to pay rent for the next eighteen months. There[20] has, unfortunately, been a change in my husband's health requiring[30] him to move to another ~~state.~~ *province*

We would like to[40] know whether it would be possible for us to be[50] released from the provisions of the lease agreement, or whether[60] you would permit us to sublet the apartment. My

336

brother[70] is willing to take over the apartment and complete the[80] terms of our lease. He would also be interested in[90] a lease for himself either at the end of our[100] present lease or as soon as we move.

Very truly[110] yours,     (111)

Mrs. Lois Hanson,
36 Albert Street,
Regina, Saskatchewan

Dear Mrs. Hanson:

We were sorry to learn of your[10] husband's poor health and its effect on his business activities.[20] Unfortunately, we cannot accept your offer to sublet the apartment[30] to your brother because that is against the terms of[40] the lease. While we have no doubt that your brother[50] would be a desirable tenant, we cannot permit you to[60] change your lease without doing the same for others. The[70] best procedure, we would suggest, is that a new lease[80] be signed between your brother and ourselves.

However, we reserve[90] the right to include a 15 per cent increase in[100] the rent because of the cost of making some necessary[110] repairs in the apartment. We wish to rebuild several of[120] the walls and to change the type of window now[130] in the apartment. If your brother will agree to these[140] terms, we shall be glad to speak further with him.[150]

Very sincerely yours,     (153)

Metropolitan Realty Corporation
504 Princess Avenue
Brandon, Manitoba

Gentlemen:

I was very much surprised at your terms for[10] permitting us to be released from our lease. In all[20] the years that we have been living in this apartment[30] you have never suggested that you were interested in making[40] such changes, and I do not see why my brother[50] should be required to pay for improvements that are of[60] value only to yourself.

I am not sure that an[70] increase in the rental would be agreeable to my brother,[80] but I shall ask him to contact you.

Yours very[90] truly,     (91)

## SPELLING

(1) obligated, unfortunately, released, sublet
(2) activities, desirable, procedure, necessary, repairs
(3) permitting

## PUNCTUATION

(1) I wish to inform you that, according to the terms of your lease, you will have to pay two months' rent in advance.
(2) I would be willing to sign the new lease either now or at the end of the year.
(3) If your brother will agree to a 10 per cent increase in the rent, together with a three-year lease, we shall be able to sign a new lease immediately.

## VOCABULARY BUILDING

*association* 1. It is a pleasure to have you as a member of our association.

*variety* 2. Our association is planning a variety of activities this year.

*encourage* 3. You should encourage them to attend the variety of functions that our association is having this year.

*interfere* 4. I do not think that your association should interfere with our plans by encouraging us to have a greater variety of activities.

*discussion* 5. You should encourage him not to interfere in the discussion of the plans of our association.

*instrument* 6. This is the best instrument you can use for a variety of purposes.

*extensive* 7. We should like to try to encourage a more extensive use of this instrument.

*installed* 8. You should encourage the members of your association to have this instrument installed because it will not require extensive repairs, and it will permit you to engage in a variety of activities.

## THEORY PRACTICE

Our association is now conducting a drive to encourage more[10] business firms to come to this city. We believe that[20] business firms will find many advantages in our city, including[30] a variety of means of transportation as well as an[40] extensive and highly skilled supply of labor. Of course, the[50] best proof of the effectiveness of doing business in this[60] city can be obtained from a discussion with people now[70] doing business here.

We are putting out some attractive advance[80] announcements encouraging business men from other cities to come down[90] and see what we have to offer. We hope that[100] we can count on you to join our drive. (109)

## SPEED BUILDING PRACTICE

Dear Sir:

It was a pleasure to receive the information[10] that we requested from you about the activities of your[20] association. It was good to know that your association is[30] going to help us in our drive.

When we have[40] a sufficient number of signatures in support of our plans,[50] we shall be able to bring the matter up for[60] discussion before the members of our committee. We hope that[70] you will continue to do all that you can to[80] encourage the members of your association to help us in[90] our work.

Cordially yours, (94)

## TRANSCRIPTION LETTERS

Provincial Trust Company
160 Borden Avenue North
Fort William, Ontario

Gentlemen:

I would like some information about your safe deposit[10] boxes. I have some valuable papers and securities which I[20] feel should not be kept around the house. Could you[30] please tell me what the cost of a safe deposit[40] box would be, and whether payment must be made in[50] advance.

I expect to make extensive use of this safe[60] deposit box, so that it will be important for me[70] to know the hours during which it may be used.[80] I also wish to know whether you must be informed[90] in advance if the box is to be used after[100] regular banking hours.

Very truly yours, (96)

339

Mr. Paul B. Franklin
64 Jackson Avenue
Toronto 18, Ontario

Dear Mr. Franklin:

It was a pleasure to receive your[10] recent letter requesting information about our safe deposit facilities.

The[20] hours during which the safe deposit box can be used[30] include the usual banking hours, as well as additional time[40] after the regular banking hours. However, if you wish to[50] use a safe deposit box after banking hours, it is[60] desirable to make arrangements at least an hour in advance.[70]

Payments for safe deposit boxes are charged to your account.[80] We have a variety of boxes. The cost of the[90] larger boxes is slightly higher, and we have only a[100] limited number available.

Our usual procedure is to furnish a[110] key which can be used only for your box. You[120] will have to sign each time that you use your[130] safe deposit box, and the bank keeps a duplicate key[140] in case you lose your key. However, the bank's key[150] cannot be used without your permission.

Sincerely yours,  (158)

Provincial Trust Company
160 Borden Avenue North
Fort William, Ontario

Gentlemen:

I have received your letter containing the information that[10] I requested about your safe deposit boxes.

According to your[20] letter, it would seem that I am the only one[30] who may use the box. As I am at work[40] during the regular hours of the banking day, I would[50] like to know whether my wife could be given permission[60] to use the box instead of myself. Please let me[70] know if such an arrangement can be made, and what[80] steps I would have to take to do this.

Yours[90] truly,  (91)

## SPELLING

(1) deposit, securities, extensive
(2) facilities, desirable, variety, procedure, duplicate, permission
(3) containing

## PUNCTUATION

(1) We believe that there are many advantages to this plan, including increased sales as well as better profits.

(2) Although we spoke to them several days ago, it was good to see that the work was going along so well.

(3) Do you know what the cost of the book would be and how I could get a copy of it soon?

# 7

## VOCABULARY BUILDING

*standard*    1. This paper comes only in the standard size.

*competent*    2. I am not competent to judge whether this paper is the standard size.

*courteous*    3. Our standard procedure is to train our employees to be competent and courteous.

*attend*    4. Many of our employees attend training classes where they are learning how to be competent and courteous.

*afford*    5. We cannot afford to have any people who are not competent and courteous attending our special training classes.

*maximum*    6. The maximum salary we can afford to pay is well above the standard wage, but we insist that these employees be competent and courteous.

*superior*    7. If you wish to obtain superior employees who are both competent and courteous, you will have to start them at the standard wage and offer them a high maximum.

*current*    8. Our current standard of wages is superior to the maximum paid in other parts of the country.

## THEORY PRACTICE

I should like to explain why we cannot afford to[10] pay more than the current wage to employees in our[20] factory. Our equipment is extremely poor and our machines are[30] not physically capable of turning out the standard amount of[40] work. The maximum salary

341

that we can afford to pay[50] is the usual standard for the industry in other parts[60] of the country.

Despite all our efforts, there has been[70] no noticeable improvement in our current production. We are sure[80] that we have obtained maximum production from our current machines. (90)

## SPEED BUILDING PRACTICE

Gentlemen:

We have been informed that the advertisements you placed[10] for us in a number of magazines were extremely difficult[20] to understand.

In view of the fact that you had[30] told us you were going to make a special effort[40] to improve the quality of our advertisements, we cannot afford[50] to continue to have you handle our account. We are,[60] therefore, giving you notice that we shall not renew our[70] contract with you when the current one expires. We are[80] sure that you will understand the reason for this action.[90]

Yours truly, (92)

## TRANSCRIPTION LETTERS

Municipal Bank and Trust Company
150 East 24th Street
New York, New York 10017

Gentlemen:

I recently received a signature card from you for[10] the purpose of opening a special checking account in your[20] bank. It was my understanding that this type of account[30] would not require any minimum balance, and that there would[40] simply be a charge of ten cents for each check.[50] I now note that there is an additional charge of[60] fifty cents a month, regardless of the number of checks[70] I make out during each month.

Could you please explain[80] the reason for this charge? I am extremely anxious to[90] open the account, but I would like to know what[100] the full cost would be.

Cordially yours, (107)

Mrs. Eileen Jansen
54 Dale Avenue
Tóronto 12, Ontario

Dear Mrs. Jansen:

We should like to explain the reason[10] for our service charge on special checking accounts.

When we[20] first installed our current system for handling special checking accounts,[30] we provided bank statements every three months. However, many of[40] our depositors found that these statements did not permit them[50] to keep their records up to date. We, therefore, changed[60] our policy and made these bank statements available every month.[70] In order to cover our bookkeeping costs, we found it[80] necessary to add a charge of fifty cents a month[90] for this service.

We regret that we cannot offer a[100] variety of charges to correspond to the number of times[110] that the special checking account is used. However, we found[120] that over a period of time there is no noticeable[130] difference in the number of occasions on which the account[140] is used. We are sure you will like this type[150] of account because it will afford you the maximum in[160] banking service at a very moderate cost.

Very truly yours,             (170)

Municipal Bank and Trust Company
150 East 24th Street
New York, New York 10017

Gentlemen:

I now understand the reason for the service charge[10] of fifty cents a month for the special checking account.[20] However, I do not usually write enough checks to make[30] it worth my while to use a special checking account.[40]

Could you tell me your requirements for opening a regular[50] checking account? I would like to know what the current[60] minimum balance would be and what other charges I would[70] have to pay. I should like to open an account[80] soon, and I would appreciate a prompt answer.

Cordially yours,             (90)

## SPELLING

(1) recently, signature, standard, minimum, anxious
(2) installed, current (currant), depositors, bookkeeping, variety, correspond, period, noticeable, occasions, afford, moderate
(3) appreciate

## PUNCTUATION

(1) In spite of our best efforts there does not seem to be any improvement in our sales of these dresses.
(2) In view of the fact that you cannot improve the quality of our advertisements, we shall not be able to continue our account with you.
(3) It was my understanding that no minimum balance would be necessary and that there would be no service charges at any time.

## VOCABULARY BUILDING

*display*      1. We shall display your goods in the front window of our store.

*protest*      2. There was no protest from them about the poor display of the goods in the store.

*interior*      3. I am sure they will make a protest about your display of their goods in the interior of the store.

*fashion*      4. I believe that many of them will protest the idea of a fashion display in the interior of the store.

*expert*      5. Although he may be a fashion expert, many people are protesting his lack of knowledge of the problems of interior display.

*delighted*      6. I shall be delighted to speak to your fashion expert and to show her our latest display of suits.

*complaining*      7. I am delighted to hear that their fashion expert has stopped complaining about the display in the interior of the store.

*competition*      8. We were delighted to know that they have stopped complaining about the competition.

## THEORY PRACTICE

Although it is now five months since we shipped our[10] last order to you, our collections have been very slow.[20] We believe that it is your intention to pay your[30] bills in full. However, we should have some explanation or[40] indication of the time of payment. Your action in this[50] matter will affect our future transactions with you.

We know[60] that you will be interested in our fall fashions, which[70] we are now ready to display in our showrooms.     (79)

## SPEED BUILDING PRACTICE

Gentlemen:

We have been informed that it is your intention[10] to make a display of your latest fashions in one[20] of your stores in this city. We would be delighted[30] to see what you have to offer, even though we[40] have never had an opportunity to make a purchase from[50] you.

If you plan to have the fashion display within[60] the next few days, please let us know so that[70] we can tell our fashion expert to be on hand.[80] We are especially interested in your line of spring dresses,[90] for we have been complaining to our buyers that we[100] do not seem to have many interesting styles.

Sincerely yours,     (110)

## TRANSCRIPTION LETTERS

National Bank and Trust Company
Three Rivers
Quebec

Gentlemen:

I am interested in obtaining a loan on my[10] clothing business. My intention in securing the loan is to[20] provide for expansion of my business so that I will[30] be in a better position to meet the competition from[40] other stores.

I wish to make certain changes in the[50] interior of the store, and to make the display windows[60] more attractive. The transaction would involve a loan of approximately[70] $10,000, to be paid back in three years.[80]

I should be glad to supply any additional information you[90] may wish to have.

Sincerely yours,     (96)

Fitwell Dresses Incorporated
Arvida
Quebec
Gentlemen:

We are always delighted to receive requests for loans[10] that indicate expansion of a business. However, before we[20] can enter into a transaction involving the loan of such[30] a large sum of money, it is necessary for us[40] to know what security you can offer for the loan.[50] We are enclosing one of our standard forms which should[60] be filled out by you and forwarded to us.

Our[70] principal concern is, of course, with the amount and type[80] of collateral you have to offer for the loan. We[90] would also be interested in seeing your financial statements for[100] the past three years. In view of the fact that[110] this loan would be used for the expansion of a[120] present building, we would also have to know the terms[130] of your lease. If you plan to purchase this property,[140] we would have to know whether you have taken out[150] any previous mortgage.

We shall be pleased to make an[160] appointment for a conference with you at any of our[170] branch offices, if you so desire.

Very truly yours,          (179)


National Bank and Trust Company
Three Rivers
Quebec
Gentlemen:

We have received your answer to our request for[10] a loan from your bank.

It would require some time[20] to gather the information you desire. We were hoping that[30] you would come to a quick decision on the transaction[40] since we are ready to offer collateral amounting to[50] $8,000. If you still require the information you mentioned[60] in your letter, we shall try to obtain the loan[70] we need from another source.[75]

Yours truly,          (77)

## SPELLING

(1) intention, securing, expansion, position, competition, interior, approximately

346

(2) transaction, security, standard, principal-ly (principle), concern, collateral, property, previous, conference

(3) mentioned

## PUNCTUATION

(1) Although you received our last order three months ago, we have not received any payments from you during that time.

(2) I wish to make certain changes in the office, including the purchase of new tables, desks, and chairs.

(3) The total bill will amount to $150, which will cover the cost of purchasing, packing, and shipping the goods.

## VOCABULARY BUILDING

| | | |
|---|---|---|
| *economy* | 1. | We cannot expect a great deal of economy from the use of this machine. |
| *distinctive* *printed* | 2. | Our advertisements are distinctive even though they are printed with a maximum of economy. |
| *identification* | 3. | We use a special kind of paper which permits economy of cost and which gives a distinctive identification to our printed materials. |
| *omit* | 4. | We shall have to omit any distinctive marks of identification on the printed material we do for them. |
| *security* | 5. | In order to provide for maximum security in the handling of your shipments, you must furnish identification marks. |
| *enlarging* *capacity* | 6. | We are enlarging the capacity of our shipping department so as to provide for greater economy. |

## THEORY PRACTICE

We have some very distinctive desks for sale which we[10] are sure will be very desirable for your office. They[20] are made so that they have more capacity than any[30] desk of a similar size. This is achieved through an[40] economy of space obtained by omitting all unnecessary features. As[50] a matter of fact, you will have 20 per cent[60] more space in this desk than in other desks of[70] a comparable size.

These desks are also guaranteed to wear[80] extremely well. They can be exposed to the most difficult[90] type of wear and tear without fear of damage. (99)

## SPEED BUILDING PRACTICE

Gentlemen:

During the past few weeks it has become impossible[10] to ship our orders on time even though we are[20] working at capacity. However, we expect to have your shipment[30] out within three days so that it will reach you[40] in time to display in your economy sale.

If we[50] can help you in any further way, we shall be[60] glad to do so. Please let us know how you[70] like these goods when you receive them.

Cordially yours, (79)

## TRANSCRIPTION LETTERS

Central Bank and Trust Company
Greenwood Shopping Plaza
Ottawa, Ontario

Gentlemen:

According to your statement of our account, the present[10] balance is $1,652.50.[20] This figure disagrees with our records by $55.[30]

Would you please check through your records again to see[40] whether there is an item of $55 which[50] you have charged to our account in error. I might[60] suggest that you check the account of a firm which[70] has a name similar to ours, Borden Brothers, of this[80] city. In the past we have sometimes received some items[90] intended for them.

Please let us know as soon as[100] possible whether this is the explanation for the difference in[110] our records.

Cordially yours, (114)

James Borden and Brothers Incorporated
P.O. Box 22
Pembroke, Ontario

Gentlemen:

We have made a careful check of our records[10] to determine whether an error has been made in our[20] handling of your account.

348

We checked carefully the account of[30] Borden Brothers of this city, but our records do not[40] show any error in their balance, as far as we[50] can find out at the present time.

We would suggest[60] that you check through your records once again to determine[70] whether you entered a deposit of $55 twice,[80] or whether you may have neglected to enter an outstanding[90] check. Our previous experience has shown that such errors may[100] be due to a duplicate entry or failure to enter[110] a particular item. If it is still impossible for you[120] to find the error, we suggest that you contact us[130] at once so that we can check further back in[140] our records and bank statements.

We hope that this matter[150] will be cleared up immediately.

Very truly yours,          (158)


Central Bank and Trust Company
Greenwood Shopping Plaza
Ottawa, Ontario

Gentlemen:

We followed your suggestion and we checked our records[10] for the past two months. We are very glad to[20] say that we have finally found the error in our[30] books. We did issue a check in the amount of[40] $55, but this check had never been entered[50] in our bank records.

Please accept our thanks for your[60] valuable help and suggestions for finding the cause of the[70] error in our balance.

We are sure that such an[80] error will not happen again.

Very truly yours,          (88)


## SPELLING

(1)  disagrees, error, similar, explanation
(2)  determine, neglect-ed, duplicate, entry, impossible
(3)  finally


## PUNCTUATION

(1)  We have some very fine items for sale which will include both office and home desks, tables, and chairs.
(2)  According to the statement which I just received, my present balance, covering purchases for the last two months, is $250.

# 10

## VOCABULARY BUILDING

| | | |
|---|---|---|
| *ambitious* *faithful* | 1. | We need someone for this job who is ambitious and faithful. |
| *supplementary* | 2. | He issued a supplementary report which showed a shortage of ambitious personnel. |
| *highlights* | 3. | His discussion of the highlights of the supplementary report showed that he was ambitious to advance in the company. |
| *assignment* | 4. | His assignment was to pick out the highlights of the supplementary report and discuss them with us. |
| *ascertain* | 5. | I would like you to ascertain whether there will be a supplementary assignment because some of the men are ambitious to start it immediately. |
| *surrounding* | 6. | Your assignment will be to ascertain whether the surrounding territory can provide any supplementary income for our company. |
| *circulation* | 7. | His next assignment will be to ascertain whether we can improve the circulation of our magazine in the surrounding territory. |

## THEORY PRACTICE

We have revised our estimate of the sales of our[10] spring styles, and it will be necessary to adjust our[20] production accordingly. This situation is due to the steady decline[30] in the circulation of the local papers in the surrounding[40] areas.

We have used every means we know of to[50] encourage the local papers to try to keep their many[60] faithful readers who have moved out of the city to[70] the surrounding areas.　　　　　　　　　　　(73)

## SPEED BUILDING PRACTICE

Gentlemen:

We have found it difficult to move our stocks[10] of your goods faster than we have in the past.[20] As a result we have a large bal-

350

ance of goods[30] on hand, and we must inform you that it will[40] be impossible for us to accept any more deliveries from[50] you until further notice. Please be good enough to inform[60] your manufacturer that he should adjust his production so that[70] he will not make more goods than he can sell.[80]

As soon as our sales improve and we can ascertain[90] our future needs, we shall be glad to inform you[100] so that you can begin shipments to us again.

Thank[110] you for your cooperation.

Very truly yours,  (117)

## TRANSCRIPTION LETTERS

Kingston Savings Bank
102 Main Street
Kingston, Ontario

Gentlemen:

I am interested in purchasing the house located at[10] 155 Main Street in this city, on which[20] your bank holds a mortgage. As this is the first[30] house that I have been interested in purchasing, I would[40] like to ascertain whether I would be allowed to take[50] over the existing mortgage from the present owners of the[60] house. I would also be interested in knowing whether I[70] can reduce the amount of the payments on the mortgage[80] by means of a down payment.

I would appreciate your[90] answers to my questions as well as any other supplementary[100] information that it might be advisable for me to have.[110]

Yours very truly,  (113)

Mr. Lawrence J. Thompson
24 Douglas Street
Woodstock, Ontario

Dear Mr. Thompson:

It is the policy of this bank[10] to assist home owners to sell their houses as easily[20] and efficiently as possible. We, therefore, make no additional charges[30] for the necessary work involved in the handling of a[40] mortgage. However, we do insist on a completely new mortgage[50] whenever a house is sold. In addition, we require that[60] the

351

face value of the new mortgage be for a[70] sum that is substantially less than that of the original[80] mortgage.

We require a down payment of at least ten[90] per cent of the present value of the mortgage. In[100] the case of the house in which you are interested,[110] this would amount to the sum of[120] $1,375. This would result in[130] a reduction in the number of payments on the mortgage, but[140] it would not affect the amount to be paid each[150] month.

We shall be happy to see you at your[160] convenience to discuss further details of the contract.

Very truly[170] yours,　　　(171)


Kingston Savings Bank
102 Main Street
Kingston, Ontario

Gentlemen:

According to the terms of your letter I would[10] have to make a down payment of[20] $1,375 in order to obtain[30] a new mortgage on the house. I would then be[40] able to reduce the number of payments without changing the[50] amount of each payment.

I would much prefer to reduce[60] the amount of each payment. Can you possibly reconsider your[70] terms so as to make it possible for me to[80] reduce the amount of each payment after making the down[90] payment on the mortgage?

Yours very truly,　　　(97)


## SPELLING

(1) locate, mortgage-d, ascertain, existing, supplementary, advisable
(2) assist, easily, necessary, original, reduction, convenience
(3) prefer


## PUNCTUATION

(1) We have made all of the changes you requested, but it will be necessary, while doing this, to go over the books again.
(2) As a result, we now find that there is a poor balance between the production, sale, and distribution of goods.
(3) I am interested in purchasing this house, but the owner does not have a mortgage on it and it is difficult for me to get one at this time.

# 11

## VOCABULARY BUILDING

*frankly*
*disappointed*

1. I was frankly very much disappointed to hear what he had to say to the members of the committee.

*situated*

2. It was obvious that he was frankly disappointed when he found out where the new house was situated.

*furnishing*

3. We are frankly disappointed with the way in which they are furnishing the new house.

*desirable*

4. It would be more desirable to continue furnishing the house than to wait for the changes you desire.

*consulted*

5. He was very much disappointed that he had not consulted him about furnishing the house, but, to put it frankly, we did not find his taste to be very desirable.

*reduction*

6. It would have been desirable to have asked for a reduction in the cost of furnishing the house, and you should have told them so frankly when you consulted them earlier.

*authorize*

7. I cannot authorize a reduction in the cost of the furnishings until I have consulted my firm, and I frankly think they will not approve it.

## THEORY PRACTICE

In response to your question about a reduction in expenses[10] in furnishing your house, I would suggest that you obtain[20] the assistance of an expert. You apparently do not seem[30] to realize that the cost of many of the materials[40] now being used in house furnishings has gone up a[50] great deal.

I frankly believe that it would be desirable[60] for you to obtain the complete figures for furnishing the[70] house before you go ahead and be disappointed when you[80] cannot afford to get just what you want. I have[90] consulted people in homes situated in your neighborhood and they[100] have told me that they had the same problems.

(109)

# SPEED BUILDING PRACTICE

Dear Sir:

Our organization is interested in opening a store[10] in this town to sell house furnishings. We are sure[20] that there are many people who would be glad to[30] have the convenience of our store in which to make[40] their purchases.

We are interested in obtaining the services of[50] someone who is familiar with the furnishing needs of the[60] people of this town. Under the circumstances, we feel that[70] you might know of someone who would be able to[80] take the position we are offering. If there are any[90] members of your firm who are interested in doing this[100] job after office hours, we should like to talk to[110] them.

Please let us know if you have anyone you[120] wish to recommend.

Yours truly,          (125)

# TRANSCRIPTION LETTERS

Mr. Arnold Black
Black and Berman
Sunnyside
Trinity Bay, Newfoundland

Dear Mr. Black:

I am in need of legal advice[10] and assistance concerning a contract in which I agreed to[20] deliver five dozen cartons of paper to a new customer[30] who has a store situated outside the city. Because of[40] the illness of several of my drivers, it was impossible[50] to make delivery of the shipment on the date agreed[60] upon.

When I finally tried to make delivery a week[70] later, the customer refused to accept the shipment. In addition,[80] he claimed that I would be responsible for the extra[90] cost of the shipment he obtained from another dealer. Should[100] I authorize my driver to make delivery of the shipment?[110]

Yours truly,          (112)

Mr. Frank Jacobs
Uptown Paper Company
161 John Street
Hamilton, Ontario

Dear Mr. Jacobs:

I have received your letter requesting advice[10] about a contract to deliver paper to one of your[20] customers.

In answering your questions, I should like to point[30] out that the most desirable way to approach your problem[40] is to examine the terms of your contract. If there[50] is a definite statement concerning damages caused by late delivery,[60] you would be bound by those conditions. However, in the[70] usual case, such items are not specifically mentioned, and it[80] is understood that delivery will be made by the date[90] specified or within a reasonable time thereafter.

Another problem is[100] whether a notice of delay in making the shipment was[110] given. If such a notice was given and your customer[120] did not say anything about this notice, then it is[130] customary to assume that he agreed to the delay. Under[140] the circumstances you have presented I would frankly say that[150] it would not be wise to authorize your driver to[160] leave the shipment at the customer's store without his definite[170] approval.

Cordially yours,     (173)

Mr. Arnold Black
Black and Berman
Sunnyside
Trinity Bay, Newfoundland

Dear Mr. Black:

I appreciate very much your assistance in[10] the problem of my delivery of paper. I shall follow[20] your advice and not authorize my driver to leave the[30] paper at the customer's store. I have been led to[40] understand that the customer is planning to go ahead with[50] a lawsuit to recover damages from our firm. Would you[60] be interested in handling the case for us? If so,[70] I shall be glad to furnish the information which you[80] mentioned in your letter.

Very truly yours,     (87)

## SPELLING

(1) legal, advice (advise), assistance, concerning, cartons, situated, finally, authorize

(2) desirable, examine, definite, specifically, mentioned, specified, reasonable, customary, frankly

(3) planning

## PUNCTUATION

(1) In response to your question about the amount of expense involved, please note that, up to now, we have not asked for an increase.

(2) I have consulted several people about this, and they have told me that they had the same problem.

(3) Because of the difficulty of making delivery on time, it was impossible to satisfy all of my customers.

# 12
## VOCABULARY BUILDING

| | | |
|---|---|---|
| *essential* | 1. | It is essential that we have a report of your progress on the job. |
| *excellent* | 2. | The excellent work of our sales force has made it essential that we increase our production. |
| *project* | 3. | I am glad to say that this is an excellent project and one that is essential to the growth of our firm. |
| *undoubtedly* | 4. | You are undoubtedly aware of this excellent project and how essential it is to our firm. |
| *adjacent* | 5. | There is a large store adjacent to our building in which you can undoubtedly find some excellent buys. |
| *designed* | 6. | They designed the project adjacent to your store, and you will undoubtedly agree that it is an excellent job. |
| *inspected* | 7. | I have inspected your project and the one adjacent to it, and they are excellent. |
| *architect* | 8. | Your architect designed the project which is adjacent to our store, and when our representative inspected it, he said that it was an excellent job in all details. |

356

## THEORY PRACTICE

We are planning to put up a project adjacent to[10] the bank building, and we are interested in obtaining the[20] services of an architect who has designed buildings similar to[30] the one that we have in mind. If you know[40] of anyone who has done such work, and you can[50] recommend him to us, we shall be grateful to you.[60]

It is essential that this architect have had enough experience[70] in this type of work to solve some of our[80] special problems. There are undoubtedly many excellent architects who have[90] the ability to do this project, but they would need[100] the special experience to do it the way we wish. (110)

## SPEED BUILDING PRACTICE

Gentlemen:

We wish to take out insurance on a new[10] building that will be completed in the near future. Our[20] architect has designed the project in what we think is[30] an excellent manner, but we are sure that you will[40] undoubtedly wish to see the plans. We are also planning[50] to make some improvements in the amount of space to[60] be provided in each office, although we know that this[70] will be an expensive job.

Please inform us whether there[80] will be any difficulty in obtaining this insurance because changes[90] are being made in the plans. It is essential that[100] we hear from you about this matter very shortly.

Very[110] truly yours, (112)

## TRANSCRIPTION LETTERS

Messrs. Harwell and Cross
748 Webster Drive
London, Ontario

Gentlemen:

I am interested in engaging an attorney to assist[10] in the collection of a debt that has been due[20] to this company for a long time. I have made[30] every effort to obtain collection in the usual way, but[40] I have not been successful. My customer claims that he[50] does not owe us any money because of a loss[60] he suffered due to defects which existed in the material[70] that we sent him. Since I inspected the material myself[80] before it was shipped, I feel that this is merely[90] an excuse to avoid payment.

I shall be glad to[100] furnish any other details which you may wish to have.[110]

Very truly yours,      (113)

Mr. Martin Randolph
Randolph and Miller Incorporated
95 Columbia Road
London, Ontario
Dear Mr. Randolph:

We shall be happy to accept your[10] case, and we shall do our utmost to obtain a[20] fair and just settlement on your claim.

From what you[30] told us in your previous letter, you have an excellent[40] chance of obtaining full recovery of your claim. It is,[50] however, essential that we be given a complete statement of[60] the facts so that we can avoid difficulty if the[70] case comes to trial. It would be our immediate intention[80] to avoid having the case go to trial. We would[90] try to obtain a settlement of your entire claim on[100] the basis of a presentation of the facts and the[110] law in the case. However, if your customer refuses to[120] agree to an amicable settlement, we would, of course, be[130] prepared to follow through and take the case to court.[140]

We would recommend that you gather together all of the[150] data related to the case, including the invoices and any[160] correspondence that passed between you and your customer.

Respectfully yours,      (170)

Messrs. Harwell and Cross
748 Webster Drive
London, Ontario

I am glad to hear that you are willing[10] to accept the case. I have now received a letter[20] from this customer informing me that he is going to[30] sue me for damages caused him by the fact that[40] I mentioned to other firms that I have been having[50] difficulty in collecting money from him. I do not know[60] whether he has a right to sue me on such[70] grounds, but I will feel better when I know that[80] you are handling the entire matter.

Cordially yours,      (88)

## SPELLING

(1) attorney, debt, successful, suffered, exist-ed
(2) excellent, recovery, essential, intention, amicable, prepared, recommend, data, correspondence
(3) damages

## PUNCTUATION

(1) If you know of anyone whom you can recommend to us, we shall be grateful for your help.
(2) There are, of course, many people who could do the job, but we would be interested in only the best man available.
(3) Since I inspected the goods myself, there is, in my opinion, no doubt that they were in good condition when we shipped them.

# 13

## VOCABULARY BUILDING

*annual*  
1. Our annual report will be ready by the end of this week.

*exceptional*  
*display*  
2. We wish to have an exceptional display for our annual show.

*gathering*  
3. We are gathering together an exceptional display for our annual fall fashion show.

*congratulate*  
4. We wish to congratulate you on the exceptional job that you did in gathering together the materials for our annual display.

*outstanding*  
5. The display of our goods was outstanding this year, and we wish to congratulate you for the exceptional job that you did in gathering and displaying our products.

*achievement*  
6. Your achievement was outstanding, and we wish to congratulate you for the excellent job that you did at our annual show.

*reputation*  
7. Your outstanding achievement in gathering together the materials for our annual display will certainly add to your reputation.

## THEORY PRACTICE

If we feel that you can display our products in[10] an outstanding way, we will be very happy to take[20] space from you. Our reputation in the field is such[30] that we would not wish to be associated with a[40] display that is not a model one.

We are attaching[50] a copy of our latest catalogue so that you can[60] see what items we offer. You will note that we[70] try to make it pleasant and easy for customers to[80] order our products.     (83)


## SPEED BUILDING PRACTICE

Dear Sir:

It is most important that we receive from[10] you in the near future a sample of the materials[20] that you plan to display in your annual fashion show.[30] We wish to prepare some dresses from this material in[40] order to have our models show them within the next[50] three weeks.

We are now going to make an attempt[60] to build up our sales of less expensive dresses, and[70] it is, therefore, very important that we use the most[80] efficient means of production. If your materials meet our needs,[90] we can prepare the dresses and put out our new[100] catalogue within the next two months.

Very truly yours,     (109)


## TRANSCRIPTION LETTERS

Messrs. Jordan and Harrison
Greystone Building
156 West Street
Woodstock, Ontario

Gentlemen:

I wish to obtain your legal advice in a[10] matter involving a purchase which I made at one of[20] the local stores. I ordered some furniture for my dining[30] room from a display in the store and gave a[40] deposit for a set like the one in the store.[50] When the furniture finally arrived, I found that several of[60] the pieces were different from those I had ordered.

When[70] I told the furniture buyer about the difference in the[80] furniture, he told me that I had not specified the[90] exact set in the store. The store has refused to[100] return my deposit or to pick up the furniture.

Cordially[110] yours,        (111)

Mrs. Rita Samuels
288 Nelson Road
Woodstock, Ontario

Dear Mrs. Samuels:

We are happy to offer our assistance[10] to you in the matter of your furniture purchase. Your[20] case is not exceptional and has occurred several times to[30] people who have done business with this store. While their[40] reputation is reasonably good, they have made it a practice[50] to stay close to the letter of the law in[60] the r business dealings.

In order to give you the maximum[70] help in this case, it will be necessary to have[80] all the information that you can give us. We would[90] like to know, first of all, whether you signed any[100] contract. Another important item is the exact difference between the[110] set which you received and the one which you saw[120] on display. If there is only a minor difference in[130] the two sets, it may be difficult to prove that[140] the store failed to carry out its part of the[150] contract. We would suggest that you make sure that no[160] one touches or uses any of the furniture.

Sincerely yours,        (170)

Messrs. Jordan and Harrison
Greystone Building
156 West Street
Woodstock, Ontario

Gentlemen:

Your letter was not very encouraging in my efforts[10] to obtain the furniture that I wished to buy. In[20] view of your excellent reputation, I felt that you would[30] be able to suggest some definite plan for settling this[40] case.

The difference between the set of furniture that I[50] wanted and the one the store delivered is very substantial,[60] and I cannot use the set I received. The set[70] has not been touched since it was delivered, but it[80] takes up too much space in my house.

Yours truly,        (90)

## SPELLING

(1)  furniture, deposit, specified, exact
(2)  exceptional, occurred, reputation, maximum, minor
(3)  definite, encouraging

## PUNCTUATION

(1)  If you feel that you can do a good job, we shall be happy to speak to you about gathering the material, having it printed, and getting it delivered.
(2)  You will note, I am sure, that sales have improved, but you should also check to see that profits have gone up as well.
(3)  When the furniture arrived, and I checked it, I found a few pieces damaged or broken.

# 14

## VOCABULARY BUILDING

*commendable*  1.  She showed commendable taste in the manner in
*decorated*  which she decorated the room.

*competent*  2.  Her competent use of a combination of plates and
*combination*  dishes to decorate the table was highly commendable.

*anticipate*  3.  We anticipate that the combination of your excellent materials and his competent designs will result in very commendable results when the house is decorated.

*expiration*  4.  At the expiration of the contract I anticipate that they will begin to look for someone more competent.

*proposed*  5.  It was proposed that we should anticipate the expiration of the contract by starting now to hire more competent men for the next job.

*uppermost*  6.  The thought that was uppermost in his mind was to anticipate trouble at the expiration of the contract by hiring competent men, and so he proposed that we keep records of commendable achievement by our employees.

## THEORY PRACTICE

I believe that we shall follow your advice in the[10] matter of the expiration of our contract with our employees[20] by making an offer now of an increase in their[30] wages. However, I presume that when the contract talks finally[40] begin, we shall be able to review the entire problem[50] of the employee who is not doing his job in[60] a competent manner.

I would not like to duplicate the[70] terms of the old contract which prevented us from doing[80] too much about employees who were not doing their job[90] properly. I can understand the need of protection for those[100] men whose work is only slightly below the standard. (109)

## SPEED BUILDING PRACTICE

Gentlemen:

We are writing to ask about the income from[10] mortgages which we purchased from you and on which we[20] were led to expect a return of eight per cent[30] on our money

At the present time the return on[40] our investment is about five per cent, and we would[50] not have invested our money with you if we had[60] known that this would be the return to be received.[70] The thought that is uppermost in our mind is whether[80] you propose to do something about this situation, of which[90] I am sure you are aware.

Please advise us as[100] soon as possible of the prospects for future returns on[110] our investments with you.

Very truly yours, (117)

## TRANSCRIPTION LETTERS

Messrs. Wilson, Greenwald and Thurston
102 Madison Avenue
Toronto 5, Ontario

Gentlemen:

I should like to engage your services in connection[10] with an accident that occurred to me recently. I was[20] a passenger on a bus which came to a sudden[30] stop and threw me against a steel rail. The bus[40] was going at a very rapid rate of speed when[50] another car came in front of it. The driver of[60] the bus did not anticipate the other car and almost[70] ran into it before he applied his brakes.

363

I did[80] not see a doctor immediately because I felt that my[90] injuries were minor, but I have been having severe pains[100] in my back for the last three days.

Yours truly,         (110)

Mrs. Arlene Simmons
946 South Street
Toronto 5, Ontario

Dear Mrs. Simmons:

We have written to the bus company[10] in reference to your accident, and their reply indicates that[20] we should anticipate a difficult case. They do not admit[30] any negligence on their part and claim that the driver[40] was going at the legal rate of speed. They state[50] that you were standing in a place which was definitely[60] marked as being not for passengers. They also claim that[70] you had been told by the driver to step back[80] beyond the line indicated for passengers, but that you had[90] not done so.

In order to prepare our case, we[100] would like to know,whether there were any witnesses who[110] could prove your side of the story. They would be[120] specifically required to testify as to whether the driver had[130] actually asked passengers to step behind this white line, and[140] whether he had said it so that everyone could hear[150] him. It would be helpful to have witnesses who could[160] testify as to the speed of the bus.

Very truly[170] yours,     (171)

Messrs. Wilson, Greenwald and Thurston
102 Madison Avenue
Toronto 5, Ontario

Gentlemen:

You have asked me to do some very difficult[10] things in connection with my accident on the bus. At[20] the time of the accident I was not particularly aware[30] of who was sitting or standing near me, although I[40] do recall one man who had commented to my friend[50] that the bus seemed to be going very fast.

I[60] can definitely say that the bus driver did not tell[70] me to stand behind a white line. Furthermore, I was[80] not the only passenger standing near the driver.

Very truly[90] yours,     (91)

364

## SPELLING

(1) connection, accident, occurred, passenger, anticipate, applied, brakes, minor
(2) reference, negligence, testify, actually
(3) particularly, commented

## PUNCTUATION

(1) However, since I do not know whether I can have the job ready on time, I must try to get some other competent manufacturer to help me.
(2) In a short time we are going to call on them, and we are sure that they will have all of the information we need.
(3) They do not admit any negligence and claim that you caused the accident, but we think we can show that they are wrong.

# 15

## VOCABULARY BUILDING

*delightful*
*pamphlet*

1. It was delightful to read your latest pamphlet because it contained so many useful items.

*literature*

2. Although our monthly pamphlet cannot be considered great literature, it will provide delightful reading for you.

*vacation*

3. We have an excellent pamphlet and other literature which tell of some delightful places to spend a vacation.

*experienced*

4. You will find their delightful pamphlet a great help in planning your vacation, and their experienced guides will add further to your pleasure.

*accommodations*

5. Our vacation accommodations are sure to prove delightful to you, and our experienced personnel will do everything they can to help you.

*agency*

6. Our agency is experienced in handling accommodations for people who wish to enjoy a delightful vacation.

*client*     7.  We have been a client of your agency for many years, during which your experienced personnel have helped us to obtain the best accommodations and to enjoy many delightful vacations.

## THEORY PRACTICE

While we cannot promise that you will have the best[10] weather on your vacation, we can guarantee that our experienced[20] personnel will assist you to the best of their ability.[30] They will help to dispose of many of the problems[40] of finding accommodations or of shopping in retail stores in[50] the various cities that you visit. They can also give[60] you practical advice on where to buy, approximately what you[70] should pay for each item, and when to expect a[80] discount.

We can recommend our agency also because each member[90] of our staff will work to his fullest capacity to[100] give you the best vacation you have ever had.                   (109)

## SPEED BUILDING PRACTICE

Gentlemen:

We have noticed lately that there has been a[10] shortage in several of the shipments that you delivered to[20] us. We are quite sure that the shortages occurred before[30] the shipments reached us, and it is, therefore, your responsibility[40] to make sure that this does not occur again.

We[50] have generally found your delivery service to be reliable, but[60] we can no longer guarantee that we shall be able[70] to continue using your service. This would depend on whether[80] or not you can correct the present shortages in deliveries.[90]

We should appreciate hearing from you further about this matter.[100]

Very truly yours,          (103)

## TRANSCRIPTION LETTERS

Mr. Walter Franklin
371 Maple Street
Owen Sound, Ontario

Dear Mr. Franklin:

My client, the East Side Real Estate Corporation,[10] has asked me to inform you that the lease on[20] your store, which is due to

366

expire within three months,[30] will not be renewed. We are expecting to remodel this[40] entire group of stores in the near future, and no[50] leases will be granted until such time as the remodeling[60] has been completed. In the meantime, you will be considered[70] a monthly tenant.

If you feel that you might be[80] interested in continuing your occupancy after the remodeling has been[90] completed, we would appreciate your letting us know how much[100] space you would be interested in acquiring.

Yours very truly,      (110)

Messrs. Hilton and Reade
229 East Street
Owen Sound, Ontario

Gentlemen:

I was surprised to hear from you to the[10] effect that within three months I would no longer have[20] a lease. My understanding of my lease was that it[30] was renewable at the same rent for a period of[40] five years. I can appreciate your desire to remodel the[50] building, but I wish to point out that my store[60] was extensively remodeled at my own expense at the time[70] I signed my lease with your client.

I presume that[80] the lease that you would be willing to sign at[90] the completion of the remodeling would call for a substantial[100] increase in rent. I do not feel that I should[110] pay an increased rent in view of the fact that[120] the value of my store will not be increased as[130] a result of your remodeling job.

I, therefore, wish to[140] inform you that I shall request a renewal of the[150] lease at the end of the present one for a[160] period of five years at the same rent I now[170] pay.

Very truly yours,      (174)

Mr. Walter Franklin
371 Maple Street
Owen Sound, Ontario

Dear Mr. Franklin:

There seems to have been a misunderstanding on[10] your part about the terms of your lease. There is[20] no written provision in the lease which gives you the[30] right to extend the lease for a period of five[40] years at the same rent. You may have discussed this[50] idea with my client, but we cannot be bound by[60] any agreement that is not in writing.

Furthermore, there is[70] a definite possibility that your store will be enlarged, thereby[80] making necessary a change in the rent.

Yours truly,      (89)

## SPELLING

(1) client, renewed, remodel, continuing, occupancy, acquiring
(2) surprised, period, extensively, presume, completion
(3) discussed, distinct, possibility, enlarged

## PUNCTUATION

(1) While we cannot promise good weather, we can promise that our people will assist you in every job you may have, big or small.
(2) We can recommend them for the job because they do careful work, charge low prices, and are well known to us.
(3) My client, who occupies a store in your building, wishes to renew his lease without an increase in rent, if possible.

# 16

## VOCABULARY BUILDING

*expires*
*compact*
1. When your present contract with them expires, I would suggest that you arrange to handle a compact model.

*obliged*
2. We are now obliged to put out a compact box, but we shall make a larger box when the present contract expires.

*determine*
3. The discount period may expire before you can determine whether you are obliged to pay the full price.

*thoroughly*
*carton*
4. We have examined thoroughly the question of whether to use the compact carton or the larger one, but we have not yet determined what to do.

*transit*       5. Since we were not obliged to examine the carton thoroughly before it was put in transit, we cannot determine why the box broke.

*assured*       6. They assured us that this carton would be thoroughly safe while it was in transit so that we were not obliged to provide insurance.

## THEORY PRACTICE

They have apparently been assured that the error in the[10] date of delivery was due to a misunderstanding, and that[20] the shipment will be in transit soon. They should now[30] be informed of the need for making arrangements for the[40] proper handling of the shipment after its arrival. We suggest[50] that you determine the date of the actual arrival of[60] the shipment by writing to the express company for the[70] information.

In order to avoid this situation in the future,[80] we would recommend that you determine by a thorough check[90] of your stock the correct number of items needed currently,[100] especially those items that may be scarce.                    (107)

## SPEED BUILDING PRACTICE

Dear Sir:

We have had a wonderful opportunity to meet[10] several people in the insurance business who seemed rather interested[20] in the difficult problem of getting better buildings for this[30] city. As a matter of fact, I am writing to[40] several of these people in the hope of having them[50] make a thorough study of the problem so that we[60] can make arrangements for financing new buildings in this city[70] We think that you will find it an advantage to[80] your company to join us in any talks we may[90] arrange on the subject of new buildings.

Very truly yours,            (100)

## TRANSCRIPTION LETTERS

Mr. George Hamilton
Southwest Merchandising Company
291 Abbott Street
Windsor, Ontario

Dear Mr. Hamilton:

We are interested in increasing the sales[10] of our products in the southwest, and we are looking[20] for someone to assume responsibility for handling our new sales[30] agency. Can you recommend someone who is thoroughly experienced in[40] the handling of children's clothing, and who is willing to[50] handle our line exclusively? You may rest assured that any[60] person who takes over this agency will be given an[70] extremely favorable salary and commission. In return we will expect[80] a strong selling campaign designed to reach parents who wish[90] their children to wear clothing that is well made, and[100] reasonable in price.

Cordially yours,  (105)

Junior Clothes Incorporated
447 Regent Street
Hamilton, Ontario

Gentlemen:

I have received your letter asking me to recommend[10] someone to handle your new sales agency for this part[20] of the country. I am very much in favor of[30] your plan because we need a strong selling campaign to[40] make parents aware of the many advances that have been[50] made in the styling of children's clothing.

I can recommend[60] three men who could do the job that you require.[70] The man that I would suggest as best qualified from[80] the selling point of view is Mr. Fred Brown who[90] is at present associated with the Green Agency. His selling[100] experience is limited to the advertising field where he has[110] done a magnificent job for us as well as for[120] many other firms. Although he is not thoroughly familiar with[130] the problems of the selling and production of children's clothing,[140] he is the type that would learn this business thoroughly[150] and quickly and would be able to improve the sales[160] of your products in a very short time.

Very truly[170] yours,  (171)

Mr. George Hamilton
Southwest Merchandising Company
291 Abbott Street
Windsor, Ontario

Dear Mr. Hamilton:

We were happy to receive your response[10] to our letter, and we wish to thank you for[20] your efforts in this matter. We are writing to Mr.[30] Brown to determine whether he would be interested in our[40] offer.

In view of Mr. Brown's lack of experience in[50] children's wear, we shall offer him a larger commission than[60] we had originally planned. If he is as good a[70] salesman as you say, he will have no trouble making[80] the best presentation of our products to the public.

Yours[90] truly,       (91)

## SPELLING

(1) interested, assume, recommend, thoroughly, experienced, exclusively, salary, commission, designed
(2) campaign, styling, associated, magnificent
(3) writing, determine, originally, planned

## PUNCTUATION

(1) As a matter of fact, I am planning to write to these people because they can, I think, make the arrangements for us.
(2) Can you recommend someone who is not only experienced but who knows our line?
(3) I am happy to say that they sell clothing that is well made and reasonable.

# 17

## VOCABULARY BUILDING

| | |
|---|---|
| **urge** **initial** | 1. I would urge you to place a small initial order with them to see how well they handle it. |
| **confidence** | 2. We have enough confidence in them to urge you to place a large initial order with them. |

*assigned* 3. We have assigned the job of placing the initial order for the goods with one of our representatives in your town, and we would urge that you place your confidence in him.

*technical* 4. The handling of the technical part of the job was assigned to our company, and I have confidence that our initial report will live up to the confidence you have in us.

*fortunate* 5. It is fortunate for us that we have not been assigned the technical problems in connection with this job, and I am confident that they will urge one of the other firms to do it.

*favorite* 6. His favorite reply to a technical question is to state that he has not been fortunate enough to have received all the necessary data, but that he is confident he will obtain it.

*gratifying* 7. It is gratifying to know that you have been fortunate enough to have been assigned to this job, and I urge you to have complete confidence in the technical ability of your men.

## THEORY PRACTICE

We had intended making an initial survey of the technical[10] problems related to the job before we submitted any estimate[20] of the cost of installing the new system. However, we[30] have confidence in the ability of our engineers to do[40] the job under present conditions, and we are going to[50] urge that our company go ahead with the job.

We[60] should also like to tell you that you did a[70] very neat and accurate job on your report of last[80] month. It should be gratifying for you to know that[90] as a result of this report we hope to get[100] this extra contract. (103)

## SPEED BUILDING PRACTICE

Gentlemen:

As the manufacturer of many of the products sold[10] in your store, we wish to bring to your attention[20] a very unusual opportunity to make greater profits. We are[30] now manufacturing a special pen which will have many advantages[40] over all others in the field. It will have many[50] technical improvements that have never

372

been put on the market[60] before. The pen can be sold for a dollar, and[70] it will bring a big profit to you.

We have[80] sent several samples of the pen to you. You may[90] keep these samples whether or not you order our pen.[100] We have confidence in your ability to sell the pen[110] because it satisfies the need for an inexpensive quality pen.[120]

Yours truly,      (122)

# TRANSCRIPTION LETTERS

Colonial Automobile Corporation
595 Westwood Avenue
Brockville, Ontario

Gentlemen:

As a dealer in Colonial Cars you will be[10] interested to know of the new sales campaign we are[20] starting early next month. In an effort to increase the[30] sales of our cars, we are placing advertisements in the[40] leading newspapers of the country urging the public to take[50] advantage of the special allowance which will be given during[60] the next two months on all cars used as a[70] trade-in for a new Colonial.

In addition, we have[80] assigned several of our salesmen to conduct a telephone campaign[90] among people in your neighborhood to make them aware of[100] these special allowances. We are sure that you will see[110] a gratifying increase in the sales of Colonial Cars.

Yours[120] truly,      (121)

Colonial Motors Incorporated
650 Forest Hill Drive
Brockville, Ontario

Gentlemen:

We wish to urge you not to engage in[10] a telephone campaign in our neighborhood to sell Colonial Cars.[20] We have conducted a survey in our neighborhood during the[30] past few months asking people about their reactions to sales[40] campaigns over the telephone. The response has been that this[50] type of sales approach is very annoying because it usually[60] occurs at a time when the man of the house[70] is not at home. The woman who receives the call[80] finds it upsetting to receive a call from a person[90] who tries to keep her on the phone long enough[100] to finish a prepared talk. The initial reaction to such[110] talks has been unfortunate in many cases because the customer[120] feels compelled to listen regardless of her interest in the[130] purchase of a car.

We are now trying a campaign[140] of selling cars by means of letters written to each[150] person in the neighborhood, showing the advantages of our cars.[160] We have confidence in the outcome of this campaign.

Very[170] truly yours,  (172)

Colonial Automobile Corporation
595 Westwood Avenue
Brockville, Ontario

Gentlemen:

We probably did not make clear to you in[10] our first letter that we intended using only the names[20] of those people who had written to us requesting information[30] about our cars.

It is our plan to make the[40] calls in the evening when the man of the house[50] is present. We also intend to gain the confidence of[60] the prospective buyer by putting no pressure on the person[70] being called. In this way we have confidence that our[80] efforts will bring about good results.

Very sincerely yours,  (89)

## SPELLING

(1) campaign, urging, allowance, assigned, neighborhood, gratifying
(2) survey, occurs, upsetting, prepared, initial, unfortunate, compelled, confidence
(3) probable-ly-ility, prospective, putting

## PUNCTUATION

(1) As the manufacturer of a new pen, I wish to tell you you can make big profits by selling it.
(2) In addition, we have several pens which are light in weight, easy to use, and inexpensive to buy.
(3) We have confidence in the outcome of this campaign, but I do not know how much it will cost us.

# 18

## VOCABULARY BUILDING

*contribution*    1. We appreciate very much your contribution to our report.

*storage*    2. We do not have enough storage space for the many contributions and gifts we received.

*hazard*    3. There is no hazard involved in the storage of these gifts and contributions.

*protection*    4. Our storage protection will avoid the hazard of loss due to fire.

*garment*    5. Any garment which has the protection of our storage facilities will avoid the hazard of fire loss.

*coverage*    6. I would hazard a guess and say that the coverage provided by your insurance policy does not provide protection for damage to garments in storage.

*respond*    7. I do not know how he will respond to the type of coverage we are offering for his garments in our policy, but I feel confident that the protection will avoid the hazard of loss due to fire.

*appearance*    8. He made an appearance in our office to respond to questions about the type of protection that would be provided under our insurance coverage for garments left in storage.

## THEORY PRACTICE

I realize that we must expect to pay a premium[10] for the shipment and storage of goods that are heavier[20] than the standard weight, but I still object to a[30] change in our previous rates because of this one shipment.[40]

When we agreed to place our garments in your storage[50] building, we did not expect to be subjected to this[60] hazard. We shall pay any additional charges which may be[70] required on this shipment, but we shall expect no change[80] in the rates on our regular shipments during the next[90] few months.      (92)

## SPEED BUILDING PRACTICE

Gentlemen:

We were not expecting to receive the shipment of[10] goods that we ordered on January 25 until the[20] end of February. We are, therefore, placed in the position[30] of having to keep these goods in storage until such[40] time as they can be put on sale. Under the[50] circumstances we cannot make our regular payment until the beginning[60] of March.

We would also like to exchange two of[70] the boxes in the shipment, as we indicated to you[80] by telephone yesterday. We have told our buyers not to[90] make any purchases until further notice from our main office.[100]

Yours truly,      (102)

## TRANSCRIPTION LETTERS

Maxwell Trading Company
298 Princess Street
Kingston, Ontario

Gentlemen:

We are introducing a new product this fall which[10] we are sure will be welcomed by the general public.[20] It is a special storage container which is guaranteed to[30] give protection to any garment which can be damaged by[40] an insect. Each of these containers will have a special[50] substance which will destroy any insect. This will make it[60] unnecessary for people to place many of their garments in[70] storage when they are not using them.

We have confidence[80] that the general public will respond to this new item[90] and that your sales will be heavy. We are enclosing[100] some display materials that you can place in your store[110] window.

Very cordially yours,     (114)

Sanitary Manufacturing Company
452 Taylor Avenue
Montreal, Quebec

Gentlemen:

We are glad to hear that you are introducing[10] a new product designed to give protection to garments that[20] are usually placed in storage. I am sure that the[30] public will respond to your product as soon as it[40] makes its appearance on the market.

However, I do not[50] feel that the methods you are using to introduce this[60] product will be effective in reaching enough people to make[70] it sell quickly. I would suggest that you use several[80] other methods of selling, such as advertisements in newspapers or[90] magazines, as well as house-to-house selling. Any product[100] that promises to help in the running of a house[110] is best sold right in the house, and the best[120] way to make the sale is to show what the[130] product can do. If this is done, I am sure[140] that the public will respond by buying it.

We realize[150] that such a campaign would be more expensive, but we[160] are sure that it will produce better sales.

Sincerely yours,        (170)

<br>

Maxwell Trading Company
298 Princess Street
Kingston, Ontario

Gentlemen:

We wish to thank you for your interest in[10] our new storage container, and for the many excellent suggestions[20] you have made. However, we do not feel that a[30] house-to-house campaign will be as effective as you[40] state, because of the fact that there is really nothing[50] about the container to show what it will do. Only[60] time will prove how effective the container is and how[70] well people like it.

We do, however, plan an extensive[80] publicity campaign in the newspapers and magazines.

Very truly yours,        (90)

## SPELLING

(1) introducing, welcomed, storage, container, guaranteed, attacked, chemical
(2) designed, appearance, magazines, realize
(3) excellent, really, publicity

## PUNCTUATION

(1) We have informed our buyers not to make any purchases or even to accept shipments until further notice from us.

(2) I would suggest that you use several methods of selling, such as newspaper advertisements, house-to-house selling, and special sales at low prices.

(3) We do, however, plan several newspaper advertisements, but only if the house-to-house sales are poor.

# 19

## VOCABULARY BUILDING

*endeavor*
*workmanship*

1. We shall endeavor to set a standard of workmanship that will be acceptable to all our customers.

*economic*

2. You should endeavor to improve your economic standard by improving the workmanship in your products.

*progressive*

3. There has been a progressive economic decline in this part of the country due to poor workmanship in the production of many items, but we are endeavoring to correct it.

*proudly*

4. They proudly announced that their economic standard had improved because of their progressive attitude and superior workmanship.

*cordial*

5. He was very cordial to everyone when he proudly announced that the company would endeavor to set progressively higher and more economic standards of production.

*invitation*

6. He sent them a cordial invitation to see the fine workmanship in the goods he is proudly displaying.

*extended*

7. They extended a cordial invitation to our firm in which they proudly announced their new styles which stress both superior workmanship and progressive fashions.

## THEORY PRACTICE

Our firm is not operating at capacity because of a[10] shortage of capital. The amount of money we have on[20] deposit is getting progressively smaller each month so that our[30] ability to buy new equipment is cut down.

We tried[40] to get a loan from our bank, but the assistant[50] manager informed us that no loan could be extended unless[60] we were able to supply more collateral. However, we have[70] been told that the money we need might be obtained[80] elsewhere if we were willing to pay a higher rate[90] of interest for it. We shall endeavor to find out[100] more about this. (103)

## SPEED BUILDING PRACTICE

Gentlemen:

We are planning to put an advertisement in your[10] paper during the first two days of next week. We[20] shall probably wish to place another advertisement towards the end[30] of the following week. We would, therefore, like to know[40] what the cost of the advertisement would be and how[50] many readers the advertisement would be expected to reach.

The[60] size of our advertisements will be governed by our opinion[70] as to the number of readers that we feel have[80] been influenced by the advertisements. If these advertisements provide the[90] number of replies that we are expecting, we shall be[100] glad to place many more advertisements in the near future.[110]

Very truly yours, (118)

## TRANSCRIPTION LETTERS

Marshall Stationery Store
1246 Sherwood Avenue
Belleville, Ontario

Gentlemen:

We are planning several changes involving the sales of[10] our pens, and we are anxious to have your opinion[20] of our plans. The most important change will be in[30] the method of making repairs, which has been done up[40] to now at each of our stores. Instead of having[50] each store handle both sales and repairs, we will set[60] up one repair agency for each part of the city.[70] Each store will be freed of the necessity of guaranteeing[80] service on the pens and will, therefore, be able to[90] concentrate on selling. However, the pens will be returned to[100] each store, which will then forward them to the central[110] repair agency.

Our service agency will be free to work[120] on repairs to its fullest capacity and we will thereby[130] give better repair service.

Very truly yours, (137)

Superior Pen Company
501 Bay Street
Toronto 2, Ontario

Gentlemen:

We were very much interested in your new plan[10] to increase the sales of your pen in our city.[20] We appreciate the cordial invitation that you extended us to[30] give our opinion of the plan.

We can certainly see[40] the advantage of having several centers specializing in the repair[50] of the pens, and we are assuming that the workmanship[60] in each of the centers would be of superior quality.[70] The part of the plan that we are not sure[80] of is whether there would be enough business for several[90] repair centers. I agree with you that we could endeavor[100] to spend more time in selling your pens if we[110] were not concerned with repairs. However, we would still have[120] to check the pen for repairs. We cannot see any[130] real difference in terms of our time and effort between[140] the new plan and the old one in this respect.[150]

You may be sure that we shall continue to sell[160] your pens to the best of our ability.

Sincerely yours,                    (170)


Marshall Stationery Store
1246 Sherwood Avenue
Belleville, Ontario

Gentlemen:

Your comments about our new repair plan were very[10] welcome, and we are glad to know of your interest[20] in this matter.

The major reason for making the change[30] to repair centers is to reduce the amount of time[40] which you have to spend in checking pens for repairs[50] before actually repairing them. Under the new plan you would[60] only take the pen and note the complaint of the[70] customer. You would do no checking of the pens. All[80] this would be done at the repair center.

Cordially yours,                    (90)


## SPELLING

(1)  necessity, guaranteeing, concentrate, assuming, capacity
(2)  appreciate, gradually, specializing, superior, endeavor, concerned
(3)  comments, actually

## PUNCTUATION

(1) We have tried to get a loan, but we have been informed that we would need more collateral or someone to guarantee the loan.

(2) If these advertisements are effective, we shall try other, more expensive, advertisements.

(3) Instead of having our store handle buying, selling, and repairing, we shall set up a new repair agency.

# 20

## VOCABULARY BUILDING

*amazed* 1. I was amazed to hear about their loss of business in this city.

*device* 2. You will be amazed at what this device can do to help you.

*accurate* 3. This device is so accurate that it has amazed all those who have used it.

*generous* 4. He gave a generous amount of his time to the development of this device so that it would be as accurate as possible.

*courteous* 5. The best device that I know of for improving sales is to have employees who are courteous to customers and accurate with their records.

*dependable* 6. We are in need of several new employees who are dependable as well as courteous, and who will keep accurate records.

*various* 7. We have various openings in our store for salesmen who are dependable and accurate.

*installments* 8. All of the various items we sell can be paid for in installments, and we offer such generous discounts that you will be amazed at how little these items actually cost.

## THEORY PRACTICE

We have available in our store several boxes of carbon[10] paper that you should find very desirable for your work.[20] When you use this paper, you have the feeling that[30] you are using the best, and when you begin filing[40] the copies that you have made, you will be amazed[50] at how difficult it is to tell the carbon copy[60] from the original.

You may elect to purchase various sizes[70] of this paper to fit any of your needs. This[80] carbon paper is now on sale at a price that[90] is well below our usual price.                    (96)

## SPEED BUILDING PRACTICE

Dear Sir:

We have had a great deal of difficulty[10] in improving our production during the last two months. In[20] particular we do not seem able to keep up with[30] the needs of our customers, although we have many of[40] our employees working overtime.

We do not wish to make[50] any special changes in our production methods because of the[60] character of our work and the fact that, in general,[70] the demand for our products does not remain steady during[80] the year. However, if we are not capable of improving[90] production, we may lose some of our customers.

                    Yours truly,          (100)

## TRANSCRIPTION LETTERS

Butler Machine Shops, Incorporated
884 St. George Street
Barrie, Ontario

Gentlemen:

During the past nine months your sales of our[10] products have gone down, and we are very much concerned[20] as to the reason for this decline. We are amazed[30] at this decline because we have reports of increased sales[40] from all other parts of the country, and we have[50] always felt that you had a good market for our[60] products. We feel that our products and our service are[70] dependable, and that the various changes we have made have[80] served to improve their value to the customer.

We would[90] very much appreciate your taking the time and trouble to[100] let us know how we can be of assistance to[110] you in increasing the sales of our products.

                    Cordially yours,          (120)

General Machine Manufacturing Company
421 Hillcrest Avenue
Toronto, Ontario

Gentlemen:

We were rather amazed to hear from you about[10] the drop in our sales of your products. Your shipping[20] department has apparently not informed you of the various difficulties[30] we have had in receiving shipments of goods on time.[40] If you will check your files, you will find that[50] we have complained several times about the fact that we[60] cannot promise an exact delivery date to a customer, and[70] have thus lost several important sales recently. In addition, we[80] have had a great deal of difficulty in getting parts[90] when a machine is in need of repairs.

It is[100] almost impossible to sell a customer a product that will[110] take an unusually long time to repair. It is also[120] difficult to prevent customers from hearing about these problems from[130] each other, and your products have been getting the reputation[140] of not being dependable because of this repair problem.

We[150] hope that this letter will finally result in some much[160] needed changes in your deliveries and repairs.

Very truly yours,    (170)

Butler Machine Shops, Incorporated
884 St. George Street
Barrie, Ontario

Gentlemen:

We must admit that we too were amazed to[10] hear of your difficulties in selling our products. We immediately[20] checked into the matter and found that you were right[30] in every respect. We can assure you that there will[40] be an immediate change in our delivery and repair service.[50]

We have been very proud of our machines because they[60] are accurate and dependable. There is no reason for delays[70] in shipment or for having customers feel that repairs will[80] be delayed due to shortages of parts.

Sincerely yours,    (89)

## SPELLING

(1) concerned, dependable, various, assistance

(2) shipping, apparently, complaint (complained), exact, impossible, unusual-ly, reputation, dependable, finally

(3) accurate, delays, delayed

## PUNCTUATION

(1) When you use this paper, you have the feeling that you are using the best, and when the members of your firm use it, they will agree.

(2) If we can improve production, we may get more customers or we may be able to cut costs.

(3) We feel that our products are well made, attractive, and low priced, but we cannot seem to sell enough of them.

# 21

## VOCABULARY BUILDING

*creditors*   1. We are making plans to pay all of our creditors within two months.

*decline*   2. We are sorry to say that there has been a decline in the amount that we can pay to each of the creditors.

*accomplish*   3. We hope to accomplish our goal of paying off each of the creditors despite a decline in sales.

*export*   4. We shall have to inform our creditors of the decline in our exports, which will make it difficult to accomplish our goal of meeting all our payments on time.

*adopted*   5. We have adopted a new plan for handling our exports which we hope will stop the decline in our business and please our creditors.

*eventually*   6. It is clear that the new export plan will eventually be adopted, and we hope that this will accomplish our goal of paying off our creditors.

*ambitious*   7. We have ambitious plans for increasing our exports, and we hope to accomplish this despite the general decline in trade.

*fault*    8. I think that we were at fault in adopting plans that were too ambitious and would, therefore, eventually fail.

## THEORY PRACTICE

We have received word from our creditors about the decline[10] in the prices of our exports. This may eventually mean[20] that we shall not be able to meet our obligations[30] on time. We had hoped to accomplish our goal of[40] increasing our export trade, and we felt that prices of[50] our goods would remain the same for at least six[60] months. It will, therefore, not be our fault if we[70] have to delay payments because of this decline in export[80] prices.

We have adopted the necessary measures to prevent too[90] much loss in our export trade.                    (96)

## SPEED BUILDING PRACTICE

Dear Sir:

We have adopted a plan in our school[10] to increase the number of subjects we offer so as[20] to take care of the large number of people who[30] are now interested in becoming capable of holding jobs in[40] the fields in which we give instruction. We are surprised[50] at this remarkable increase in the number of people who[60] wish to come to our school, because we had expected[70] a decline in some subjects due to the fact that[80] we felt business had been slow in these lines.

We[90] shall, of course, do our very best to take care[100] of everyone who wishes to come to our school, although[110] it will mean that we shall have to add many[120] special classes.

                    Respectfully yours,        (124)

## TRANSCRIPTION LETTERS

Adams Publishing Company
106 Cumberland Road
Halifax, Nova Scotia

Gentlemen:

I am interested in securing copies of the books[10] I have listed on the enclosed paper. These books are[20] to be used in my classes by students who are[30] making a study of available books in the field, to[40] decide which book should be adopted for this course. In[50] view of the fact that your books may eventually be[60] the ones to be used for this course, I would[70] appreciate your sending an examination copy of each book. I[80] cannot expect my students to purchase these books since they[90] are doing this project at my suggestion to aid in[100] selecting the best book for the course.

Thank you for[110] your kind assistance in this matter.

Very sincerely yours,     (119)

Dr. Charles Parker
Maritime College
490 Oakland Street
Truro, Nova Scotia

Dear Dr. Parker:

We are always happy to cooperate in[10] the selection of books for a course by making available[20] an examination copy. However, we cannot grant your request for[30] copies of each of the books because of our standing[40] rule to provide only one copy to the teacher of[50] a particular course. We recognize how worth while is your[60] project of having students involved in the selection of books,[70] but we cannot change our rule in your case.

We[80] might suggest another way in which you can obtain the[90] copies of the books you desire. We would be happy[100] to sell to your library at a discount copies of[110] each of these books if you could obtain from the[120] librarian of the college a formal purchase order requesting them.[130] It is our policy to allow discounts to the school[140] library on all textbooks.

We hope that these arrangements will[150] be satisfactory to you. Please let us know if we[160] can be of further help to you in any way.[170]

Cordially yours,     (172)

Adams Publishing Company
106 Cumberland Road
Halifax, Nova Scotia

Gentlemen:

I have your letter indicating that you cannot send[10] us copies of the books we requested. I am trying[20] to obtain the approval of the college librarian for a[30] formal request to purchase these books for use in this[40] class project. I shall take whatever steps may be necessary[50] to get her approval, but I am not too sure[60] that I shall be successful.

We hope that we shall[70] be able to consider your books for adoption in the[80] near future.

Very truly yours,      (85)

## SPELLING

(1) securing, adopted, eventually, assistance
(2) cooperate, particular, recognize, library, formal
(3) approval, successful, adoption

## PUNCTUATION

(1) If we have to delay payments, it will not be our fault, but we shall try to make them on time.
(2) Although we shall have to add several new classes, we shall, of course, do our best to take care of everyone.
(3) In view of the fact that we may use your book, we would appreciate getting a copy of it.

# 22

## VOCABULARY BUILDING

*accurate*
*excessive*

1. Although the report seems to be accurate, it took an excessive amount of time to prepare.

*bookkeeping*

2. Your bookkeeping procedures may be accurate, but you require an excessive amount of time to provide statements of profit and loss.

*analysis*

3. We shall need an accurate analysis of their bookkeeping methods to see if there is an excessive loss of time or effort.

*injustice*

4. His analysis of their bookkeeping records shows that their procedures were accurate, but that they worked an injustice on many firms.

| | |
|---|---|
| *margin* | 5. Your bookkeeping records show that you are adding an excessive margin of cost and this works an injustice on many firms. |
| *appropriate* | 6. It would be more appropriate to have your bookkeeping records show a lower margin of profit so as to avoid an excessive mark-up. |
| *hereafter*<br>*prevent* | 7. We shall try hereafter to take appropriate steps to prevent a repetition of the injustice done to our students by the excessive prices they were charged for books. |

## THEORY PRACTICE

You indicated in your letter that our last shipment contained[10] many damaged boxes. We have checked all of the boxes,[20] and the damage totaled $82, which we have[30] deducted from your bill.

I believe the damage could have[40] been prevented if we had labeled the boxes in such[50] a way as to indicate that they were to be[60] handled carefully. Hereafter, we shall take appropriate steps to prevent[70] excessive damage by making an accurate record of the contents[80] of the boxes on the outside. In this way we[90] are sure that we shall be able to keep to[100] a minimum the margin of loss due to such damage.                                             (110)

## SPEED BUILDING PRACTICE

Gentlemen:

We agree with you that it is an important[10] problem to have the public understand why it is difficult[20] to give a particular date and time for deliveries of[30] orders.

In our opinion it would be best for you[40] to set up a regular plan for making deliveries in[50] each part of the city. There could be deliveries every[60] other day during the week. This would be better than[70] yards and yards of advertising copy because it would speak[80] for itself. The public would soon become familiar with the[90] idea of seeing your delivery trucks on the same day[100] each week, and in this way they would not have[110] to worry about not being at home when a delivery[120] is made.

Yours truly,                    (124)

# TRANSCRIPTION LETTERS

Mrs. Pearl Anderson
52 Belmont Avenue
Hull, Quebec

Dear Mrs. Anderson:

We are happy to announce a reduced rate[10] on subscriptions to our magazine. Instead of the usual rate of[20] $5 a year, we are making available, for a[30] limited time only, a special subscription of $3 a[40] year. The purpose of this reduced subscription rate is to[50] encourage our readers to send us the names of persons[60] who might wish to subscribe to our magazine.

If you[70] will sign the subscription form below and list the name[80] of one person who might be interested in our magazine,[90] we shall be happy to send you the magazine for[100] another year at the lower rate. You will be billed[110] at a later date for the subscription.

Cordially yours,     (110)

Russell Publishing Company
St. Catharine Street
Montreal 3, Quebec

Gentlemen:

I am not in a position to comply with[10] the request you made in your recent letter for the[20] names of friends who would be interested in a subscription[30] to your magazine. I do not believe it a wise[40] policy to have my friends subjected to unnecessary annoyance by[50] a magazine. My friends know of the fact that I[60] am a subscriber to your magazine, and they have had[70] ample opportunity to look through the magazine when they have[80] been in my home. If that has not been sufficient[90] to convince them of the value of your magazine, I[100] am sure that nothing further would help. In addition, I[110] am certain that they would recognize the source of your[120] letter because I have frequently mentioned how much pleasure I[130] obtained from reading your magazine.

I shall be happy to[140] take advantage of your offer for a subscription at the[150] reduced rate of $3, and I am filling out[160] the form for the subscription and enclosing it with this[170] letter.

Very truly yours,     (174)

Mrs. Pearl Anderson
52 Belmont Avenue
Hull, Quebec

Dear Mrs. Anderson:

Thank you for your prompt answer to[10] our recent letter. We can understand and appreciate your feelings[20] in the matter. We wish to thank you for your[30] kind comments about our magazine. It is good to know[40] that our readers think enough of the magazine to encourage[50] their friends to read it.

Although our offer for the[60] reduced subscription was based on the sending in of the[70] name of a prospective subscriber, we are allowing your subscription[80] at the reduced rate without sending the name.

Sincerely yours,       (90)

## SPELLING

(1) subscriptions, purpose, encourage, billed
(2) position, friends, unnecessary, source, frequently, mentioned, advantage
(3) comments, prospective

## PUNCTUATION

(1) We shall hereafter take steps to prevent damage, but we cannot be sure of the results.
(2) Instead of our usual rate, we are making available, for a short time only, a special rate for all of our books, magazines, and newspapers.
(3) I am happy to accept your offer, and I shall send my check within three days, if possible.

# 23

## VOCABULARY BUILDING

*obvious*  1. It is obvious that he is not very popular with the
*popular*  members of the office staff.

*majority* 2. The vast majority of your products are obviously very popular in this part of the country.

*qualified* 3. It was obvious that he was the popular choice of the majority of the people, even though he was not the best qualified.

*reliable* 4. It is obvious that this study was made by a person who was well qualified and reliable, and who knew the popular choices of the majority of the people.

*folly* 5. It is obvious that it would be folly to accept him for the job without checking on his qualifications and reliability.

*seemingly* 6. It would seemingly be folly to go against the popular choice of the majority of the members, but he wants to make sure that they have a reliable and qualified person for the job.

*technical* 7. This job is seemingly too technical for you, and it would be folly for you to go ahead and make obvious errors.

## THEORY PRACTICE

We have obtained an excellent machine that can be used[10] to improve the cleaning of your apartment. It has been[20] approved by many experts in the field, and has proved[30] to be popular and reliable with those who have used[40] it. Because the machine is so popular, we are extending[50] the time during which it will be on sale. We[60] have observed that many people wish to buy this machine[70] as a gift for their friends.

Although this machine does[80] not need any special handling or treatment, we have a[90] repair department that is qualified to give service as well[100] as technical assistance.          (103)

## SPEED BUILDING PRACTICE

Dear Sir:

We believe that you will remember that we[10] wrote to you recently about getting some younger men to[20] increase the efficiency of our office staff. We have had[30] altogether too many delays in getting out the work, and[40] we felt that this was due to the influence of[50] the older members of our staff who usually cannot work[60] quickly for a long period of time.

We would greatly[70] appreciate any information you may have about the problem, together[80] with the names of any people who would be qualified[90] to give us some help in the matter.

Very truly[100] yours,        (101)

# TRANSCRIPTION LETTERS

Mr. James Bailey
342 Beverly Place
Regina, Saskatchewan

Dear Mr. Bailey:

We are interested in publishing a series of[10] articles on current problems in business. We feel that there[20] is a popular demand among a majority of business men[30] for such a series of articles.

We have been informed[40] that you are well qualified to handle such an assignment,[50] and we are, therefore, making an offer to you to[60] do this series of articles. We would like the articles[70] to be reliable without having too much technical material, and[80] we would prefer to have the kind of treatment that[90] would receive the approval of intelligent business men.

Would you[100] be interested in undertaking the writing of such a series[110] of. articles?

Sincerely yours,        (114)

Spencer Publishing Company
196 Gardner Street
Winnipeg, Manitoba

Gentlemen:

I am definitely interested in your offer to write[10] a series of articles on current problems in business. However,[20] before I can give you a definite answer, I would[30] like to clear up certain important points. First, I would[40] like to know whether these articles would be published each[50] week in your magazine, or whether they would appear whenever[60] you felt they were appropriate to current happenings in the[70] field of business. I would like to know whether these[80] articles would be expected to reach your regular subscribers or[90] whether they would be designed to interest new readers in[100] subscribing to your magazine. I would also like to know[110] whether each article should be complete for each issue, or[120] whether **they** would be continued from one issue to the[130] next.

I do not believe that any of these problems[140] will cause any particular difficulty in coming to an agreement,[150] and I look forward to writing the articles for your[160] magazine.

Cordially yours,        (163)

Mr. James Bailey
342 Beverly Place
Regina, Saskatchewan

Dear Mr. Bailey:

We cannot, at this time, give you[10] definite answers to the questions you raised about the articles[20] we are interested in having you write.

Our handling of[30] the articles will depend upon the topics they cover, how[40] long they are, and their particular interest to our readers.[50] If we feel that they would be of sufficient interest[60] to encourage new subscribers, we would give them publicity along[70] those lines. Until we see the articles, it would be[80] folly for us to make plans about them.

Sincerely yours,        (90)

## SPELLING

(1) series, articles, current (currant), popular, assignment, technical, writing
(2) definitely, importance-ant, appropriate, designed, continued
(3) handling, topics, publicity, folly

## PUNCTUATION

(1) We would appreciate your sending the information you may have, together with a copy of the letter you received from our New York office.
(2) We have been informed that you will be able to do the job, and we are, therefore, sending a copy of the articles we have just received.
(3) Before I take the job, I would like to know, first of all, how much I would be paid.

# 24

## VOCABULARY BUILDING

*endeavor*  
*delinquent*  

1. We should appreciate it if you would endeavor to get them to pay their delinquent account.

*discretion*  

2. We would suggest that you use discretion when you endeavor to collect delinquent accounts.

*indebtedness*  

3. The amount of indebtedness on delinquent accounts is so small that you should endeavor to proceed with discretion in trying to collect them.

*describe*  

4. In our next letter we shall endeavor to describe the condition of our delinquent accounts and the amount of indebtedness involved in them.

*disposition*  

5. I shall endeavor to describe the methods we use in the disposition of delinquent accounts where the amount of indebtedness is so small as to call for special discretion.

*inclined*  

6. I am inclined to believe that we shall not be able to make a satisfactory disposition of our delinquent accounts using our present practices; and I shall endeavor to describe a new plan.

*persuade*  

7. I am inclined to believe that you can persuade them to make a satisfactory disposition of their delinquent account provided you use the proper discretion.

## THEORY PRACTICE

I am prepared to cooperate with you in the handling[10] of the delinquent accounts as indicated in the letter you[20] mailed two weeks ago. Even under ordinary circumstances we would[30] suggest that you use a great deal of discretion in[40] trying to settle the indebtedness of these customers. However, these[50] customers can well afford to make an early disposition of[60] their indebtedness. I am inclined to believe that their unwillingness[70] to cooperate is due to some extraordinary circumstances of which[80] we are not aware.

(84)

# SPEED BUILDING PRACTICE

Gentlemen:

It is necessary that we have the electrical repairs[10] completed and the bill in our hands at the end[20] of this month. We expect to have a meeting of[30] several very important people in our office at that time,[40] and we wish to have everything in the best possible[50] condition. We would have no objection to having your men[60] work in the evenings to finish the job quickly, and[70] we are prepared to pay whatever costs would be involved.[80]

We would be willing to make payment for the job[90] within thirty days after it is finished. Whenever you feel[100] that it has become necessary to make changes in your[110] plans, please let us know as soon as possible.

Yours[120] truly,          (121)


# TRANSCRIPTION LETTERS


Ingram Publications Incorporated
444 Jasper Avenue
Edmonton, Alberta

Gentlemen:

I have been a subscriber to your magazine for[10] the past five years, and during that time I have[20] renewed my subscription three times because I felt that your[30] magazine was providing interesting and reliable coverage of the news.[40] During the past three weeks I have received three letters[50] from you asking me to renew my subscription even though[60] it is not due to expire for another five months.[70]

Furthermore, I have felt lately that many of your articles[80] are written to attract new readers rather than to present[90] the news. You also seem to write each story as[100] though it were of great significance, even though many of[110] them are given little attention in the newspapers.

Yours truly,          (120)

Mr. Lester Hopkins
47 West 15th Street
Calgary, Alberta

Dear Mr. Hopkins:

We are indebted to you for your frank[10] and honest letter. We are inclined to agree that we[20] have been delinquent in our handling of your account, for[30] we have checked our records and we find that your[40] subscription is not due to expire for another five months.[50] Please accept our apologies for this error. We endeavor to[60] avoid giving annoyance to our subscribers, while at the same[70] time reminding them when their subscriptions should be renewed, so[80] as to prevent their missing a single issue. As far[90] as our articles are concerned, we always make it a[100] policy to present to our readers what we think is[110] the most important and interesting news. We sincerely feel that[120] it is not our purpose to follow along with what[130] the newspapers may consider to be the most important news.[140] If an article is given greater attention in our magazine[150] than it gets in the newspapers, it merely means that[160] we think it is more important.

Cordially yours,      (168)

Ingram Publications Incorporated
444 Jasper Avenue
Edmonton, Alberta

Gentlemen:

Your explanation about the handling of articles in your[10] magazine was not completely satisfactory. I have been reading your[20] magazine during the past few years because I felt that[30] your handling of the news was based on a clear[40] description and careful understanding of the events of the day.[50] I do not believe that you should edit the news[60] by selecting those articles that you think are important and[70] giving them greater coverage.

However, I recognize your right to[80] describe events from your own point of view.

Yours truly,      (90)

## SPELLING

(1) subscriber, renewed, reliable, coverage, expire, attract, significance
(2) indebted, frank, delinquent, apologize, error, endeavor, annoyance, concerned, sincerely, merely
(3) explanation, articles, satisfactory, interpretation, description, events, edit, completely, recognize, describe

## PUNCTUATION

(1) These customers can well afford, as far as I know, to take care of their indebtedness, but I do not know when they will do it.
(2) With respect to payment for the job, would you prefer cash, check, or credit for future purchases?
(3) Whenever any changes become necessary, please let us know as soon as possible or we may not be able to make them.

# 25

## VOCABULARY BUILDING

*renewal*
*routine*
1. We shall handle the renewal of the contract in the routine way.

*document*
2. This document calls for a renewal of the terms of the contract with only a few routine changes.

*signature*
3. You missed one part of the routine in the renewal of the contract when you failed to get his signature on the document.

*devote*
4. I should like to devote some time to the routine matters involved in the renewal of the document before I put my signature on it.

*survey*
5. We must devote a good deal of time to a survey of the routine changes before we can put our signature to a renewal of the document.

*eliminating*
6. As a result of the survey we have just completed, we shall devote a good deal of time to ways of eliminating unnecessary routine work in our office.

*elaborate*
7. He devoted a great deal of time in his survey to methods of eliminating some of the elaborate routines in our office in the handling of such matters as the renewal of contracts.

## THEORY PRACTICE

You are undoubtedly aware of the fact that our books[10] will be audited some time about the middle of next[20] month. We have assumed in the past that the books[30] of each branch would always be ready to be audited.[40] However, this procedure has not worked too well, and we[50] shall try to devote some time this year to eliminating[60] the delays that have occurred.

We should like to indicate,[70] therefore, that instead of following the usual routine of having[80] each branch bring its books up to date in time[90] for the audit, we shall send our accountant down to[100] each branch to make a survey of the books.               (109)

## SPEED BUILDING PRACTICE

Dear Sir:

We wish to acknowledge receipt of your letter[10] of May 15. Although we are glad to see that[20] you are interested in improving the efficiency of our company,[30] we cannot agree with you that this is the time[40] to make a general survey of our company. Any such[50] arbitrary step now would cause many of our people to[60] lose their enthusiasm for increasing sales. Most of our people[70] are capable of increasing their sales this year if they[80] are able to work without having to worry about the[90] level of efficiency of their paper work.

We shall undoubtedly[100] make an efficiency survey in the near future so as[110] to eliminate any poor practices.

                              Yours truly,               (117)

## TRANSCRIPTION LETTERS

Mrs. Alberta Chase
49 Oxford Road
Swift Current, Saskatchewan
Dear Mrs. Chase:

Many women subscribe to several different magazines because[10] they feel that no one publication gives them all the[20] information they wish to have. For this reason, we are[30] now in the process of publishing a new magazine that[40] will provide women with a digest of most of the[50] news that appears during the week.

Our "Women's Digest" will[60] devote most of its pages to those items that help[70] women to live better. We will eliminate the purely routine[80] items that are not of lasting interest and will include[90] a survey of those articles that are undoubtedly of value[100] to women. We are sure that you will find our[110] new "Women's Digest" of great interest to you.

Yours truly, (120)

Rogers Publishing Company
281 Dexter Boulevard
Vancouver, British Columbia

Gentlemen:

When I received your letter announcing your publication of[10] the "Women's Digest," I was interested, but not surprised. There[20] have been so many publications recently in digest form that[30] it is difficult to tell one from the other.

However,[40] if your magazine will do what it is supposed to[50] do, I will be happy to subscribe to it. I[60] am sure that many of my friends would be as[70] interested as I am in a magazine that surveys the[80] entire field of published material and prepares a digest of[90] those items that can be of help to women like[100] myself. I hope that you are talking about such fields[110] as women's styles and house furnishings. I know that it[120] is difficult for me to keep up with the latest[130] developments in these fields because no one magazine on the[140] market now gives a complete picture.

Please send me your[150] first copy so that I can see how closely your[160] magazine lives up to its claims.

Cordially yours, (168)

Mrs. Alberta Chase
49 Oxford Road
Swift Current, Saskatchewan

Dear Mrs. Chase:

In answer to your letter asking us to[10] send you the first issue of our new magazine, we[20] are sorry to say that we cannot send copies to[30] your home because we are planning to have the first[40] issue sold only at news stands. We will, however, be[50] happy to send all other issues to your home.

We[60] are enclosing a subscription blank which you can use at[70] any time. Please do not send any money with the[80] subscription; we will bill you later.

Sincerely yours, (88)

399

## SPELLING

(1)  women, difference-t, publications, process, digest, eliminate, routine, undoubtedly
(2)  surprised, recently, surveys, furnishings, developments
(3)  answer

## PUNCTUATION

(1)  We should like to indicate, however, that, instead of doing it our way, they used a different procedure.
(2)  Some women read this magazine because they like the stories in it, but they do not look at the advertisements.
(3)  When I received your recent letter, I was interested, but not surprised.

# 26

## VOCABULARY BUILDING

*annoyance*  1.  We regret very much the annoyance that has been caused you.

*expression*  2.  His expression of annoyance told us that he was not pleased with the report.

*anxiety*  3.  His expression changed to one of anxiety as he heard the details of the business activities for the year.

*management*  4.  Their poor management of the business caused much annoyance and anxiety to the officers of the firm.

*compiled*  5.  As they read the report of the profits compiled by the management, the officers of the company lost their expressions of anxiety and annoyance.

*postpone*  6.  Despite the annoyance and anxiety of some members of the firm, it was decided to postpone changes in the management until more evidence had been compiled.

*inferior*  7.  We have compiled a list of cases in which your service was inferior, and the annoyance and anxiety that has been caused us compels us to postpone any future orders.

*remainder*   8.  The management of the company decided to postpone any future orders as an expression of their
annoyance over the fact that the remainder of the
goods delivered was of inferior quality.

## THEORY PRACTICE

We have recently compiled figures showing that the decline in[10]
our sales has been due to poor methods of delivery[20] and the inferior
quality of goods. We are preparing all[30] of the evidence to support
this belief, and we are[40] putting it in a folder which we are planning
to[50] send to each of our branch offices. When you receive[60] your copy
of the folder, please attach your signature to[70] it and read especially
those chapters that concern you.

In[80] the center of the report we have put a summary[90] of sales
compiled on the basis of the first six[100] months of the year.    (104)

## SPEED BUILDING PRACTICE

Gentlemen:

We are interested in finding out what the cost[10] would be for
an office in your building. We are[20] planning to use it as our execu-
tive office because we[30] wish to establish a branch of our company in
this[40] city. We are not familiar with the cost of an[50] office in your
building. We should inform you that our[60] expenditure for this purpose is limited. For this reason, we[70] would not be able to take an
expensive office.

We[80] should like to take the office as soon as possible[90] and have
it for the remainder of the year on[100] a month-to-month basis. After
that we would be[110] willing to sign a lease for a year.

Very truly[120] yours,      (121)

## TRANSCRIPTION LETTERS

Morrison Automobile Agency
1242 Cartier Street
Quebec, Quebec

Gentlemen:

As you may recall, I recently purchased a car[10] from you. At
that time, you told me that you[20] would guarantee the car for one
year.

During the past[30] six months I have had to bring in the car[40] for repairs on four different occasions. It is true that[50] you did the repairs each time and made no charge.[60] However, the car is again in need of repairs, and[70] I feel that I have had enough annoyance and anxiety[80] about it. It is certainly an inferior car, and I[90] cannot continue to use it knowing that it might break[100] down at any time.

I should like to return this[110] car and get back the remainder of my payment.

Yours[120] truly,        (121)

Mr. George Jennings
322 Chandler Place
Quebec, Quebec

Dear Mr. Jennings:

When you put your signature on the contract[10] of sale for the car which you purchased from us[20] recently, you understood that the guarantee would cover only normal[30] wear and tear. As you know, we have repaired your[40] car four times for damages that were not due to[50] normal wear and tear. When a car is driven at[60] high speeds for a long period of time during the[70] hot summer months, it is impossible to guarantee how long[80] it will continue to perform properly. The car that you[90] purchased was four years old and had been driven[100] 52,000 miles. The conditions under which you drove this[110] car were not ordinary, and no car could be expected[120] to stand up under the treatment you gave it. High[130] speeds and quick stops will, of course, wear out the[140] brakes in a very short time.

We are sorry to[150] inform you that we cannot take back the car and[160] return the remainder of your payment. We trust that you[170] will understand our position in this matter.

Yours truly,        (179)

Morrison Automobile Agency
1242 Cartier Street
Quebec, Quebec

Gentlemen:

I have purchased many cars in the past, and[10] I have never had so much difficulty as I have[20] had with this one.

When I bought the car, I[30] told you that I intended driving it for long distances[40] during the summer months, and that I liked a car[50] that would stop quickly. You told me that this car[60] would do exactly that, and that I would have no[70] annoyance or anxiety about it. This car has definitely not[80] performed as you said it would.

Yours truly,   (88)

## SPELLING

(1) guarantee, occasions, annoyance, anxiety, inferior, remainder
(2) signature, contract, normal, repaired, period, properly, ordinary
(3) exactly

## PUNCTUATION

(1) When you receive the folder please read it, sign two copies, and return one copy to me.
(2) In the center of the report, near the summary of sales, we have given some information about our profits for the year.
(3) As you may recall, I wrote to you recently, but, at that time, you could not give me the information I wanted.

# 27
## VOCABULARY BUILDING

*marvelous*
*reputation*
1. He built a marvelous reputation on the basis of good service and prompt delivery.

*simplicity*
2. The simplicity of their organization is responsible to a large extent for their marvelous reputation.

*justify*
3. We cannot justify the extreme simplicity of these garments in view of our reputation for having only the latest in fashions.

*fortunate*
4. You are fortunate in not having to justify the extreme simplicity of your styles because you do not have a reputation for any particular kind of styles.

*tendency*
5. There is a tendency today to try to justify simplicity in dress by calling it good styling, but we have not built our marvelous reputation in that way.

*gradual*    6. We have noted a gradual tendency by many concerns of marvelous reputations to get away from extreme simplicity in style.

*wisdom*    7. I question the wisdom of trying to justify the tendency to get away from simplicity of style, and it is fortunate for us that other firms are gradually doing the same thing.

## THEORY PRACTICE

For the past several years we have been studying the[10] wisdom of a change in the arrangement of our sales[20] offices throughout the United States. We have felt that it[30] was an error to have a separate territory for each[40] salesman. We cannot justify such an arrangement.

Our current advertising[50] campaign is emphasizing the tendency of many women to desire[60] garments that can be used for many purposes. This is[70] apparently due to the influence of the woman who owns[80] her home and who may wish to buy many things[90] besides clothing, but who is on a fixed salary or[100] income.    (101)

## SPEED BUILDING PRACTICE

Dear Sir:

In answer to your letter about the problems[10] involved in the building of several independent companies throughout the[20] United States to handle your products, I would like to[30] say that I think it would be very inconvenient to[40] do so at this time. One reason for this belief[50] is that it would be necessary to have each of[60] these companies incorporated under the laws of the different states.[70] This would mean that any identification of these companies with[80] your office in New York City would be lost.

In[90] addition, under the circumstances it would be very difficult to[100] handle all of the financial problems at this time.

Cordially[110] yours,    (111)

# TRANSCRIPTION LETTERS

Phillips Car Company
110 Bank Street
Ottawa 5, Ontario

Gentlemen:

When I bought my car from you, I felt[10] that it would be better to buy it and make[20] time payments so that I would not have to wait[30] until I had saved enough to purchase the car. At[40] the present time I am able to make the remainder[50] of the payments on the car at one time, and[60] I would like to arrange to do this as soon[70] as possible. I would also like to cancel the insurance[80] policy which I took out with you on the car.[90]

The car is performing in such a way as to[100] justify your reputation for fine cars, and I have recommended[110] several of my friends to you.

Very truly yours,     (119)

Mr. Harold Porter
404 Fourth Avenue
Ottawa 3, Ontario

Dear Mr. Porter:

In answer to your letter requesting us to[10] change the terms of our contract so as to permit[20] you to pay the remainder of your balance at this[30] time, we are sorry to say that we cannot comply[40] with your wishes. The financing for the car was handled[50] by another firm, and we have no control over the[60] matter once the contract has been signed. In addition, we[70] cannot make any change in the terms of the insurance[80] because that, too, is handled by our finance company.

We[90] might add that we do not think it wise for[100] you to pay off the remainder of your obligation because[110] the terms of the contract provide for a penalty in[120] cases of pre-payment. Furthermore, the insurance protection that you received[130] under our contract gives the best type of coverage at[140] the lowest price.

We appreciate very much your kind words[150] about our reputation, and thank you very much for sending[160] your friends to see us. We shall be happy to[170] assist you in any way we can.

Very sincerely yours,     (180)

Phillips Car Company
110 Bank Street
Ottawa 5, Ontario

Gentlemen:

I was thoroughly surprised to hear from you that[10] I could not pay off the remainder of my obligation,[20] and that I should not change my insurance policy on[30] the car.

Despite the fact that I could obtain interest[40] at a bank on the money I wish to use[50] to pay off the loan, I do not like to[60] do business that way. When I purchased the car, I[70] told you that I intended to pay off the remainder[80] of the balance as soon as possible.

Yours truly,   (89)

## SPELLING

(1) remainder, cancel, insurance, policy, justify, reputation, recommended
(2) financing, handled, current (currant), obligation, protection
(3) thoroughly, surprised

## PUNCTUATION

(1) In answer to your question, may I ask why you think it would be inconvenient for us to do the job at this time?
(2) Would it be very difficult to handle this special job in addition to your regular work?
(3) When I bought my car from you, you told me that under no circumstances would I have to spend money on repairs for at least a month.

# 28
# VOCABULARY BUILDING

*activity*
*comparatively*
*burden*

1. The level of business activity in this town has been comparatively high during the past year.
2. The burden of increasing the level of activity of our organization rests on a comparatively small number of people.

|              |    |                                                                                 |
|--------------|----|---------------------------------------------------------------------------------|
| *fundamental*    | 3. | Our fundamental problem is to increase business activity by a comparatively large amount without adding any additional financial burden. |
| *characteristic* | 4. | The fundamental characteristic of our method is that we are trying to increase business activity while making a comparatively small profit. |
| *acquainted*     | 5. | There are several fundamental characteristics of our business with which you must become acquainted before you can begin any activity to lower our comparatively heavy financial burdens. |
| *classification* | 6. | We make a classification of our goods on the basis of several fundamental characteristics which are comparatively difficult to notice unless you are acquainted with our activities. |
| *ignorant*       | 7. | If you find that your customers are ignorant of the fundamental characteristics of our products, you should try to have them become acquainted with the comparatively small difference between our products and others. |

## THEORY PRACTICE

We appreciate your efforts to make our annual sale as[10] successful as possible. However, because of the comparatively small burden[20] that this sale places on the members of our staff,[30] we feel sure that we can finish our preparations on[40] time.

You also mentioned that you are planning to cancel[50] your annual sale because of a lack of some essential[60] goods. We are exceedingly anxious to help you in any[70] way possible. We can definitely guarantee to supply many of[80] the items that you are evidently missing, and we believe[90] we can get many of the other items from members[100] of our association.          (103)

## SPEED BUILDING PRACTICE

Gentlemen:

We have found during the past few years that[10] the introduction of new products to the general public does[20] not always bring about immediate success. We have made an[30] investigation of the problem of how to introduce new products,[40] and we believe that it is indispensable to have members[50] of your company make individual calls on prospective customers.

407

When[60] a customer has a chance to inspect the products that[70] you are trying to sell, he can make an intelligent[80] choice. Many people who receive a letter in the mail[90] do not take the trouble to read it carefully enough[100] to understand what you are trying to offer them.

Yours[110] truly,      (111)

## TRANSCRIPTION LETTERS

Simmons Auto Rental Agency Incorporated
330 Hudson Street
Victoria, British Columbia

Gentlemen:

I would appreciate receiving information about the rental of[10] a car. Several of my friends and business associates have[20] told me that there are some fundamental advantages in this[30] type of arrangement for a man in my position. I[40] am a salesman for a firm that does most of[50] its business in this state. While I travel comparatively short[60] distances to each of my accounts, the number of miles[70] I travel is quite large on an annual basis.

I[80] would like to know whether rental charges include insurance and[90] repairs, and what arrangements can be made for a particular[100] model and type of car. I would be interested in[110] having a new model car each year.

Yours truly,      (119)

Mr. Harold Prescott
412 Auburn Place
Victoria, British Columbia

Dear Mr. Prescott:

We were happy to receive your letter of[10] inquiry about our car rental service.

On the basis of[20] your problems and the type of driving you do, we[30] would strongly recommend the use of a rented car on[40] an annual basis. You can make any type of arrangement[50] you wish relative to the year and make of car,[60] and you may have a new model each year. These[70] new models are usually available within a month after they[80] appear on the market.

The charge for a car will[90] depend upon the make of the car,

408

and each car[100] can be obtained on the basis of full insurance and[110] repairs. However, these repairs do not include those due to[120] an accident or to some special occurrence. We take care[130] of the repairs due to wear and tear.

The charge[140] for these cars will run from $80 a month[150] for the lowest priced cars to $150[160] a month for the more expensive cars. There is a[170] small additional charge for a new model each year.

Sincerely[180] yours,     (181)

Simmons Auto Rental Agency Incorporated
330 Hudson Street
Victoria, British Columbia

Gentlemen:

You answered most of the questions I asked relative[10] to the rental of your cars, and I am glad[20] that I took the trouble to become acquainted with your[30] rental service. I am definitely interested in going ahead with[40] a rental plan, but I wish to know whether it[50] is essential that I give you a definite answer now[60] about the change of models each year, since I do[70] not know yet whether I will be able to do[80] this.

Thank you very much for your assistance.

Yours truly,     (90)

## SPELLING

(1) rental, associates, fundamental, advantages, position. comparatively, distances, annual, basis, model
(2) inquiry, strongly, recommend, relative, accident, occurrence, expensive
(3) answered, acquainted, definitely, essential, assistance

## PUNCTUATION

(1) However, because of our comparatively small sales, we cannot expect large profits for this year.
(2) Do you believe that, at this time of the year, an investigation of the company would be necessary, profitable, or of value to us?
(3) Although I have asked my friends about the rental of a car, could you tell me what the advantages of such an arrangement would be to me?

# 29

## VOCABULARY BUILDING

*illustrate*   1. I shall try to illustrate the value of this machine when I see you.

*permanent*  2. He will try to illustrate the value of a permanent change in the selling methods of your company.

*economy*   3. The way to illustrate the economy of this machine is to keep a permanent record of its performance.

*machinery*  4. I can best illustrate the economy of this machinery by showing you permanent records of its production at other firms.

*patent*   5. In order to get permanent benefit from this machinery, you should take out a patent on it.

*solution*   6. If you patent this idea, I think that you will have a permanent solution to the problem of economy in the operation of your machinery.

*overcome*  7. If we can overcome the lack of economy in the use of this machinery, we will have a permanent solution to our production problems.

*specific*   8. Although there is no specific solution to the problem of economy in the operation of this machinery, I think that my plan will illustrate how you can overcome many of these problems.

## THEORY PRACTICE

I am somewhat surprised and annoyed at the manner in[10] which the machinery that we recently bought from you has[20] been performing. To illustrate my point, I might mention the[30] specific problem of poor economy in operating the machines. Although[40] the loss of economy in the machines is not great[50] now, I am worried about the future after there has[60] been a good deal of wear and tear on the[70] machinery.

I would, therefore, like to have someone from your[80] organization come down and look over the machines as soon[90] as possible.

(92)

410

# SPEED BUILDING PRACTICE

Gentlemen:

We have made a rather large investment in your[10] company in the hope that we would be able to[20] obtain a maximum return on our money. However, the returns[30] have been irregular, and there seems to be no justification[40] for this in view of the fact that your company[50] is making large profits. We know that you do not[60] have any direct jurisdiction over the distribution of the profits[70] of your company, but we feel sure that you are[80] in a position to make an investigation of the matter[90] for us.

We would be happy to have your opinions[100] on the matter, and we should be glad to get[110] together with you to talk over the matter.

Cordially yours,　　　　　(120)

# TRANSCRIPTION LETTERS

Douglas Auto Service Incorporated
306 South Drive
Lachine, Quebec

Gentlemen:

We wish to obtain some information about your truck[10] service. For the past five years we have been using[20] our own trucks, and we are not completely satisfied with[30] their efficiency or economy. Also, our drivers have not given[40] the type of service that we wish to offer to[50] our customers.

We have felt that the solution to the[60] problem might be to hire a public carrier to take[70] over all of our deliveries. We would need at least[80] two trucks three days a week during the month, and[90] three trucks during the rush periods at the end of[100] each month.

Please let us know whether you can provide[110] economy and service, without loss of efficiency.

Yours truly,　　　　　(119)

Fisher Manufacturing Company
186 Butler Street
Montreal, Quebec

Gentlemen:

We believe that we can satisfy all of your[10] needs and requirements for trucking service. As a matter of[20] fact, the principal advantage of our trucking service is the[30] efficiency and economy we provide. There are no problems of[40] upkeep of machinery and equipment because we take care of[50] that ourselves. We are able to do it with greater[60] economy because of the large number of trucks we use.[70] We are enclosing a schedule of rates for the use[80] of our service, and we shall be happy to discuss[90] any specific points with you.

In reference to your question[100] about the quality of our service, here too we have[110] the solution to your problems. Our drivers are specifically trained[120] to give the best possible type of service, and they[130] have had many years of experience doing this. We are[140] confident that once you begin using our trucking service you[150] will make a permanent change and drop all of your[160] own trucks. You will have no worry about deliveries once[170] you begin to use our service.

Yours truly,        (178)

Douglas Auto Service Incorporated
306 South Drive
Lachine, Quebec

Gentlemen:

I am glad to see that you mentioned the[10] problem of economy in the rental of your trucks, because[20] that is of maximum importance to us. We do not[30] wish to make an investment in a trucking service if[40] the cost is going to be too high for us.[50]

On the basis of the comments in your letter, we[60] believe you have overcome most of the objections that we[70] raised. We are planning to get together with you to[80] talk over specific details somewhat later this month.

Yours truly,        (90)

## SPELLING

(1) completely, satisfied, economy, solution, carrier, deliveries, periods

(2) satisfy, principal-ly (principle), machinery, equipment, schedule, specific, reference, specifically, confident, permanent

(3) maximum, comments

## PUNCTUATION

(1) I am somewhat surprised and rather annoyed at the loss of time, money, and effort we have had with this machine.

(2) As a matter of fact, in spite of what they may say, this arrangement will make the upkeep of your car much more efficient.

(3) As a result of your recent letter, we believe you have overcome most of our objections, but we cannot do anything until later on.

# 30

## VOCABULARY BUILDING

*enormous*  
*foreign*
1. We have shipped an enormous amount of material to foreign countries during the past few years.

*adequate*
2. We do not feel that our foreign trade balance is adequate despite the enormous increase in shipments during the past year.

*hitherto*
3. Although we have hitherto done an adequate business with foreign countries, we feel that there is still an enormous market for our goods in many of these countries.

*eventually*
4. We shall eventually try to increase our share of the enormous amount of business done with foreign countries even though we have hitherto made an adequate profit from our local trade.

*assortment*
5. Although we now sell an assortment of goods to foreign countries, we eventually expect an enormous increase in the sales of some goods that have hitherto not been selling adequately.

*adopt*
6. We shall eventually have to adopt a policy of selling an assortment of goods to foreign countries although we have hitherto received an adequate profit from our sales in this country.

*ascertain*
7. We should like to ascertain eventually whether we should adopt a different policy in our dealings with foreign countries by handling an assortment of goods.

413

# THEORY PRACTICE

We would suggest that you do not hesitate to give[10] up the idea of building a hotel in the location[20] that you have selected. The principal reason for this is[30] that there are too many hospitals in the neighborhood, which[40] would eventually tend to discourage people from coming to the[50] hotel. I would suggest that you drop your plans, even[60] though it hurts to admit that an idea that you[70] have thought about for a long time is not a[80] practical one.

I have an assortment of properties that I[90] think would be far more suitable for your hotel.                    (99)

# SPEED BUILDING PRACTICE

Gentlemen:

We must inform you that your mortgage will have[10] to be renewed at this time. In order to obtain[20] a renewal of the mortgage, it will be necessary for[30] you to make a minimum payment of $10,000[40] and to make some improvements in the building itself. These[50] improvements would include mechanical work as well as several items[60] that are necessary because of neglect on the part of[70] the previous owners.

We are sending you by messenger a[80] complete list of the improvements that will have to be[90] made in the building in order to obtain a renewal[100] of the mortgage.

Very truly yours,          (106)

# TRANSCRIPTION LETTERS

Bryant Garage Company
196 Main Street
Thunder Bay, Ontario

Gentlemen:

I have been using your garage service for the[10] past three years, and during that time I have complained[20] to you on several occasions about the long delays in[30] getting my car. Yesterday when I took out my car,[40] I had to wait more than half an hour, and[50] when I finally received the car I noticed that my[60] left fender was damaged. I am positive that the damage[70] was done by your men because I always look at[80] my car before and after I bring it to your[90] garage.

414

I shall try to ascertain the cost of the[100] repairs and send you an estimate. If you wish to[110] make the repairs yourself, I will have no objection.

Yours[120] very truly,        (122)

Mr. Peter Hopkins
156 Westree Avenue
Thunder Bay, Ontario

Dear Mr. Hopkins:

We have checked your car carefully in[10] order to determine how the damage to your fender occurred,[20] and we find that it could not possibly have been[30] our fault because the damage is too high on the[40] fender. Such damage could have occurred only as a result[50] of a collision with a truck. It is possible that[60] a truck might have run into your car while it[70] was parked.

In reference to your complaint about the time[80] it takes to receive your car, we wish to remind[90] you that you do not give us adequate time in[100] which to get your car down to the street. You[110] can avoid delay by calling us in advance and telling[120] us when you will need your car. In this way[130] we can put the car in a spot where it[140] will be available when you are ready to use it.[150]

We are sure that if you adopt this procedure you[160] will avoid any difficulty in getting your car without delay.[170]

Yours truly,        (172)

Bryant Garage Company
196 Main Street
Thunder Bay, Ontario

Gentlemen:

I am glad that you mentioned the advisability of[10] calling you in advance when I need my car. I[20] have done just that on many occasions, but I have[30] found that it was impossible to get an answer on[40] the phone. Your men are either busy bringing down cars,[50] or they are outside and do not hear the phone.[60]

I would be glad to cooperate with you in this[70] way to obtain better service, but I cannot always ascertain[80] in advance when I shall need the car.

Yours truly,        (90)

415

## SPELLING

(1) garage, complaint (complained), occasions, yesterday, damaged, positive, ascertain, estimate
(2) occurred, collision, reference, complained (complaint), adequate, adopt, procedure
(3) mentioned, advisability, occasions, cooperate

## PUNCTUATION

(1) In answer to your letter, may I suggest that you do not build a hotel at this or any other location in this part of the city.
(2) In order to obtain a mortgage on your store, it will be necessary to make some improvements, a few repairs, and a large down payment.
(3) Yesterday, when I took out my car, I noticed that my fenders on the front, back, and side were damaged.

# 31

## VOCABULARY BUILDING

*argument*    1. We do not wish to have any argument about the contract.

*facilities*    2. The argument between them involved the use of storage facilities by both companies.

*chiefly*    3. The argument was concerned chiefly with the use of the same facilities by both firms.

*hardest*    4. The hardest problem to solve was that of the use of our storage facilities, chiefly because of an argument over the price.

*collateral*    5. The hardest problem we face in the purchase of their facilities is the amount of collateral to be given.

*insisted*    6. In order to avoid an argument, he insisted that they provide more collateral, and he based his request chiefly on the poor facilities they had in the factory.

*debit*    7. I cannot debit their account for the full value of the collateral chiefly because of the fact that we insisted on using only the present market value of their facilities.

*impression* 8. I got the impression that they insisted on having us debit their account for the original value of their facilities chiefly because they had no other collateral to offer.

## THEORY PRACTICE

We are planning to hold a conference with members of[10] the local community concerning the complaint that we have received[20] regarding our facilities. We are insisting on this meeting because[30] we feel that we must have the confidence of local[40] business men in order to develop our plans adequately.

The[50] complaints that we have received claim that our contract with[60] the community is contrary to their best interests chiefly because[70] they have the impression that we plan to reduce our[80] production in this area. We can recognize the feeling of[90] some people in this community toward such a plan, and[100] that is why we are recommending that you communicate with[110] us as soon as you know more about the content[120] of their complaints. (123)

## SPEED BUILDING PRACTICE

Gentlemen:

We have received a complaint from a passenger on[10] one of our buses who says that he was injured[20] because of the negligence of our driver. The circumstances in[30] this case seem peculiar because of the fact that this[40] person had sent in a complaint like this before, notwithstanding[50] the fact that we were able to prove that there[60] had been no negligence on our part. Nevertheless, we shall[70] follow up this matter so as to avoid any difficulty[80] at a later date.

At this time we would like[90] to have a statement from the driver of the bus[100] so that we can get together the full story of[110] what happened. In this way we shall not have to[120] rely on the impressions of the other passengers on the[130] bus.

Yours truly, (133)

# TRANSCRIPTION LETTERS

Mrs. Doris Ross
124 Main Street
Halifax, Nova Scotia

Dear Mrs. Ross:

I have completed my examination of your brother,[10] and I can now give you some definite information about[20] his condition.

His problem is chiefly that of the removal[30] of a growth on his leg. This growth is not,[40] at the present time, dangerous, but it is located in[50] such a place as to be a constant source of[60] irritation. It may, therefore, develop into something far more serious[70] if it is not taken care of soon. I would[80] recommend an operation for the removal of this growth, and[90] I would suggest that the operation be done within the[100] next three months. If there is any delay, the growth[110] may spread to other parts of his body.

Cordially yours,      (120)

Dr. Harold Owen
226 Governor Road
Victoria, British Columbia

Dear Dr. Owen:

Thank you very much for your prompt[10] reply concerning the condition of my brother.

I agree fully[20] with your recommendations, and I have tried my hardest to[30] get my brother to agree to go through with the[40] operation. His argument is that it is unwise to have[50] an operation on such a small growth because of the[60] possibility that it will go away by itself. He does[70] not have confidence in your expectation that the growth will[80] become larger because he says that it has been the[90] same for the past three years. I have insisted that[100] he cannot be sure of his statement because he did[110] not have it checked by a doctor in the past.[120] However, he is satisfied to let things stand as they[130] are. He has agreed to go through another series of[140] tests within six months to determine whether there has been[150] any additional growth during that time.

I shall get in[160] touch with you in a month or two to use[170] your examination facilities once again.

Sincerely yours,      (177)

Mrs. Doris Ross
124 Main Street
Halifax, Nova Scotia

Dear Mrs. Ross:

I was surprised to hear of your[10] brother's decision not to go through an operation at this[20] time for the removal of the growth on his leg.[30] He apparently does not recognize the value of preventing a[40] serious operation later by going through a simple one now.[50] However, his argument is similar to that of many people[60] in his condition.

I recommend that he continue to use[70] the medicines that I prescribed. These medicines will keep the[80] area around the growth free from infection.

Very truly yours,             (90)

## SPELLING

(1) completed, examination, chiefly, removal, dangerous, irritation, serious, recommend
(2) concerning, argument, possibility, confidence, expectation, insisted, facilities
(3) decision, apparently, recognize, medicines, prescribed, infection

## PUNCTUATION

(1) I have now completed the examination you requested, but I cannot give you any definite information at this time.
(2) Since his condition is serious, but not dangerous, I do not, at the present time, recommend an operation.
(3) I agree with you fully, and I have tried my hardest to have the operation taken care of, but my brother does not wish to do it at this time.

# 32
## VOCABULARY BUILDING

*assurance*    1. I have his assurance that the goods will be delivered by the end of the week.

| | | |
|---|---|---|
| *complaint* | 2. | You have our assurance that we shall handle your complaint to your complete satisfaction. |
| *worthless* | 3. | You have my assurance that we shall investigate his complaint and let you know whether or not his claim is worthless. |
| *authorize* | 4. | I cannot authorize you to make a complaint against them until I have some assurance that their claims are worthless. |
| *compromise* | 5. | I cannot authorize you to agree to a compromise plan to settle their complaint until I have some assurance that they will give up their almost worthless claims. |
| *confer* | 6. | We cannot authorize you to confer with them about a settlement of your complaint until we have your assurance that you are willing to compromise to settle the issue. |
| *voluntary* | 7. | I shall be glad to confer with them on a voluntary basis if they can give me some assurance that they are willing to reach a compromise on their complaint. |
| *sympathize* | 8. | While I sympathize with their complaint, I cannot confer with them on a voluntary basis unless I know that you will support me if a compromise is agreed upon. |

## THEORY PRACTICE

I am attaching a copy of their letter containing the[10] complaint about our delivery service. I am sure that their[20] complaint is worthless, but I have no assurance as yet[30] that they have told me the complete story. I shall[40] be staying in touch with them as long as necessary[50] to find out all the facts in the case. That[60] is the only thing preventing me from telling them that[70] we do not expect to pay them any money on[80] their claim or that we are willing to enter into[90] any sort of compromise. (94)

## SPEED BUILDING PRACTICE

Gentlemen:

We are interested in having our building project finished[10] as soon as possible. We realize that it is not[20] practicable at this time to ask you to give us[30] a definite date by which you can perform your part[40] of the contract. However, it will be helpful if you[50] can

420

give us a preliminary idea of the amount of[60] time you will probably need.

We are attaching a copy[70] of a letter we received from one of our representatives[80] in which he asks us to confer with you in[90] order to form an idea of when we can begin[100] using the new building.

Yours truly,      (106)

# TRANSCRIPTION LETTERS

Dr. Leo J. Snell
206 High Street
Montreal, Quebec

Dear Dr. Snell:

We are happy to announce the development[10] of a new type of X-ray machine that should prove[20] of great help to you. This machine is a smaller[30] model of the type that you are now using, but[40] it includes many of the advances in the field of[50] X-ray work during the past few years. We feel confident[60] that your patients will especially appreciate this machine because it[70] will make the taking of X-rays possible without long periods[80] of discomfort.

We shall be happy to give you a[90] demonstration of the machine at your office at any time[100] convenient to you. We look forward to being of service[110] to you.

Very truly yours,      (115)

Mr. Henry Holmes
122 Dundas Street
London, Ontario

Dear Mr. Holmes:

Your description of your new X-ray machine[10] interests me, and I will be glad to arrange to[20] have you demonstrate the machine to me. However, I would[30] like to know whether this machine will provide the standard[40] sizes of X-rays or whether it contains the new type[50] of adjustable size picture about which I have read in[60] some medical journals. I have found that the problem of[70] storing a large number of X-rays is becoming quite serious[80] to me.

421

The advantages that you mentioned about the size[90] of the machine are almost worthless to me because of[100] the fact that I do not move my X-ray equipment[110] about since I have the room to keep it in[120] one place. I am, however, interested in the possibility that[130] your machine may avoid some of the discomforts to patients,[140] and may cut down the time required to take X-rays.[150] Would it also reduce the time needed to develop the[160] X-rays?

Please call my office to make an appointment to[170] demonstrate the machine.

Yours truly,          (175)


Dr. Leo J. Snell
206 High Street
Montreal, Quebec

Dear Dr. Snell:

In answer to your questions about our[10] new X-ray machine, we should like to say that we[20] do not have the type of machine that permits the[30] taking of pictures of different sizes. The article to which[40] you referred was concerned with an experimental model that is[50] being developed by our research department. We do not expect[60] to have this type of X-ray machine ready for at[70] least five years.

We are sure that our present machine[80] has many advantages that will interest you.

Very truly yours,          (90)


## SPELLING

(1) tremendous, compact, patients, discomfort, demonstration, convenient
(2) description, standard, adjustable, medical, journals, becoming
(3) article, referred, experimental, research


## PUNCTUATION

(1) Your description of the machine interests me, and, although it is difficult for me to purchase one now, I shall be glad to look at it.
(2) Would this machine reduce the time needed to develop the X-ray, or is that not possible with this machine?
(3) In answer to your questions, please let me inform you that, although the machine is the best on the market, it does not take pictures of different sizes.

# 33

## VOCABULARY BUILDING

*ashamed*  
*departure*

1. We are ashamed to say that we came too late to see him before his departure from the station.

*calendar*

2. We are ashamed to say that our departure has been delayed because we did not check our calendar before making this appointment.

*behavior*

3. We are ashamed to say that we made no note on our calendar to write them about his behavior at the time of his departure.

*notation*

4. I made a notation on my calendar about the time and date of your departure, but I am ashamed to say that I overlooked it.

*contemplate*

5. If you contemplate leaving next week, you should make a notation of the time of your departure on your calendar.

*journal*

6. I am ashamed to say that although I did contemplate making a notation in my journal about the date of his departure, I forgot to do it.

*fortnight*

7. According to the notation on your calendar he is scheduled to leave in a fortnight, but I am ashamed to say that I did not make a notation in my journal of the date of his departure.

## THEORY PRACTICE

We should like to suggest that you arrange to have[10] someone from our office accompany you on your trip. We[20] are sure that you will be able to accomplish your[30] goal better if someone from our firm is with you.[40] It will take a great deal of self-control to[50] conduct the conferences of which you are in charge, and[60] it will be difficult to give instructions to your assistants[70] if you become involved in discussions over a long period[80] of time. As you requested, we have made the necessary[90] inquiries, and we have learned that the conference room will[100] be large enough to accommodate at least thirty people. (109)

# SPEED BUILDING PRACTICE

Dear Sir:

We take great satisfaction in informing you that[10] we have been able to make significant progress in your[20] case. We are sure that the significance of our progress[30] will be realized when a settlement of your claim is[40] made. However, I feel that we should be sensible in[50] our handling of the case by not asking for a[60] settlement that would be impossible to pay. I believe that[70] a spirit of fairness will help a great deal to[80] bring about a settlement without the necessity of taking the[90] matter to court.

We shall, of course, keep in touch[100] with you and let you know if there are any[110] significant developments.

Very truly yours, (115)

# TRANSCRIPTION LETTERS

Dr. Alvin Baker
68 Haro Avenue
Vancouver, British Columbia

Dear Dr. Baker:

You recently had occasion to treat a[10] patient by the name of Helen Smith who was suffering[20] from pains in her back. At the time of her[30] visit to your office, she probably told you that she[40] did not know how these pains had started, but that[50] they had been troubling her more and more during the[60] past few months. Mrs. Smith did not tell you that[70] the pains in her back began soon after she was[80] involved in an automobile accident. Immediately after the accident she[90] said she felt no pain and refused medical help.

Would[100] you please re-examine her and let me know whether her[110] condition could have resulted from the automobile accident.

Yours truly, (120)

Mr. Samuel Smith
22 James Street
Montreal, Quebec

Dear Mr. Smith:

It is difficult for me to answer[10] your letter concerning the condition of Mrs. Helen Smith. In[20] the first place, you did not indicate whether you are[30] Mrs. Smith's husband or whether you are related to her[40] in any way. Secondly, it is now four months since[50] the time of the accident, so that the condition of[60] her back might have changed a great deal by now.[70]

According to my records, Mrs. Smith came for one visit,[80] and refused to return to keep her second appointment. She[90] informed my nurse that she felt so much better that[100] another visit was unnecessary. On the basis of her actions[110] in this case, I would be inclined to think that[120] it would not be possible to determine at this time[130] whether there was any connection between the accident and the[140] condition of her back. I shall be glad to make[150] another examination, but I cannot promise any definite conclusions as[160] to the cause of her condition.

Please call my office[170] to make an appointment for the examination.

Yours very truly,      (180)

Dr. Alvin Baker
68 Haro Avenue
Vancouver, British Columbia

Dear Dr. Baker:

Your letter concerning the condition of my[10] wife, Mrs. Helen Smith, was not very encouraging. As you[20] may have gathered from my letter, I am in the[30] process of bringing a law-suit against the taxi company[40] with whose cab my wife was involved in the accident.[50] My wife should have told you the real cause of[60] her difficulty at the time she first came to you,[70] but she is the type that believes in self-control[80] even though she may suffer because of it.

Very truly[90] yours,      (91)

## SPELLING

(1) suffering, probable-ly-ility, troubling, accident, re-examine
(2) behavior, inclined, connection, conclusions
(3) encouraging, process

## PUNCTUATION

(1) At the time of her visit, which was some time in April, she did not tell me that she had been in an accident.

425

(2) You did not indicate, in the first place, whether you are this woman's husband, or, as a matter of fact, whether you are related to her at all.

(3) Your letter concerning the condition of my wife's brother, Mr. Harold Smith, did not indicate the real cause of his difficulty.

# 34

## VOCABULARY BUILDING

*ordinarily*   1. We do not ordinarily permit exchanges of items purchased at this store.

*certified*   2. We do not ordinarily ask for payment by a certified check, but we shall have to do so in this case.

*peculiar*   3. It is peculiar for them to ask for a certified check when they ordinarily accept any kind of payment.

*background*   4. Because of his peculiar background, I would not have ordinarily certified him for the job, but he did very well on his tests.

*briefly*   5. I should like to tell you briefly about some of the peculiar features of his background which would not ordinarily come to your attention.

*pertaining*   6. We shall outline briefly all the facts pertaining to his background, and we shall include certain peculiar items which would not ordinarily appear in such a report.

*phase*   7. I shall report briefly on one peculiar phase of the background of this company which would not ordinarily come to your attention.

*awkward*   8. I can briefly answer some of your questions pertaining to his peculiar background and experience by saying that he is now going through an awkward phase which would not have ordinarily occurred.

## THEORY PRACTICE

I have received your announcement concerning the new membership drive.[10] While I have ordinarily not been particularly interested in increasing[20] the number of our members, I do have one good$^{30}$ possibility for membership. However, before I submit his name, I$^{40}$ would like to investigate his background briefly so as to$^{50}$ make sure that he has the fundamental characteristics for member-ship$^{60}$ in our organization.

I believe that once a man has$^{70}$ been certified for membership by a majority of our members,$^{80}$ there should be no trouble in get-ting him elected. I$^{90}$ also believe in avoiding problems due to care-lessness in the$^{100}$ selection of members.      (103)

## SPEED BUILDING PRACTICE

Gentlemen:

We are interested in obtaining a substantial number of$^{10}$ new subscriptions to our magazine. We believe that we do$^{20}$ not have a sufficient number of people in the southern$^{30}$ states reading our magazine, and we think that there are$^{40}$ many who would be sympa-thetic to the material we publish.$^{50}$

We are thinking of putting out special issues of the$^{60}$ magazine for different parts of the country. In this way$^{70}$ we believe that we can increase the number of subscriptions$^{80}$ in the southern as well as the northern states.

Very$^{90}$ truly yours,      (92)

## TRANSCRIPTION LETTERS

Dr. Morris Jaffe
Box 29
Swift Current, Saskatchewan

Dear Dr. Jaffe:

I am writing to you at the$^{10}$ suggestion of one of your patients, Mrs. Mary Green. My$^{20}$ son, who is five years of age, has been losing$^{30}$ weight due to his extremely poor eating habits. Mrs. Green$^{40}$ told me that you treated her son for a similar$^{50}$ problem with excel-lent results. Mrs. Green also told me that$^{60}$ you prescribed a medi-cine which gave her child the necessary$^{70}$ energy to improve his eating habits, and I wondered if$^{80}$ I could get the same prescription for my son.

I$^{90}$ should be glad to come to your office with my$^{100}$ son, but we are away from the city, and we$^{110}$ shall not be back for another month.

Very truly yours,      (120)

Mrs. Caroline Johnson
39 Sommerville Avenue
Oakville, Ontario

Dear Mrs. Johnson:

I have received your letter pertaining to[10] the condition of your son and requesting a prescription to[20] help improve his condition. However, the prescription that Mrs. Green[30] mentioned was not given to build up her son's appetite,[40] but to prevent infection due to a cut that he[50] had received while playing. I gave her a list of[60] foods which were designed to improve her son's eating habits.[70] They apparently had the desired result, for her boy is[80] now doing very nicely.

I would not ordinarily give a[90] diagnosis or a prescription without seeing the child, but the[100] type of treatment that I recommended for Mrs. Green's child[110] could be given to your son without any danger. I[120] am, therefore, enclosing the same list of foods that I[130] suggested for Mrs. Green's boy. If these do not work[140] to your satisfaction, I would suggest that you bring your[150] boy in to see me when you return to the[160] city. There is a possibility that his condition has resulted[170] from other causes.

Yours truly,      (175)

Dr. Morris Jaffe
Box 29
Swift Current, Saskatchewan

Dear Dr. Jaffe:

Your letter was forwarded to me and[10] I was pleased to receive the prescription for foods that[20] you included.

I have tried all of these foods with[30] my son, but he has refused to eat them. Since[40] I realize how awkward it is for you to prescribe[50] for him through the mail, my son and I will[60] make a special trip in to see you this week.[70] I also want to check on the possibility that his[80] condition may be due to other causes.

Very truly yours,      (90)

# SPELLING

(1) losing, wondered
(2) pertaining, appetite, infection, designed, apparently, ordinarily, diagnosis, possibility
(3) awkward

428

## PUNCTUATION

(1) My son, who is now five years old, has been losing weight because of his poor eating, playing, and sleeping habits.

(2) Mr. Green's child had a poor appetite only after the operation, but your son's appetite has been poor for a long time.

(3) I would not ordinarily give a diagnosis, or even suggest a prescription, without observing the child's eating habits, but there is no danger in his taking the prescription I am enclosing.

# 35

## VOCABULARY BUILDING

*data* 1. We are sure that we have all of the data you require.

*concrete* 2. You should try to put all of your data in concrete form so that it can be used in the report.

*evidence* 3. The data we have gathered should provide concrete evidence of how poorly the company was managed.

*habit* 4. We make it a habit to include only concrete data in any evidence we present.

*bonus* 5. We do not make it a habit to give a bonus, but your work contained such good concrete evidence to support the data, that we feel you deserve it.

*brilliant* 6. He did such a brilliant job gathering concrete evidence and data for the report that we are considering giving him a bonus.

*heartily* 7. We heartily approve your plan to give him a bonus for the brilliant job he did in gathering concrete data for the report.

*preserve* 8. They heartily approve your plan to preserve all concrete evidence and data for possible future use.

## THEORY PRACTICE

We are forwarding to you all of the data we[10] have received concerning the desirability of establishing an office in[20] this city.

We have found the people to be friendly[30] and interested in your products, but we still feel that[40] we do not have enough concrete evidence to support the[50] plan to open a branch of your business here. We[60] think that your best procedure would be to build friendships[70] in this area first, and afterwards try to set up[80] a small branch in a rented office so as to[90] see how the people will react to your sales campaign.[100] Later on, you can decide whether or not to take[110] a permanent place for your company.     (116)

## SPEED BUILDING PRACTICE

Gentlemen:

We are sorry to have to inform you that[10] we have found your products to be defective in recent[20] months. We have had to send back several items from[30] each of the last three shipments. Our complaint has been[40] that the quality of the goods is not uniform, so[50] that we do not know what to expect when we[60] receive a shipment from you.

We could continue sending back[70] the defective goods that we receive from you, thus increasing[80] your expense for delivery, but we do not believe that[90] this is the best way to do business. In the[100] future we shall send you a telegram if any of[110] the goods that we receive from you are defective, so[120] that you will have a written record for your files.[130.]

Yours truly,     (132)

## TRANSCRIPTION LETTERS

Dr. Howard Stone
1 Markland
Hamilton, Ontario

Dear Dr. Stone:

I am in urgent need of advice[10] on what to do about my father who has been[20] suffering for several years from pains in his stomach. I[30] recently took him to our local doctor, who referred me[40] to a specialist. The specialist said that my father needed[50] an operation to correct some internal difficulties. In order to[60] be sure, I took my father to another doctor who[70] told me that all he needed was a series of[80] treatments which would remove the cause of his pains.

I[90] thought it might be best to obtain some additional advice,[100] and I would like to bring my father in for[110] a thorough physical examination some time this week.

Very truly[120] yours,     (121)

430

Mr. Gilbert Tyler
35 Thornridge Drive
Thornhill, Ontario

Dear Mr. Tyler:

Your father came to my office yesterday,[10] and I have now completed my examination and diagnosis of[20] his condition. In my opinion, your father's condition is such[30] that an operation is necessary provided he is willing to[40] go away for a period of at least three months[50] for a complete rest after the operation. It is possible[60] that the operation may not cure his illness completely, but[70] I am sure that leaving it to treatment alone will[80] not produce any improvement in the future. While there are[90] cases on record of people with your father's condition who[100] have recovered through a long series of treatments, these cases[110] are unusual, and there are many others where this type[120] of treatment did not result in any concrete improvement.

If[130] you decide to have your father go through with the[140] operation, please make sure that he arranges to be away[150] from his present position for at least three months. It[160] would be extremely poor procedure to go through the operation[170] without making provision for a full recovery afterwards.

Yours truly,   (180)

Dr. Howard Stone
1 Markland
Hamilton, Ontario

Dear Dr. Stone:

While I heartily agree with your proposal[10] to perform an operation on my father, I find that[20] I cannot get him to agree to take the time[30] off that you feel would be necessary for a complete[40] recovery. He seems to feel that it is worth a[50] try to go through the series of treatments that have[60] been proposed. However, he says that if these fail, he[70] will be willing to go through the operation and take[80] the time off for recovery that you suggest.

Yours truly,   (90)

## SPELLING

(1)  urgent, advice (advise), stomach, referred, specialist, internal, physical

431

(2) diagnosis, period, concrete, recovery
(3) heartily, proposal, perform-ed

## PUNCTUATION

(1) I took him to a local doctor who referred me to a specialist who, in turn, referred me to you.
(2) Would you say that, in your opinion, my father's condition is difficult, dangerous, and unusual?
(3) While I heartily agree that an operation is necessary for your father's condition, can you be sure that he will go through with it?

# 36

## VOCABULARY BUILDING

*budget*    1. We shall present our budget for the year at our next meeting.

*capital*    2. Our budget for capital expenses will be higher than ever before.

*inability*    3. Their inability to cut their capital budget will force them to reduce some of their services.

*deduct*    4. Your inability to deduct some of these items from your capital budget may cause some difficulty.

*comparison*    5. A comparison of your capital budgets for the past five years will show you the effect of your inability to deduct certain unnecessary items.

*liability*    6. It is impossible for us to make a comparison of your liability under the new capital budget because of our inability to compare the effect of certain deductions that you made before.

*expiration*    7. We shall try to deduct our liability for some of these items at the expiration of the present capital budget.

*negotiations*    8. At the expiration of our negotiations we shall be able to submit a capital budget which will show the comparisons of liabilities for the past five years.

## THEORY PRACTICE

In view of the fact that you are not acquainted[10] with our equipment, we shall endeavor to send to you[20] as promptly as possible a book giving the correct pattern[30] of activities for the best use of our equipment.

It[40] has also occurred to us that you should get some[50] advance information on some of the changes that we are[60] planning in our new equipment.

At the expiration of your[70] present repair contract we shall be glad to give you[80] our special renewal contract in which you will have the[90] privilege of deducting 10 per cent from the cost of[100] the contract if the number of calls for repairs is[110] below our standard.

(113)

## SPEED BUILDING PRACTICE

Gentlemen:

Your representative in this building called on us yesterday[10] to tell us about the advantages of signing a new[20] lease with your company at this time. From the information[30] that he gave us, it would not be difficult for[40] us to make an immediate decision in the matter. However,[50] we cannot sign a contract without the approval of our[60] home office, and it is not their policy to sign[70] a new lease until the expiration of the old one.[80]

It has occurred to us that we can get in[90] touch with them within the next few days and ask[100] them to make an exception in this case.

Very truly[110] yours,　　　(111)

## TRANSCRIPTION LETTERS

Mrs. Florence Gilmore
31 Hewitt Avenue
Windsor 8, Ontario

Dear Mrs. Gilmore:

We are now conducting a survey sponsored by[10] the American Association for the Advancement of Television to determine[20] the listening habits of the public during the afternoon hours.[30] We are interested in knowing whether you follow a particular[40] pattern of listening, or whether you simply tune in any[50] television station that provides the type of entertainment you wish[60] to see at the moment.

We hope to be able[70] to present recommendations for the improvement of the programs now[80] being offered. We shall endeavor to make the results of[90] our survey available to the public as promptly as possible.[100] If you do not wish your name to be used,[110] please indicate that in the space below.

Yours truly,   (119)

Emerson and Franklin Incorporated
2489 Broadway
New York 61, New York

Gentlemen:

Although I do not listen to television very frequently[10] during the afternoon, I have looked at it often enough[20] during those hours to have formed an opinion about the[30] quality of the programs.

It is my honest opinion that[40] most of the programs follow a similar pattern in which[50] the impression given is that all people wish to escape[60] from the world of reality. There seems to be a[70] definite tendency to present plays and stories that are not[80] related to life as it actually is. While I can[90] understand the need for some people to get away from[100] their difficulties and problems by seeing shows that make them[110] forget the present, I feel that there is so much[120] of this type of entertainment during the afternoon hours that[130] it is almost useless for a serious listener to look[140] at TV at that time.

It has occurred to[150] me that the people who produce the TV programs[160] are thinking in terms of the radio programs that were[170] presented many years ago at that time of the day.[180]

Yours truly,   (182)

Mrs. Florence Gilmore
31 Hewitt Avenue
Windsor 8, Ontario

Dear Mrs. Gilmore:

Your very interesting comments about the type[10] of programs shown on television during the afternoon brought up[20] some very fundamental issues in the television industry today. The[30] television industry is always faced with the problem of whether[40] to arrange

434

its programs for the person who wishes only[50] pure entertainment or to present programs principally for those persons[60] who wish to learn something from TV.

We should[70] like to thank you for the care, time, and trouble[80] you took in preparing your answers to our questions.

Very[90] truly yours,       (92)

## SPELLING

(1) conducting, survey, sponsored, association, pattern, entertainment, offered, endeavor, promptly

(2) frequently, similar, reality, tendency, actually, serious, occurred

(3) fundamental, preparing

## PUNCTUATION

(1) We shall endeavor to make the results available as promptly as possible, but we cannot be sure that they will appear in next month's issue of the magazine.

(2) Although I do not listen to television very frequently, I have looked at it often enough, in my opinion, to have formed conclusions about the quality of the programs.

(3) We should like to thank you for the care, time, and trouble you took, but we cannot pay you for your expenses.

# 37

## VOCABULARY BUILDING

*recover*
*outstanding*

1. We are trying to recover most of our outstanding loans by the end of this year.

*pending*
*economic*

2. No move will be taken to recover outstanding obligations pending a report on economic conditions in the area.

*partial*

3. We have a partial list of accounts still outstanding, and we expect to recover them as soon as economic conditions improve.

| | |
|---|---|
| *entitled* | 4. We cannot offer you a partial recovery of your outstanding obligations, even though you may be entitled to it, pending a report on economic conditions. |
| *reduction* | 5. You will not be entitled to a partial recovery of your outstanding obligations pending the outcome of a suit by other creditors for a reduction of the amount due to them. |
| *compensation* | 6. I think that he should be entitled to some sort of compensation for any partial reduction in the amount of his outstanding obligations. |

## THEORY PRACTICE

In response to your recent letter, I should like to[10] explain why it took so long for us to give[20] you an answer on your offer to deliver the goods[30] we requested.

We had no indication that your sales representative[40] would be so interested in the transaction. We revised our[50] plans several times in accordance with his request to adjust[60] the contract to give him more desirable terms. We could[70] not expose ourselves to the possibility of making an error,[80] and we needed the assistance of our home office.

We[90] are extremely sorry about the delay, and we are sure[100] that the transaction will go ahead quickly now.     (108)

## SPEED BUILDING PRACTICE

Gentlemen:

Our company is interested in making several improvements in[10] our office, and we have been informed that your organization[20] has done many jobs like this in the past in[30] an efficient manner.

We had expected to have the job[40] done at the end of this year, but circumstances made[50] it impossible for us to begin building up to the[60] present time.

As we are in the advertising business, it[70] will be necessary to have some of the work done[80] after office hours during the week, and the balance over[90] the weekend. If these conditions are satisfactory to you, and[100] you can obtain the necessary insurance, we shall be ready[110] to go ahead with the job immediately.

Very truly yours,     (120)

# TRANSCRIPTION LETTERS

Central Broadcasting Company
312 Madison Avenue
New York 3, New York 10017

Gentlemen:

Our company is anxious to place several advertisements over[10] your radio and TV stations, and we would like[20] to obtain some information from you about the cost and[30] time of such advertisements.

We would like to have an[40] advertisement shown on TV twice a day for approximately[50] one minute. We would like to have the advertisements seen[60] by people in the metropolitan New York area only since[70] we do not have delivery facilities for customers outside the[80] metropolitan area. We would also like to have at least[90] three announcements a day made over the radio at a[100] time when the audience would contain a large number of[110] housewives.

Please let us know whether you can place these[120] advertisements.

Very truly yours,          (124)

Carter Manufacturing Company          d
64 Hastings Street
Vancouver, British Columbia

Gentlemen:

It is difficult to explain in a letter all[10] of the details involved in obtaining radio and TV[20] time on our stations. We would suggest that you permit[30] us to send one of our representatives to discuss some[40] of the details with you.

We can, however, offer certain[50] general comments about our facilities and fees. You are apparently[60] interested in what is called a "spot" announcement. Such announcements[70] are usually given during station breaks, and there is no[80] relationship between the program being presented and the product being[90] advertised. Hence, the cost of such announcements would be less[100] than those having a direct connection between the program and[110] the advertisement. The amount charged for an announcement would depend[120] upon the number of people who are seeing the show[130] or listening to it over the radio. The largest audience[140] would be reached during the evening hours on television and[150] the afternoon and morning hours on radio.

Our representative will[160] give you exact costs for a particular time when you[170] see him.

Cordially yours, (174)


Central Broadcasting Company
312 Madison Avenue
New York 3, New York 10017

Gentlemen:

Thank you for your prompt reply to our questions[10] concerning advertising over your television and radio stations. We shall[20] be happy to speak with your representative about the details[30] of cost and time.

Since writing our previous letter to[40] you, we have been thinking further about the problem, and[50] we have decided that it would not be to our[60] advantage to have these advertisements placed over the radio because[70] the products we wish to advertise are new and would[80] be best advertised if they could be seen.

Yours truly, (90)


## SPELLING

(1) anxious, approximately, metropolitan, facilities, audience
(2) apparently, connection
(3) concerning, writing, previous, decided


## PUNCTUATION

(1) We should like to place two advertisements for approximately one minute each, provided they are given in the morning and in the afternoon.
(2) It is difficult to tell you about the length, time, and cost of television announcements in a letter, but our representative can give you this information in one hour's time.
(3) Since we wrote our previous letter we have decided to place advertisements in newspapers, magazines, and over TV, but we do not wish to advertise over the radio.

438

# 38

## VOCABULARY BUILDING

*confirm*      1. This letter will confirm the existence of the contract
*existence*       which was signed in our office today.

*consult*      2. I should like to consult with them about the exist-
                  ence of the debts before I confirm the new contract.

*liable*       3. I am not liable for any debts that may have been in
                  existence before I took over the firm, and I would
                  suggest that you confirm this by consulting your
                  lawyer.

*mechanical*   4. We cannot be held liable for the existence of any
                  mechanical defects unless we confirm such liability
                  in advance.

*extensive*    5. We should like to consult with you about whether
                  we are liable for the existence of any extensive
                  mechanical defects in the operation of the machine.

*induce*       6. We are trying to induce them to make some exten-
                  sive mechanical changes in their machines, but they
                  will not confirm the existence of any responsibility
                  on their part and so they cannot be liable for any
                  damages.

*miserable*    7. Their miserable experience with the extensive me-
                  chanical problems involved in the handling of the
                  machine may induce them to ask us to be liable for
                  all repairs.

## THEORY PRACTICE

We presume from your letter that you are anxious to[10] dispose of some of your property through our agency. We[20] are assuming that you realize that there is very little[30] property available at the present time, and that you can[40] probably make arrangements to sell your property at a substantial[50] premium.

As far as we can see, there is apparently[60] no reason for delay in putting the property up for[70] sale at this time. If you had intended waiting for[80] a better price for your property, we believe

439

that there[90] is absolutely no chance of getting a better price in[100] the future. A buyer would have to pay almost twice[110] the sum that you are asking to duplicate the property[120] that you wish to sell.   (125)

## SPEED BUILDING PRACTICE

Gentlemen:

I have been informed that the present shortage of[10] houses represents an unusually fine opportunity for investment in mortgages.[20] I would, therefore, like to make a small investment at[30] this time. At the present time I have some money[40] invested, but the character of these investments is such that[50] in my opinion they will never bring a large return.[60] I hope that I will be able to exchange my[70] present investments for those in mortgages which are generally expected[80] to pay a larger return.

I should like to know[90] the regular terms for investment in your firm so that[100] I may know whether I wish to become a member[110] of your group. Please let me know as soon as[120] possible whether you have any particular investment opportunities for me.[130]

Yours truly,            (132)

## TRANSCRIPTION LETTERS

Atlantic Broadcasting System
73 Ontario Street
Stratford, Ontario

Gentlemen:

As you know, we have been placing a considerable[10] amount of advertising with your television station. While we have[20] not sponsored any particular programs, we have made extensive use[30] of your "spot" announcements. The cost of these programs has[40] been higher than we had expected, but the results from[50] our first few programs were encouraging.

However, we have found[60] that there has been a sharp drop during the past[70] three months in the number of inquiries about our products.[80] While we admit that we cannot completely measure the success[90] of our advertisements by the number of inquiries received, we[100] feel that it is extremely unlikely for people to buy[110] our products without writing for further details.

Very truly yours,            (120)

440

Griffith Carpet Company Incorporated
25 Caledonia Road
Toronto, Ontario

Gentlemen:

We can understand your reaction to the decreased number[10] of inquiries you have been receiving from your television announcements[20] on our station. We have made a careful check of[30] the effect of your advertisements on the television listener. Our[40] conclusion is that the programs lack variety and interest for[50] the listener.

While the expense of changing your announcements more[60] frequently would be fairly high, our experience has shown that[70] the TV public wishes as much variety as it[80] can get. We would suggest that you change your advertisements[90] at least once a week so as to increase the[100] interest of the listener in your products. We realize that[110] we cannot confirm our conclusions by any absolutely reliable data,[120] but we do feel that it is worth your while[130] to look into the possibility of a more frequent change[140] of advertisements.

We should be happy to arrange to have[150] you speak with one of our program supervisors about your[160] problem. We are sure that he can be of great[170] help to you in planning your future advertising activities.

Very[180] truly yours,        (182)

Atlantic Broadcasting System
73 Ontario Street
Stratford, Ontario

Gentlemen:

We were quite surprised to hear your suggestion that[10] we change our advertisements at least once a week in[20] order to continue listener interest in our products. You have[30] apparently forgotten that your program supervisor specifically assured us that[40] it would not be necessary to change programs more than[50] twice a month because of the changing audience which would[60] see our advertisements. Furthermore, if you have made inquiries about[70] the effect of our advertisements on the public, why did[80] we not receive such information for our consideration?

Sincerely yours,        (90)

## SPELLING

(1) considerable, sponsored, extensive, encouraging, inquiries, success, unlikely

(2) reaction, decreased, variety, realize, confirm, absolutely, supervisors, activities, data

(3) quite, forgotten, specifically, assured, audience

## PUNCTUATION

(1) As you know, it is extremely unlikely that they will buy our products, but we shall try our best to sell to other customers.

(2) While the expense would be high, our feeling is, on the basis of past experience, that we could still make a profit.

# 39

## VOCABULARY BUILDING

*opposed*
*preliminary*

1. He told us that he was opposed to the recommendations contained in the preliminary report of the committee.

*intense*
*publicity*

2. He opposed the idea of having an intense publicity campaign before the preliminary announcement from the president of the company.

*indulge*

3. I do not think it wise to indulge in any preliminary publicity about our plans because of the intense competition that we have to face.

*finance*

4. In order to finance the entire operation, we must indulge in an intense publicity campaign to obtain preliminary approval of our plans.

*questionnaire*

5. We cannot indulge in any unnecessary expense to finance your publicity campaign, but we can prepare the questionnaire for you.

*interval*

6. We suggest that you allow a rather long interval between the beginning of your preliminary publicity and the sending out of the questionnaire.

## THEORY PRACTICE

When we totaled our sales for the month we found[10] that we had many customers who did not pay their[20] bills early enough to deduct a discount. There are undoubtedly[30] many reasons for this, but we are not prepared to[40] accept the idea that our customers cannot afford to take[50] advantage of a cash discount. Furthermore we are interested in[60] extending our discount period and we are prepared to give[70] an additional two per cent discount beyond the standard figure[80] of two per cent.

We feel that the matter is[90] urgent, and we are, therefore, sending all of our figures[100] to you in a folder which you may keep for[110] further reference.                    (112)

## SPEED BUILDING PRACTICE

Dear Sir:

I was surprised to hear that you had[10] some objection to our plan for the expenditure of money[20] to build a number of stores in this part of[30] the city. You are probably not familiar with the fact[40] that there is a great need to establish stores in[50] this part of the city to avoid the inconvenience that[60] people now have in getting to stores. We are sure[70] that you will see the value in building these stores,[80] and that is why we are anxious to have you[90] talk the matter over with us.

You may remember that[100] we talked about our plan to several people whom you[110] recommended as being capable and who enjoyed the respect of[120] business men all over the city. We hope that you[130] will use your influence to obtain additional financial support for[140] the plan.

Cordially yours,                    (141)

## TRANSCRIPTION LETTERS

Empire Broadcasting System
109 Walker Street
Boston 16, Massachusetts 10019

Gentlemen:

I have been asked to communicate with you about[10] the possibility of introducing educational television in the schools. It[20] is the feeling of many members of our staff that[30] the tremendous appeal

443

of television should be used to improve[40] educational work as well as for entertainment for commercial purposes.[50] Before we proceed any further with our plans, we would[60] like to have reactions of television stations towards the use[70] of part of their time for educational purposes.

There is[80] an intense interest in the subject here at the college,[90] and we feel that many people would give their support[100] and time to educational TV. We would appreciate any[110] preliminary comments or remarks you may have about the problem.[120]

Cordially yours,  (122)

Dr. Harry Perkins
24 Herser Street
Los Angeles, California 21956

Dear Dr. Perkins:

We are very happy to give you[10] some of our experiences and thoughts on the subject of[20] educational TV.

We agree with you that the possibilities[30] of television for influencing the public mind are very great[40] and that if TV can be used to improve[50] education, it should be done without the slightest delay. However,[60] many people are often carried away by the possibilities of[70] television without realizing that there is actually only a small[80] difference between live television and films. While we do not[90] deny the fact that television is much more alive and[100] up to date than films, we cannot indulge in any[110] wide use of our facilities for educational purposes unless there[120] are no other ways in which the same service can[130] be performed by present facilities. Frankly, in our opinion, the[140] only real advantage of live TV is that it[150] could be used to reduce the number of teachers needed[160] in a particular school. One teacher can undoubtedly handle far[170] larger groups by means of live TV.

Very truly[180] yours,  (181)

Empire Broadcasting System
109 Walker Street
Boston 16, Massachusetts 10019

Gentlemen:

The point of view you expressed in your letter[10] seems to indicate that you are not interested in the[20] idea of educational TV at

444

this time. We do[30] not believe that the only purpose of educational TV[40] is to make up for a shortage of teachers. It[50] is obvious that the wholesale substitution of TV instruction[60] for the regular classroom teaching would result in a lowering[70] of educational standards. We are interested in the use of[80] educational TV to assist in the improvement of student[90] learning.

Very truly yours,      (94)

## SPELLING

(1) communicate, introducing, proceed, intense, preliminary
(2) influencing, slightest, carried, realizing, actually, indulge, facilities, frankly, undoubtedly
(3) substitution, lowering, standards, student

## PUNCTUATION

(1) Before we proceed with these plans, we should like to know how long the job will take, how much it will cost, and how much we can expect to make.
(2) While we do not deny that films are useful, they can never be as interesting as live TV.
(3) Can you assist us in using TV to improve student learning, or do you feel that TV would cost too much?

# VOCABULARY BUILDING

**compel**
**artificial**

1. We cannot compel people to accept artificial products without lowering our prices.

**distinct**
**genuine**

2. We have a distinct feeling that we can sell the genuine articles much better than the artificial ones even if the price is higher.

**outcome**

3. There is a distinct advantage in having genuine articles placed in the window since we know what the outcome would be if we used artificial items.

**beneficial**

4. I am sure that the outcome of our special campaign will be distinctly beneficial if we can compel them to give us the genuine figures on their production.

445

*controversy*    5. I have a distinct feeling that there may be some beneficial outcomes from the controversy even if they compel him to give them his genuine sales figures.

*reality*    6. The controversy was in reality the outcome of their genuine desire to compel him to hire more competent people for the job.

## THEORY PRACTICE

We hesitated to make any recommendations to you about the[10] desirability of transferring your office to another part of the[20] city because we are somewhat uncertain about the future areas[30] of development in this city. We definitely do not want[40] to overlook the possibility of an increase in business in[50] your present location, and we do not want to lose[60] your confidence, particularly since you have been recommended to us[70] by an exceedingly good friend of ours.

We are, therefore,[80] attaching a report that we made of business opportunities in[90] this area. When you have read the report, we feel[100] that you will have enough information to make a decision[110] that will enable you to accomplish the most beneficial results. (120)

## SPEED BUILDING PRACTICE

Gentlemen:

We have made the investigation of business opportunities in[10] this area that you requested, and we find that there[20] are many opportunities to make substantial investments within the next[30] few years. We have found that many business firms have[40] neglected the opportunities that are present by making only a[50] minimum effort to sell their goods.

We believe that you[60] can achieve maximum profits by trying to encourage people from[70] outside the city to come to town to make their[80] purchases. Nevertheless, we realize that many of these ideas may[90] not be practicable at this time. We have, therefore, inspected[100] several locations outside the city.

We trust that our report[110] gives you sufficient opportunities to select a location to your[120] satisfaction. We shall be happy to perform any other service[130] you may wish.

Cordially yours,      (135)

# TRANSCRIPTION LETTERS

Southern Broadcasting System
15 Rosemount Avenue
Rochester, New York 20136

Gentlemen:

I have been looking at your show called "Name[10] and Price" ever since it first came on television over[20] two years ago, and I have found the show to[30] be very interesting. I should like to know if there[40] is any possibility of my appearing on the show in[50] the future. I have been able to answer most of[60] the questions that were asked, and my friends have suggested[70] that I appear on the show.

I am attaching a[80] brief summary of my background since I am sure that[90] you select your contestants for the show only after careful[100] checking of their backgrounds.

Very truly yours,        (107)

Mr. Alvin Moore
109 King Street
London, Ontario

Dear Mr. Moore:

Thank you very much for your letter[10] in which you requested information about our program "Name and[20] Price."

We are always anxious to obtain contestants who will[30] continue the high level of performance of the show. However,[40] we cannot give you a definite decision in the matter[50] until we have more information about you and have made[60] an investigation of your background. We are, therefore, enclosing one[70] of our regular application forms. Please fill in all of[80] the required information and mail the form to us.

You[90] will note that we request the right to investigate your[100] background and that you agree that we shall not be[110] held responsible for the outcome of our investigation. This provision[120] is necessary in order to avoid a possible law-suit[130] from those people who are not accepted on the program[140] and who claim that we have damaged them because of[150] our investigation.

We hope that we may find it possible[160] to have you appear on the program in the near[170] future.

Sincerely yours,        (173)

Southern Broadcasting System
15 Rosemount Avenue
Rochester, New York 20136

Gentlemen:

I had expected a certain amount of checking and[10] investigating of my background when I wrote asking to appear[20] on your program, but I did not realize how much[30] would be involved in such an undertaking.

My purpose in[40] writing to you originally was to appear on the program[50] within two or three weeks from now. It seems likely[60] that your investigation would require several months. Since I will[70] not be in town after this month, it will be[80] necessary for me to withdraw my application.

Very truly yours,      (90)

## SPELLING

(1) attaching, summary, contestants
(2) anxious, performance (performs), decision, investigate, provision
(3) expect-ed, originally

## PUNCTUATION

(1) The show is called "Pay the Price," but it has not been on TV long enough to reach a large audience.
(2) We are, therefore, enclosing an application form which, you will notice, gives us the right to investigate your background.
(3) I had expected a certain amount of checking, but do you realize how much information they are asking me to give them?